Harmony of Nodes: Exploring Distributed Systems in Operating Systems

Table of Content

Chapter 1: The Foundations of Distributed Systems

- Defining distributed systems and their role in modern computing.
- Overview of the key principles guiding distributed system design.
- Exploring essential concepts such as nodes, communication, and shared resources.
- Understanding the challenges and advantages of distributed architectures.
- Examining common architectural patterns, including tiered architectures.
- Discussion on microservices and their impact on distributed system design.
- Overview of different models such as client-server, peer-to-peer, and hybrid models.
- Exploring the characteristics and use cases for each model.
- The role of communication in distributed systems.
- Understanding message-passing and remote procedure call (RPC) mechanisms.

Chapter 2: Networked Architectures: A Deep Dive

- Basics of computer networking and its relevance to distributed systems.
- Understanding protocols, IP addressing, and subnetting.
- In-depth exploration of the client-server architectural pattern.
- Role of servers and clients in distributed systems.
- Characteristics and advantages of peer-to-peer architectures.
- Challenges in maintaining connectivity and data consistency.
- The role of middleware in abstracting communication complexities.
- Different types of middleware: message-oriented, object-oriented, and transactional.
- Understanding scalability challenges in distributed systems.
- Techniques for load balancing to distribute work effectively.

Chapter 3: Concurrency and Parallelism in Operating Environments

- Defining concurrency and its relevance in distributed environments.
- Challenges and benefits of managing concurrent processes.
- Understanding parallel processing and its significance.
- Techniques for parallelizing tasks in distributed systems.
- Exploring synchronization challenges in distributed systems.
- Overview of synchronization mechanisms: locks, semaphores, and barriers.
- Overview of different distributed computing models: shared-memory vs. message-passing.
- Examining the advantages and limitations of each model.
- Real-world examples of distributed systems effectively utilizing concurrency and parallelism.
- Challenges faced and lessons learned in implementing concurrent and parallel solutions.

Chapter 4: Communication Protocols: Building Bridges in Distributed Systems

- Understanding the crucial role of communication protocols in distributed systems.
- Overview of common communication protocols: TCP/IP, HTTP, and more.
- Importance of standardized message formats in distributed communication.
- Exploring serialization techniques for efficient data transmission.
- Defining RPC and its role in distributed computing.
- Implementing RPC in different programming paradigms.
- Overview of RESTful architecture in distributed systems.
- Design principles for creating scalable and maintainable APIs.
- Understanding event-driven communication in distributed systems.
- Exploring messaging queues, publish-subscribe models, and event-driven architectures.

Chapter 5: Fault Tolerance and Resilience Strategies

- Defining fault tolerance and its significance in distributed computing.
- Types of faults and their impact on system reliability.
- Exploring replication as a strategy for enhancing fault tolerance.
- The role of redundancy in ensuring continuous system operation.
- The concept of checkpointing to ensure data consistency.
- Strategies for efficient checkpointing and recovery in distributed environments.
- Techniques for detecting failures in distributed systems.
- Designing robust handling mechanisms for various failure scenarios.
- Overview of distributed consensus algorithms.
- Examining consensus protocols like Paxos and Raft.

Chapter 6: Scalability Challenges and Solutions

- Defining scalability and its critical role in distributed system design.
- Understanding the difference between horizontal and vertical scalability.
- Strategies for scaling databases in distributed environments.
- Sharding, partitioning, and replication techniques.
- The importance of load balancing in maintaining system performance.
- Overview of load balancing algorithms and strategies.
- Understanding the role of caching in improving system responsiveness.
- Techniques for distributed caching in large-scale systems.
- Exploring the relationship between microservices architecture and scalability.
- Design principles for creating scalable microservices.

Chapter 7: Security Measures in Distributed Operating Systems

- Identifying unique security challenges in distributed computing.
- Overview of potential vulnerabilities and attack vectors.
- Strategies for authenticating users and entities in distributed systems.
- Implementing authorization mechanisms for secure access control.
- The role of encryption in securing data during transmission.
- Strategies for implementing end-to-end encryption.
- Designing distributed firewall systems for network security.
- The role of intrusion detection systems in distributed environments.
- The importance of regular security audits in distributed systems.
- Ensuring compliance with industry standards and regulations.

Chapter 8: Future Horizons: Emerging Trends in Distributed Systems

- Exploring the rise of edge computing and its impact on distributed systems.
- Architectural considerations for distributed edge environments.
- Understanding the paradigm shift towards serverless computing.
- The role of serverless architectures in distributed environments.
- Exploring the intersection of blockchain and distributed systems.
- Applications of distributed ledger technologies beyond cryptocurrencies.
- The integration of machine learning for intelligent decision-making.
- Enhancing distributed systems with predictive analytics and pattern recognition.
- Addressing ethical considerations in the development and deployment of distributed systems.
- Balancing technological advancements with social responsibility.

Introduction

In the dynamic and ever-evolving landscape of computer science, the orchestration of distributed systems within operating environments emerges as a critical frontier, shaping the very foundation of modern computing. "Harmony of Nodes: Exploring Distributed Systems in Operating Systems" embarks on a comprehensive journey, immersing readers in the intricate world where nodes collaborate seamlessly, and data traverses a complex web of connections to achieve unprecedented levels of efficiency and scalability.

As the guide unfolds, it meticulously unravels the complexities inherent in distributed systems, providing a nuanced exploration of the challenges and innovations that define this captivating domain. The term "Harmony of Nodes" encapsulates the essence of distributed systems—a symphony of interconnected entities working in unison, creating a harmonious orchestration that goes beyond the capabilities of a single computing unit. The guide sets the stage by delving into foundational concepts, elucidating the principles that underpin the design and functionality of distributed systems.

The exploration begins with an in-depth examination of the fundamentals, unraveling the core concepts that distinguish distributed systems from their centralized counterparts. The historical context and evolution of distributed computing provide valuable insights into the trajectory of its development, offering a panoramic view of the journey that has led to the sophisticated systems in use today.

The architectural patterns in distributed systems take center stage, shedding light on the various models that define their structure. Whether through the client-server paradigm, peer-to-peer networks, or the microservices architecture, each model contributes to the symphony of distributed computing, offering unique advantages and posing distinct challenges. Real-world examples illustrate the successful implementation of these architectural patterns, bringing theoretical concepts to life.

Networking architectures form a crucial segment of the exploration, as the guide delves deep into the intricacies of computer networking. From the basics of protocols and IP addressing to the complexities of client-server and peer-to-peer architectures, the guide navigates through the intricacies of creating connections that enable the seamless flow of information across distributed systems.

The exploration of concurrency and parallelism in operating environments unfolds as a captivating chapter, as the guide navigates the challenges and benefits of managing concurrent processes. Synchronization mechanisms, distributed computing models, and real-world case studies provide a comprehensive understanding of how systems handle simultaneous tasks, ensuring efficient resource utilization.

Communication protocols emerge as the bridges that facilitate seamless interaction among nodes, forming the essence of the distributed symphony. The guide navigates through the role of communication protocols, emphasizing the importance of standardized message formats, remote procedure calls (RPC), and RESTful APIs. Event-driven communication takes its place in the narrative, showcasing how distributed systems leverage messaging queues and publish-subscribe models for efficient event handling.

The guide's exploration extends into the realm of fault tolerance and resilience strategies, acknowledging the inevitability of faults in distributed systems and detailing strategies to mitigate their impact. Replication, redundancy, checkpointing, and distributed consensus algorithms become integral components in ensuring the robustness and reliability of distributed systems.

Scalability challenges and solutions take center stage in the exploration, reflecting the imperative need for systems to adapt and expand in the face of growing demands. Database scaling strategies, load balancing techniques, and microservices architecture come into focus, demonstrating how distributed systems evolve to meet the scalability requirements of modern applications.

Security measures in distributed operating systems become a critical consideration, as the guide addresses the unique challenges posed by the distributed nature of computing. Authentication, authorization, encryption, distributed firewalls, and intrusion detection systems form the arsenal of tools to safeguard against potential threats. Security audits and compliance ensure that distributed systems adhere to industry standards and regulations, safeguarding sensitive data and maintaining the trust of users.

As the guide progresses towards its concluding chapters, it casts a gaze into the future horizons of distributed systems. Emerging trends such as edge computing, serverless computing, blockchain integration, machine learning, and the ethical considerations in the development of distributed systems paint a visionary landscape. The integration of machine learning for intelligent decision-making, the rise of edge computing, and the intersection of blockchain with distributed systems provide a glimpse into the transformative potential that awaits.

Throughout the narrative, "Harmony of Nodes" maintains a delicate balance between theoretical insights and practical considerations. Real-world case studies, examples, and lessons learned from both successes and failures enrich the exploration, providing readers with a tangible and applicable understanding of distributed systems. The guide's forward-looking approach, coupled with ethical considerations, underscores the importance of responsible innovation in this ever-evolving domain.

In essence, "Harmony of Nodes: Exploring Distributed Systems in Operating Systems" stands as a beacon in the realm of computer science literature. It invites readers on a captivating journey, where the symphony of interconnected nodes creates a harmonious orchestration that defines the contemporary era of computing. As the guide concludes, readers are equipped not only with a profound understanding of distributed systems but also with the visionary insights needed to navigate the uncharted territories of tomorrow's computing landscape.

Chapter 1: The Foundations of Distributed Systems

Defining distributed systems and their role in modern computing.

Distributed systems represent a pivotal paradigm in modern computing, embodying an architectural approach where the processing, storage, and communication components of a computer system span multiple interconnected nodes. This departure from traditional monolithic structures offers a scalable, fault-tolerant, and flexible framework that underpins various contemporary applications and services. In the realm of distributed systems, each constituent node operates independently, often communicating with others to collectively fulfill computational tasks. The fundamental objective is to harness collective computing resources efficiently, accommodating the increasing demands posed by data-intensive applications and the exponential growth of digital information.

One defining characteristic of distributed systems lies in their spatial dispersion, with nodes geographically distributed across diverse locations. This spatial distribution enables the harnessing of resources from different geographical regions, promoting redundancy and minimizing the impact of localized failures. As a consequence, distributed systems exhibit enhanced resilience, ensuring the continued functionality of the system even in the face of component failures or external disruptions. This fault-tolerant nature is particularly crucial in today's computing landscape, where uninterrupted availability and reliability are non-negotiable requirements for applications and services.

The architecture of distributed systems is intricately linked with the concept of decentralization, where no single node assumes sole control. This decentralized structure facilitates efficient resource utilization and scalability, allowing the system to seamlessly adapt to varying workloads. The absence of a central authority distributing tasks among nodes engenders a level of autonomy and agility that is conducive to the dynamic nature of modern computing environments. It also mitigates the risks associated with single points of failure, thereby enhancing the overall robustness and reliability of the system.

Communication forms the lifeblood of distributed systems, with nodes relying on networks to exchange information and collaborate on tasks. The network infrastructure connecting these nodes must be designed with considerations for latency, bandwidth, and reliability to ensure optimal performance. Communication protocols, such as the Transmission Control Protocol (TCP) and User Datagram Protocol (UDP), play a crucial role in facilitating seamless interaction between distributed components. This intricate interplay of communication mechanisms is essential for orchestrating complex distributed applications, ranging from cloud computing platforms to internet-scale services.

The advent of cloud computing has further propelled the prominence of distributed systems, offering on-demand access to a shared pool of configurable computing resources. Cloud platforms leverage distributed architectures to deliver services such as Infrastructure as a Service (IaaS), Platform as a Service (PaaS), and Software as a Service (SaaS). This paradigm shift in computing has revolutionized the way organizations approach resource provisioning, enabling them to scale their operations dynamically in response to changing requirements without the burden of managing physical hardware.

Big Data processing represents another domain where distributed systems have become indispensable. The sheer volume, velocity, and variety of data generated in the digital age necessitate distributed approaches for storage and processing. Distributed file systems like Apache Hadoop Distributed File System (HDFS) and distributed processing frameworks like Apache Spark exemplify the distributed systems' role in managing and analyzing vast datasets. These technologies facilitate parallel processing, enabling efficient handling of data-intensive tasks and empowering organizations to derive valuable insights from their data.

Distributed databases also underscore the importance of distributed systems in modern computing. With the proliferation of data-driven applications, the need for scalable and distributed storage solutions has become paramount. Distributed databases, such as Apache Cassandra and Amazon DynamoDB, distribute data across multiple nodes, ensuring high availability, fault tolerance, and efficient retrieval. This approach aligns with the evolving data management requirements of applications ranging from e-commerce platforms to social media networks.

Security and privacy considerations are integral aspects of distributed systems, particularly as they deal with sensitive data and diverse communication channels. The decentralized nature of these systems introduces challenges related to authentication, authorization, and data encryption. Ensuring the confidentiality and integrity of data across distributed environments requires robust security measures, and advancements in cryptographic techniques play a pivotal role in addressing these concerns.

In conclusion, distributed systems constitute a cornerstone of modern computing, offering a versatile and scalable framework to meet the evolving demands of today's technology landscape. From cloud computing to Big Data analytics and distributed databases, the pervasive influence of distributed systems is evident across a myriad of applications. As the digital ecosystem continues to evolve, the role of distributed systems will likely expand, providing the foundation for innovative solutions that push the boundaries of what is achievable in the realm of computing.

Overview of the key principles guiding distributed system design.

Designing distributed systems involves a multifaceted approach, guided by several key principles that collectively shape the architecture, functionality, and reliability of these complex systems. At the forefront lies the principle of fault tolerance, emphasizing the system's resilience in the face of failures, be they hardware malfunctions, network issues, or software errors. This necessitates the incorporation of redundancy, replication, and error recovery mechanisms to ensure uninterrupted operation and graceful degradation under adverse conditions. Scalability stands as another pivotal principle, addressing the system's ability to efficiently handle growing workloads by seamlessly accommodating additional resources. Achieving scalability often involves the adoption of horizontal scaling, where the system's capacity expands by adding more nodes or components.

Interwoven with fault tolerance and scalability is the principle of consistency, dictating that all nodes within the distributed system present a coherent view of the data despite potential delays or network partitions. The CAP theorem, which posits the trade-offs between Consistency, Availability, and Partition tolerance, serves as a foundational guideline in navigating these challenges. Ensuring data consistency also involves careful consideration of distributed transactions, with mechanisms like two-phase commit protocols or optimistic concurrency control strategies being implemented to manage the coordination of operations across multiple nodes.

The principle of performance optimization underscores the importance of efficient resource utilization to deliver optimal response times and throughput. This often entails load balancing mechanisms to distribute work evenly among nodes, as well as the utilization of caching strategies and compression techniques to minimize latency. Additionally, the principle of modularity encourages the design of distributed systems as a composition of loosely coupled components, allowing for easier maintenance, updates, and extensibility. The adoption of microservices architecture exemplifies this principle, promoting the development and deployment of small, independent services that can be scaled and updated independently.

Security remains a paramount consideration in distributed system design, emphasizing the protection of data, communication channels, and access controls across the network. Encryption, authentication, and authorization mechanisms play pivotal roles in safeguarding sensitive information and mitigating potential vulnerabilities. Moreover, the principle of simplicity advocates for straightforward, comprehensible designs, as complexity often introduces potential points of failure and hinders system understanding, troubleshooting, and maintenance.

Distributed systems also grapple with the challenge of ensuring effective communication between nodes, leading to the principle of communication transparency. This principle urges designers to abstract the complexities of communication, shielding developers from the intricacies of network protocols and infrastructure details. Techniques such as Remote Procedure Call (RPC) or Message Queues facilitate transparent communication, allowing components to interact seamlessly while encapsulating the underlying complexities.

Adherence to the principles of decentralization and autonomy is crucial to promoting system flexibility and resilience. Decentralization distributes control and decision-making authority across nodes, reducing the risk of a single point of failure and enhancing the system's adaptability. Autonomy empowers individual components to operate independently, fostering fault isolation and enabling more efficient resource utilization.

As data plays a central role in distributed systems, the principle of data locality advocates for storing and processing data close to where it is most needed. This approach minimizes latency and reduces the reliance on long-distance communication, aligning with the broader goal of optimizing system performance. The rise of edge computing exemplifies the practical application of this principle, pushing data processing closer to the source.

Finally, the principle of observability emphasizes the need for robust monitoring, logging, and debugging capabilities within a distributed system. Given the inherent complexities and potential for emergent behaviors, effective observability ensures quick detection and resolution of issues, facilitating ongoing system improvement and optimization.

In conclusion, the design of distributed systems is a nuanced endeavor guided by a set of interrelated principles. Fault tolerance, scalability, consistency, performance optimization, modularity, security, simplicity, communication transparency, decentralization, autonomy, data locality, and observability collectively form the cornerstone of effective distributed system design. The careful application and integration of these principles enable the creation of resilient, efficient, and adaptive systems capable of meeting the challenges posed by the distributed computing landscape.

Exploring essential concepts such as nodes, communication, and shared resources.

In the realm of distributed systems, the concept of nodes serves as a fundamental building block, representing individual computational entities within the network. Nodes can take various forms, ranging from physical machines to virtual instances, and collectively form the infrastructure that executes the distributed system's operations. These nodes communicate and collaborate to achieve common goals, often emphasizing fault tolerance and scalability. The interactions between nodes are governed by communication mechanisms that facilitate the exchange of information and coordination of tasks.

Communication in distributed systems is a critical aspect that defines the flow of data, commands, and status updates between nodes. Various communication models and protocols exist to enable effective interaction, each with its strengths and trade-offs. Remote Procedure Call (RPC), for instance, allows nodes to invoke procedures or methods on remote machines as if they were local, abstracting the complexities of network communication. Message-oriented communication, on the other hand, involves the exchange of messages between nodes, offering flexibility in terms of communication patterns and data serialization formats.

Shared resources play a pivotal role in distributed systems, reflecting the collaborative nature of these environments. Resources can include data stores, computing power, and services that multiple nodes may access concurrently. The effective management of shared resources is essential for ensuring consistency and avoiding conflicts. Distributed databases, such as those utilizing the principles of sharding or replication, exemplify strategies to provide scalable and reliable access to shared data across multiple nodes. Resource allocation and scheduling mechanisms also play a key role, ensuring fair and efficient utilization of computational resources among competing nodes.

Nodes in distributed systems often engage in parallel and concurrent processing, allowing tasks to be executed simultaneously across multiple entities. This concurrency introduces the challenge of synchronization to maintain consistency and coherence in shared data and resources. Locking mechanisms, such as mutexes or semaphores, and advanced concurrency control strategies, like optimistic or pessimistic locking, are employed to regulate access and modification of shared data. The careful design of concurrency control mechanisms is crucial to prevent race conditions, deadlocks, and other pitfalls associated with parallel execution.

The concept of distributed consensus is integral to achieving agreement among nodes in the presence of failures and communication delays. Consensus algorithms, such as the Paxos or Raft algorithms, provide a framework for nodes to reach a common decision, even when faced with failures or partitions in the network. By ensuring that nodes agree on a particular value or state, consensus mechanisms underpin the consistency and reliability of distributed systems, serving as a foundational concept in their design.

Fault tolerance is another core concept that addresses the inevitability of failures within distributed systems. Nodes can experience hardware malfunctions, network disruptions, or software errors, necessitating mechanisms to detect, isolate, and recover from faults. Redundancy and replication are commonly employed to mitigate the impact of failures, allowing the system to continue functioning even in the presence of faulty nodes. Checkpointing and rollback recovery mechanisms further contribute to fault tolerance by enabling the system to revert to a consistent state following a failure.

The concept of eventual consistency acknowledges that achieving immediate consistency across all nodes in a distributed system may be impractical or inefficient. Instead, systems may adopt eventual consistency, where all nodes converge to a consistent state over time, even in the face of network partitions or delays. This approach balances the trade-off between consistency and availability, acknowledging that strict consistency may be unattainable in certain scenarios.

Distributed transactions represent a critical concept in ensuring data integrity and consistency across multiple nodes. Coordinating transactions that involve multiple operations on distributed data sources requires careful consideration of atomicity, consistency, isolation, and durability (ACID) properties. Two-phase commit protocols, distributed locking mechanisms, and optimistic concurrency control are employed to manage the complexities of distributed transactions and ensure their reliable execution.

The concept of load balancing addresses the need to distribute computational workloads evenly across nodes to optimize resource utilization and avoid bottlenecks. Load balancers, whether implemented as dedicated components or integrated into the system's architecture, dynamically allocate tasks to nodes based on factors such as current resource availability and processing capacity. Load balancing enhances system scalability by preventing individual nodes from becoming overwhelmed and ensures efficient utilization of computational resources.

In summary, the essential concepts of nodes, communication, and shared resources form the bedrock of distributed systems. Nodes represent the individual entities within the system, communication governs the interactions between these nodes, and shared resources encapsulate the collaborative nature of distributed computing. Concepts such as concurrency, distributed consensus, fault tolerance, eventual consistency, distributed transactions, and load balancing further contribute to the holistic understanding of the intricacies involved in designing and maintaining robust distributed systems.

Understanding the challenges and advantages of distributed architectures.

Distributed architectures, while offering a plethora of advantages, also present a unique set of challenges that shape their design and implementation. One of the foremost advantages lies in scalability, as distributed architectures empower systems to expand their capacity seamlessly by adding more nodes or resources. This scalability is crucial for accommodating growing workloads and ensuring optimal performance as demand fluctuates. Additionally, distributed architectures enhance fault tolerance by dispersing system components across multiple nodes. Redundancy and replication mechanisms can be leveraged to mitigate the impact of hardware failures, network issues, or software errors, contributing to the overall reliability and resilience of the system.

However, scalability and fault tolerance come with their own challenges, and achieving a balance between them is a delicate task. As the number of nodes in a distributed system grows, managing communication and coordination becomes more complex. Ensuring consistency across distributed nodes can be challenging, especially in the presence of network partitions or delays. The trade-offs embodied in the CAP theorem (Consistency, Availability, Partition tolerance) exemplify the challenges associated with achieving strong consistency, high availability, and fault tolerance simultaneously. Striking the right balance requires careful consideration of the specific requirements and characteristics of the distributed system in question.

Communication in distributed architectures, while essential for collaboration among nodes, introduces its own set of challenges. Network latency and bandwidth limitations can impact the speed and efficiency of communication, affecting the overall performance of the system. As the distance between nodes increases, the potential for communication delays rises, necessitating strategies such as data locality or caching to optimize response times. Furthermore, ensuring the security of communication channels becomes paramount in distributed architectures to protect against potential threats, emphasizing the need for robust encryption, authentication, and authorization mechanisms.

The management of shared resources is another critical aspect of distributed architectures, and it brings both advantages and challenges. Shared resources, such as databases or storage systems, facilitate data access and utilization across multiple nodes. This fosters collaboration and allows for the centralized management of data. However, ensuring the consistency and integrity of shared resources poses challenges, particularly when multiple nodes attempt to access or modify the same data concurrently. Concurrency control mechanisms, such as locking or transaction coordination, are essential for maintaining data consistency and avoiding conflicts.

Concurrency, a core advantage of distributed architectures, enables parallel and simultaneous processing of tasks across multiple nodes. This concurrent execution enhances the system's throughput and efficiency. However, managing concurrency introduces complexities related to synchronization, as multiple nodes may contend for access to shared resources. Race conditions, deadlocks, and other concurrency-related issues require careful consideration and the implementation of robust concurrency control strategies to ensure data integrity and system stability.

Distributed architectures also embrace the concept of decentralization, distributing control and decision-making authority across nodes. This decentralization enhances system flexibility, adaptability, and fault isolation. Nodes can operate autonomously, contributing to overall system resilience. Nevertheless, managing a decentralized system requires sophisticated coordination mechanisms to ensure coherent decision-making and consistent states across nodes. Achieving a balance between decentralization and coordination is crucial to prevent conflicts and maintain system integrity.

Fault tolerance, while advantageous, introduces challenges related to the detection, isolation, and recovery from failures. Redundancy and replication mechanisms aim to mitigate the impact of node failures, but the implementation of these strategies must be carefully orchestrated to avoid overloading the system or introducing inconsistencies. Additionally, the complexity of fault-tolerant systems may increase the difficulty of debugging and troubleshooting, requiring advanced monitoring and observability mechanisms to quickly identify and address issues.

Distributed architectures also face challenges related to data consistency. The concept of eventual consistency acknowledges that achieving immediate consistency across all nodes may be impractical, leading systems to opt for a model where consistency is reached over time. This introduces complexities in managing divergent states and resolving conflicts, requiring careful consideration of trade-offs between consistency and availability.

Despite these challenges, distributed architectures offer significant advantages, including improved performance, fault tolerance, scalability, and flexibility. The ability to harness the power of multiple nodes in parallel enables the efficient processing of large datasets and complex computations. Scalability allows systems to adapt to varying workloads, ensuring optimal resource utilization. The distributed nature of these architectures also aligns well with modern cloud computing paradigms, where resources are often geographically dispersed.

In conclusion, understanding the challenges and advantages of distributed architectures is paramount for designing robust and effective systems. Scalability, fault tolerance, communication efficiency, shared resource management, and decentralization are key advantages that drive the adoption of distributed architectures. However, achieving a balance between these advantages and addressing associated challenges such as data consistency, concurrency, and fault management requires careful consideration and thoughtful design. Ultimately, a well-designed distributed architecture can unlock the potential for high-performance, resilient, and scalable systems that meet the demands of modern computing environments.

Examining common architectural patterns, including tiered architectures.

Architectural patterns provide proven solutions to recurring design problems, offering a structured approach to building robust and scalable systems. One common architectural pattern is the tiered architecture, which organizes a system into distinct layers or tiers, each responsible for specific functionalities. The three-tier architecture, consisting of presentation, application, and data tiers, is a prevalent example. The presentation tier handles user interface interactions, presenting information to users and collecting their input. This separation of concerns enhances maintainability and allows for different presentation technologies to be employed without affecting the underlying logic. The application tier, often referred to as the business logic layer, contains the core functionality and processing rules. This tier acts as an intermediary between the presentation and data tiers, orchestrating the flow of information and business operations. The data tier, also known as the persistence layer, manages the storage and retrieval of data. This division facilitates scalability and flexibility, enabling the modification of one tier without significantly impacting the others.

Microservices architecture represents a more contemporary approach, emphasizing the development and deployment of small, independently deployable services. Each microservice encapsulates specific business capabilities and communicates with others through well-defined APIs. This pattern enhances agility, allowing teams to develop, deploy, and scale services independently. Microservices promote fault isolation, as the failure of one service does not necessarily affect others. However, managing the interactions between microservices, handling data consistency, and ensuring effective communication introduce challenges that require careful consideration and implementation of appropriate patterns and technologies.

Service-Oriented Architecture (SOA) is another architectural pattern centered around the idea of organizing software components as services. These services communicate over a network and can be loosely coupled, promoting interoperability and reusability. SOA aligns well with distributed systems, fostering the development of modular and scalable applications. The use of standards like Simple Object Access Protocol (SOAP) or Representational State Transfer (REST) for communication between services enhances flexibility and allows for the integration of diverse technologies. However, the governance of services, ensuring compatibility, and managing the lifecycle of services pose challenges that need to be addressed for successful SOA implementation.

Event-Driven Architecture (EDA) is characterized by the asynchronous communication of events between components. Events, representing significant occurrences in the system, trigger reactions in other components. This decoupling of components through events enables scalability and responsiveness. Message queues, publish-subscribe systems, and event sourcing are common mechanisms in EDA. Event-Driven Architecture is particularly well-suited for systems requiring real-time processing, adaptability to changing conditions, and support for event-driven workflows. However, maintaining consistency, handling event delivery failures, and debugging complex event-driven systems require careful design and implementation.

Layered architecture, also known as n-tier architecture, extends the tiered approach by introducing additional layers for specific functionalities. This pattern fosters separation of concerns, modularity, and ease of maintenance. Each layer represents a distinct level of abstraction, with well-defined interfaces between them. Common layers include the presentation layer for user interface interactions, the business logic layer for processing, the service layer for encapsulating business services, and the data access layer for managing data storage. While layered architecture offers clarity and maintainability, excessive layering can lead to increased complexity, and the rigid separation may not suit all types of applications.

Model-View-Controller (MVC) is an architectural pattern that divides an application into three interconnected components: Model, View, and Controller. The Model represents the data and business logic, the View handles the user interface and presentation, and the Controller manages user input and updates the Model accordingly.

MVC promotes modular development, code reusability, and separation of concerns. Changes in one component do not necessarily affect others, facilitating easier maintenance and updates. This pattern is widely employed in web development frameworks and graphical user interface applications. However, enforcing strict separation can lead to increased complexity, and adapting MVC to specific requirements may necessitate variations of the traditional pattern.

Component-Based Architecture involves building systems by assembling pre-built, reusable components. Components encapsulate specific functionalities and can be easily integrated into different applications. This pattern fosters modularity, code reuse, and accelerates development by leveraging existing components. However, effective component management, versioning, and ensuring compatibility between components from different sources pose challenges. Additionally, choosing the appropriate granularity of components and maintaining a balance between flexibility and standardization require careful consideration.

The Hexagonal Architecture, also known as Ports and Adapters or Onion Architecture, focuses on the independence of the application's core business logic from external concerns such as databases, user interfaces, or external services. The core is encapsulated within the innermost layer, while external concerns are treated as adapters connected to the core through defined interfaces or ports. This pattern enhances testability, flexibility, and maintainability by allowing the replacement of adapters without affecting the core logic. However, properly designing and managing the interfaces between the core and adapters, as well as avoiding overcomplication, are essential aspects of successful Hexagonal Architecture implementation.

The Repository Pattern is commonly used for managing data access and storage in a structured manner. It abstracts the logic for retrieving and storing data, providing a uniform interface for the application to interact with the underlying data storage mechanisms. This pattern enhances testability and allows for easy replacement or modification of the data storage technology without affecting the application's business logic. However, the appropriate design of repository interfaces, managing complex data relationships, and ensuring optimal performance are considerations that should be addressed when applying the Repository Pattern.

In conclusion, architectural patterns serve as guiding principles for designing and organizing software systems, offering solutions to recurring challenges. Tiered architectures provide a structured separation of concerns, while microservices, SOA, and EDA emphasize distributed and modular approaches. Layered architectures, MVC, and component-based architectures promote modularity and maintainability, each with its own trade-offs. The Hexagonal Architecture focuses on decoupling the core business logic from external concerns, and the Repository Pattern provides a standardized approach to data access. Choosing the right architectural pattern depends on the specific requirements, constraints, and goals of the application, requiring a thoughtful and informed decision-making process during the design phase.

Discussion on microservices and their impact on distributed system design.

Microservices have emerged as a transformative architectural paradigm, significantly impacting the design and development of distributed systems. Unlike traditional monolithic architectures where all components are tightly coupled into a single unit, microservices architecture advocates for the decomposition of applications into small, independently deployable services. Each microservice encapsulates a specific business capability and communicates with others through well-defined APIs, fostering modularity, agility, and scalability.

One of the central tenets of microservices architecture is the principle of service autonomy. Each microservice operates as an independent entity, with its own database and business logic. This autonomy enables teams to develop, deploy, and scale services independently, fostering rapid and decentralized development. This stands in contrast to monolithic systems, where changes to one component often require retesting and redeploying the entire application, impeding agility and innovation.

The modular nature of microservices facilitates continuous integration and continuous deployment (CI/CD) practices. Teams can develop, test, and deploy microservices independently, allowing for more frequent and granular updates. This accelerates the release cycle, enabling organizations to respond rapidly to changing requirements and market dynamics. Additionally, the ability to scale individual microservices independently enhances resource utilization and cost-effectiveness, as organizations can allocate resources based on specific service demands rather than the overall application's requirements.

Microservices architecture also aligns well with cloud computing and containerization technologies. Containers, such as Docker, provide a lightweight and consistent environment for deploying microservices, simplifying the deployment process and promoting consistency across different stages of the software development lifecycle. Cloud-native infrastructure further complements microservices, offering scalable and dynamic resources that adapt to the varying demands of microservices-based applications.

While microservices bring significant advantages, they introduce unique challenges to distributed system design. One critical challenge is managing the complexity of interactions between microservices. As the number of microservices grows, orchestrating their communication, ensuring data consistency, and maintaining system-wide coherence become intricate tasks. Designing effective communication patterns, employing service discovery mechanisms, and implementing resilient communication strategies are essential aspects of addressing this challenge.

Distributed transactions pose another challenge in microservices architecture. In a monolithic system, transactions often involve operations on a single database, ensuring atomicity, consistency, isolation, and durability (ACID). However, in a microservices environment, transactions may span multiple services with their independent databases. Achieving consistency across distributed transactions becomes complex, necessitating the implementation of distributed transaction management mechanisms. Two-phase commit protocols, compensation transactions, and eventual consistency models are among the strategies employed to address this challenge.

Ensuring data consistency in microservices architecture is a nuanced task. As each microservice manages its own data, maintaining consistency across the system becomes a distributed coordination challenge. Event-driven architectures, eventual consistency models, and strategies like CQRS (Command Query Responsibility Segregation) are commonly employed to manage data consistency. These approaches prioritize responsiveness and partition tolerance, acknowledging that achieving immediate consistency across all microservices may be impractical.

Service discovery and load balancing are critical components in a microservices ecosystem. With services dynamically scaling up or down, the ability to discover and connect to available instances becomes crucial. Service discovery mechanisms, often integrated with container orchestration platforms like Kubernetes, enable dynamic updates to service locations. Load balancing ensures efficient distribution of incoming requests across multiple service instances, preventing individual microservices from becoming overloaded.

Microservices security is a paramount concern in distributed system design. The decentralized nature of microservices, with each service potentially exposed to the external network, necessitates robust security measures. Implementing secure communication channels, enforcing access controls, and managing authentication and authorization across multiple services are critical aspects of microservices security. Additionally, the adoption of API gateways and identity management solutions enhances security by providing a centralized point for managing and enforcing security policies.

Observability and monitoring are indispensable in microservices architecture. With numerous independent services contributing to the overall system functionality, detecting, diagnosing, and resolving issues become challenging. Advanced monitoring tools, logging, and centralized observability platforms are essential for gaining insights into the performance, health, and behavior of individual microservices. This visibility aids in identifying bottlenecks, detecting failures, and optimizing the overall system.

Despite these challenges, the benefits of microservices architecture have led many organizations to adopt this paradigm, particularly in dynamic and rapidly evolving environments. The modularity, scalability, and agility provided by microservices empower organizations to innovate, scale, and respond to market changes with unprecedented speed. Furthermore, microservices architecture aligns well with modern development practices, such as DevOps, enabling seamless collaboration between development and operations teams and fostering a culture of continuous improvement.

In conclusion, microservices have significantly reshaped distributed system design, offering a modular, scalable, and agile approach to application development. The autonomy of microservices allows for independent development and deployment, fostering rapid innovation and adaptability. However, the challenges associated with communication complexity, distributed transactions, data consistency, security, and observability require careful consideration and thoughtful design decisions. As organizations continue to embrace microservices, finding a balance between the advantages and challenges is crucial for harnessing the full potential of this architectural paradigm.

Overview of different models such as client-server, peer-to-peer, and hybrid models.

The landscape of network architectures is diverse and dynamic, with various models designed to fulfill specific requirements and address particular challenges. The client-server model is a fundamental paradigm in distributed computing, characterized by the segregation of roles between clients and servers. In this model, clients, which can be individual devices or applications, make requests for services or resources, while servers respond to these requests by providing the necessary data or functionalities. This clear distinction facilitates scalability, centralized resource management, and a hierarchical structure that simplifies maintenance and updates. However, the client-server model also introduces potential bottlenecks at the server, and its dependency on continuous server availability can impact the overall system's robustness.

Contrasting with the client-server model is the peer-to-peer (P2P) model, which decentralizes the architecture by allowing all participating nodes, or peers, to act both as clients and servers. Peers collaborate by directly sharing resources, services, or information with one another, without relying on a central server. P2P networks are often associated with file-sharing systems, where each peer can contribute and retrieve data. This model inherently supports scalability, fault tolerance, and resilience, as the network's strength increases with the number of participating peers. However, managing security, maintaining consistency, and ensuring efficient resource utilization in P2P networks pose challenges, particularly as the scale of the network grows.

The hybrid model combines elements of both client-server and peer-to-peer architectures to leverage their respective advantages. In a hybrid model, certain components or functions may be centralized in a client-server fashion, while others operate in a peer-to-peer manner. This amalgamation allows for a flexible and adaptable architecture that can accommodate diverse requirements within a single system. For instance, a hybrid cloud infrastructure may have centralized servers for critical processing tasks while incorporating peer-to-peer communication for data sharing among distributed nodes. This hybrid approach seeks to optimize the benefits of both models while mitigating their individual limitations.

Within the client-server model, variations exist that cater to specific needs. The three-tier architecture is a noteworthy extension, segregating the system into presentation, application, and data tiers. This design promotes modularity, flexibility, and easier maintenance. The presentation tier handles user interfaces, the application tier manages business logic, and the data tier is responsible for data storage and retrieval. This tiered approach enhances scalability and supports the development of distributed systems. However, it may introduce complexity and potential bottlenecks in communication between tiers.

Another crucial model is the microservices architecture, an evolution of the client-server model that emphasizes the development and deployment of small, independently deployable services. Microservices encapsulate specific business functionalities and communicate through well-defined APIs. This model enhances modularity, accelerates development cycles, and facilitates continuous integration and deployment practices. The autonomy of microservices enables independent scaling, fault isolation, and adaptability to diverse technologies. However, managing the interactions between microservices and ensuring data consistency in a distributed environment present notable challenges.

The characteristics of each architectural model contribute to its suitability for different scenarios and applications. The client-server model, with its centralized structure, often finds application in scenarios where control, security, and ease of maintenance are paramount. The peer-to-peer model excels in scenarios where decentralization, scalability, and fault tolerance are essential, such as in distributed file-sharing systems or certain blockchain networks. Hybrid models offer a middle ground, allowing organizations to strike a balance between centralized control and decentralized collaboration, catering to specific needs within a unified framework.

In conclusion, the diverse landscape of network architectures, encompassing client-server, peer-to-peer, and hybrid models, reflects the need for adaptable solutions in the ever-evolving realm of distributed computing. Each model brings unique strengths and trade-offs, with considerations for scalability, fault tolerance, security, and adaptability shaping their applicability. As technology continues to advance, the choice of architectural model becomes a critical decision, influencing the efficiency, resilience, and success of distributed systems in various domains.

Exploring the characteristics and use cases for each model.

The characteristics and use cases of various architectural models play a pivotal role in shaping the design and deployment of distributed systems. The client-server model, a foundational paradigm in distributed computing, is characterized by a clear separation of roles between clients and servers. Clients initiate requests for services or resources, and servers respond by providing the requested data or functionalities. This model exhibits a hierarchical structure that simplifies maintenance, scalability, and centralized resource management. Common use cases for the client-server model include web applications, where clients interact with central servers to retrieve dynamic content, and enterprise systems, where centralized databases manage and distribute data to multiple clients. The clear division of responsibilities facilitates efficient resource utilization and supports a variety of client types, making it suitable for diverse applications.

Contrastingly, the peer-to-peer (P2P) model decentralizes the architecture by allowing all participating nodes, or peers, to act as both clients and servers. Peers collaborate by directly sharing resources, services, or information without relying on a central server. The P2P model exhibits characteristics of scalability, fault tolerance, and resilience, making it well-suited for scenarios where the strength of the network increases with the number of participating peers. File-sharing systems, such as BitTorrent, exemplify P2P use cases, where peers contribute and retrieve data directly from one another, reducing dependence on central servers. Additionally, certain blockchain networks adopt a P2P approach, enabling distributed consensus and decentralization in validating transactions across nodes.

The hybrid model combines elements of both client-server and peer-to-peer architectures, offering a flexible and adaptable approach. This hybridization allows for a more nuanced design that can accommodate diverse requirements within a single system. Cloud computing exemplifies a common use case for the hybrid model, where centralized servers manage critical processing tasks, while peer-to-peer communication may be employed for data sharing among distributed nodes. Hybrid models enable organizations to optimize the benefits of both client-server and P2P architectures while mitigating their individual limitations, offering a tailored solution that aligns with specific use cases and operational needs.

Within the client-server model, the three-tier architecture introduces additional layers, further refining the distribution of responsibilities. The presentation tier handles user interfaces, the application tier manages business logic, and the data tier is responsible for data storage and retrieval. This tiered approach enhances modularity, flexibility, and ease of maintenance. Use cases for the three-tier architecture span across various domains, including web development, where the separation of concerns simplifies development and facilitates independent scaling of each tier. Enterprise applications, such as customer relationship management (CRM) systems, benefit from the modular structure of three-tier architecture, allowing for easier updates and scalability.

Microservices architecture represents an evolution of the client-server model, emphasizing the development and deployment of small, independently deployable services. Each microservice encapsulates specific business capabilities and communicates through well-defined APIs. The autonomy of microservices enables independent scaling, fault isolation, and adaptability to diverse technologies, making them well-suited for use cases requiring agility and rapid development cycles. Cloud-native applications often adopt microservices, enabling continuous integration and deployment practices. E-commerce platforms, content management systems, and online banking applications leverage microservices to manage specific functionalities independently, contributing to easier maintenance, updates, and scaling.

Each architectural model comes with its strengths and trade-offs, aligning with specific characteristics that make them suitable for particular use cases. The centralized nature of the client-server model is advantageous in scenarios where control, security, and ease of maintenance are paramount. Its hierarchical structure and clear separation of roles make it applicable to a broad range of applications, from web development to enterprise systems. Peer-to-peer models excel in decentralized scenarios where scalability, fault tolerance, and resilience are essential. File-sharing systems, blockchain networks, and certain collaborative applications benefit from the inherently distributed nature of P2P architectures.

Hybrid models find their place in scenarios where a balanced approach is required, combining the advantages of both client-server and peer-to-peer architectures. Cloud computing, with its centralized servers for critical tasks and distributed nodes for data sharing, exemplifies the adaptability of hybrid models to diverse requirements. Three-tier architecture refines the client-server model, introducing modularity and ease of maintenance, making it suitable for web development and enterprise applications. Microservices architecture, with its emphasis on independence and agility, meets the demands of modern cloud-native applications, such as e-commerce platforms and content management systems.

In conclusion, the exploration of architectural models reveals a nuanced landscape where characteristics and use cases play a crucial role in guiding the design choices of distributed systems. The client-server model, peer-to-peer model, hybrid model, three-tier architecture, and microservices architecture each contribute to the diversity of approaches, addressing specific needs and challenges across various domains. As technology continues to advance, the selection of an appropriate architectural model becomes a strategic decision, shaping the efficiency, resilience, and success of distributed systems in evolving and dynamic environments.

The role of communication in distributed systems.

Communication is the lifeblood of distributed systems, serving as the vital conduit through which diverse components, nodes, or processes collaborate to achieve common objectives. The complexity and scale of distributed systems necessitate effective communication mechanisms to enable seamless coordination, data exchange, and collaborative computation. At its core, communication in distributed systems involves the exchange of messages or information among entities, transcending geographical or logical boundaries. The role of communication is multifaceted, influencing the system's architecture, performance, fault tolerance, and overall functionality.

In the realm of distributed systems, one of the primary objectives of communication is to facilitate the coordination and synchronization of activities among disparate components. Whether it be nodes in a network, microservices in a cloud-native application, or processes in a parallel computing environment, effective communication ensures that these entities operate in concert to achieve shared goals. Coordination mechanisms such as message passing, remote procedure calls (RPC), and publish-subscribe systems enable entities to exchange information, update states, and collectively progress towards the desired outcomes. This collaborative communication is essential for the success of distributed systems, as it orchestrates the flow of information and actions across the distributed landscape.

Furthermore, communication plays a pivotal role in ensuring data consistency and integrity within distributed systems. As data is distributed across multiple nodes or components, maintaining a coherent and consistent view of information becomes a critical challenge. Consistency models, such as strong consistency, eventual consistency, or causal consistency, guide the design of communication protocols to align with specific application requirements. The trade-offs between consistency and availability, often encapsulated in the CAP theorem (Consistency, Availability, Partition tolerance), underscore the importance of thoughtful communication strategies in achieving the desired balance based on the system's objectives and constraints.

In the context of fault tolerance, communication becomes a linchpin in mitigating the impact of failures within distributed systems. Redundancy, replication, and distributed consensus mechanisms rely on effective communication to detect and respond to faults. The ability of distributed nodes to communicate and reach a consensus, even in the presence of failures or network partitions, contributes to the resilience of the system. Protocols like the Raft consensus algorithm or the Paxos protocol exemplify the intricate communication patterns that underpin fault-tolerant distributed systems, ensuring that the system can continue to operate even when individual components experience failures.

Scalability, a fundamental requirement in modern distributed systems, is intricately linked to communication efficiency. The ability to scale horizontally by adding more nodes or components hinges on the system's communication infrastructure. Scalable communication patterns, such as sharding, partitioning, or load balancing, distribute the workload across multiple entities, preventing bottlenecks and optimizing resource utilization. Additionally, communication protocols that support parallelism and asynchronous interactions contribute to the scalability of distributed systems, enabling them to handle increasing workloads and adapt to changing demands.

Security is another crucial aspect of communication in distributed systems. The inherently open and interconnected nature of distributed environments exposes them to potential security threats, ranging from unauthorized access to data interception and malicious attacks. Secure communication protocols, encryption mechanisms, and authentication mechanisms are imperative to safeguard sensitive information and ensure the confidentiality and integrity of messages. As distributed systems often span across networks with varying levels of trust, securing communication channels becomes paramount to prevent unauthorized access and protect against potential vulnerabilities.

Real-time responsiveness and adaptability are key drivers for the design of communication in distributed systems. Applications such as online gaming, financial trading platforms, or collaborative editing tools demand low-latency communication to provide users with a seamless and interactive experience. Messaging patterns like publish-subscribe or event-driven architectures enable real-time communication, allowing distributed components to react promptly to changes or events. Adaptive communication protocols, which dynamically adjust to varying network conditions, contribute to the resilience of distributed systems, ensuring that they can deliver optimal performance in dynamic and unpredictable environments.

The advent of cloud computing further underscores the significance of communication in distributed systems. Cloud-native architectures leverage distributed communication patterns to harness the power of elastic scalability, allowing applications to dynamically scale resources up or down based on demand. Communication between microservices, a core tenet of cloud-native design, enables the development of modular and independently deployable services. Application Programming Interfaces (APIs), another facet of communication in the cloud, provide standardized interfaces for diverse services to interact, fostering interoperability and enabling the composition of complex distributed systems from modular building blocks.

In conclusion, communication stands as the linchpin in the intricate tapestry of distributed systems, influencing their architecture, performance, fault tolerance, and overall functionality. The collaborative nature of distributed systems relies on effective communication to synchronize activities, maintain data consistency, and facilitate fault tolerance. As scalability, security, real-time responsiveness, and adaptability become increasingly crucial in modern distributed systems, the design and implementation of communication mechanisms play a pivotal role in shaping the success and resilience of these complex and interconnected environments. Thoughtful consideration of communication patterns, protocols, and security measures is essential for architects and developers seeking to navigate the intricate landscape of distributed systems in a rapidly evolving technological landscape.

Understanding message-passing and remote procedure call (RPC) mechanisms.

Message-passing and Remote Procedure Call (RPC) mechanisms are fundamental communication paradigms that play a pivotal role in distributed computing, enabling interactions between different entities, processes, or systems. Message-passing is a communication model where entities communicate by sending and receiving messages. Each entity, often referred to as a process or node, can independently execute its tasks and communicates with others by exchanging messages. This model fosters decentralization and asynchronous communication, allowing entities to operate independently while coordinating through message exchanges. Message-passing is commonly used in various distributed systems, including message-oriented middleware, publish-subscribe systems, and actor-based concurrency models.

In the context of message-passing, one prominent model is the Actor model. In this model, entities called actors encapsulate both state and behavior, and communication occurs through the exchange of messages. Actors can create new actors, send messages to other actors, and modify their own internal state upon receiving messages. This model promotes modularity, as actors can operate independently, communicating solely through messages, and encapsulating their state. The Actor model is used in systems like Erlang and Akka, providing a scalable and fault-tolerant approach to distributed computing. Message-passing, in the context of the Actor model, offers a natural way to express concurrency and parallelism, allowing actors to communicate without shared state and minimizing the need for locks and synchronization mechanisms.

On the other hand, Remote Procedure Call (RPC) mechanisms provide a more procedural and synchronous approach to communication in distributed systems. RPC allows a program or process to invoke procedures or functions on a remote server as if they were local, abstracting the complexities of distributed communication. This paradigm simplifies the development of distributed applications, making it appear as if the invocation of a remote function is the same as calling a local one. Underlying the abstraction of RPC is the serialization of function parameters, transmission of the request to the remote server, execution of the function, and the return of results.

Technologies like gRPC and XML-RPC exemplify the use of RPC mechanisms in distributed systems.

Message-passing and RPC mechanisms cater to different communication requirements and scenarios. Message-passing, with its asynchronous and decentralized nature, is well-suited for systems that emphasize loose coupling, fault tolerance, and scalability. In scenarios where components operate independently, exchanging messages to achieve coordination or to share information, message-passing becomes an effective and natural choice. This approach aligns well with event-driven architectures and is often employed in systems that prioritize responsiveness and adaptability to dynamic conditions.

RPC mechanisms, with their synchronous and procedural nature, are advantageous in scenarios where a more tightly coupled and procedural interaction is required between distributed components. The abstraction provided by RPC allows developers to design and implement distributed applications with a familiar, function-call-like interface, making it easier to reason about the distributed behavior of the system. RPC is often used in situations where the distributed components need to collaborate in a more tightly coordinated manner, such as in client-server architectures or when integrating different services in a distributed environment.

One challenge in distributed systems is dealing with failures and ensuring robust communication. In message-passing systems, failure detection and recovery mechanisms become crucial, as entities may fail independently, and ensuring message delivery in the face of node failures requires careful design. Techniques like acknowledgments, retries, and distributed consensus protocols are often employed. In RPC systems, fault tolerance mechanisms need to consider issues such as network failures, server crashes, and idempotency of operations. Transactional models and approaches like the idempotent

RPC design pattern are used to enhance the resilience of RPC-based systems.

The choice between message-passing and RPC depends on the specific requirements and characteristics of the distributed system. Message-passing is favored in scenarios where a more decentralized, asynchronous, and loosely coupled interaction is desired. It aligns well with event-driven architectures, microservices communication, and scenarios where fault tolerance and scalability are paramount. RPC, on the other hand, provides a more structured, synchronous, and procedural approach, making it suitable for scenarios where a more tightly coordinated interaction is required, such as in traditional client-server architectures, tightly coupled systems, or when a simple and familiar programming model is preferred.

As distributed systems evolve and adopt new architectural paradigms, the lines between message-passing and RPC mechanisms can blur. Modern frameworks often combine elements of both paradigms to provide a holistic approach to communication. For example, gRPC, a remote procedure call framework, incorporates features such as bidirectional streaming and support for different serialization formats, embracing some aspects of message-passing. Similarly, actor-based systems may incorporate RPC-like mechanisms to enable more procedural communication between actors when needed.

In conclusion, message-passing and RPC mechanisms represent two fundamental approaches to communication in distributed systems, each catering to specific requirements and scenarios. Message-passing excels in asynchronous, decentralized, and fault-tolerant systems, promoting loose coupling and scalability. RPC, with its synchronous and procedural nature, simplifies the development of tightly coordinated interactions in distributed applications. The choice between these mechanisms depends on the architectural goals, communication patterns, and system requirements, showcas-

ing the versatility and adaptability required in the diverse landscape
of distributed computing.

Chapter 2: Networked Architectures: A Deep Dive

Basics of computer networking and its relevance to distributed systems.

Computer networking serves as the backbone of modern communication and connectivity, forming the foundation for a wide array of applications and services. At its core, networking involves the interconnection of computers and devices, enabling them to exchange data, share resources, and collaborate. The relevance of computer networking to distributed systems is profound, as distributed systems leverage networking principles to facilitate seamless communication and cooperation among distributed entities. The basics of computer networking encompass a spectrum of concepts, including protocols, topologies, addressing, and communication models, each playing a crucial role in the design, implementation, and functionality of distributed systems.

Protocols form the cornerstone of computer networking, defining the rules and conventions governing communication between devices. The Internet Protocol Suite, commonly known as TCP/IP, is a fundamental set of protocols that underpins the global network infrastructure. TCP/IP encompasses protocols such as Transmission Control Protocol (TCP) and Internet Protocol (IP), providing reliable, connection-oriented communication and addressing, respectively. These protocols facilitate end-to-end communication over networks, ensuring that data is transmitted reliably, and devices can be identified and addressed. In distributed systems, adherence to communication protocols is vital, as it establishes a common language and set of rules that enable disparate components to exchange information seamlessly.

The topology of a network defines the physical or logical arrangement of its components and their interconnections. Common topologies include star, bus, ring, and mesh, each with its advantages and limitations. In the context of distributed systems, the network topology influences the communication patterns and fault tolerance. For example, a mesh topology, where each node is connected to every other node, can enhance fault tolerance by providing multiple communication paths. Understanding and selecting an appropriate network topology is crucial for distributed systems architects, as it directly impacts the reliability, scalability, and performance of the distributed infrastructure.

Addressing plays a pivotal role in networking by providing a means to uniquely identify devices on a network. In the context of the Internet, devices are assigned IP addresses, enabling them to communicate across the global network. IP addresses are structured hierarchically, with each device having a unique combination of network and host identifiers. The Domain Name System (DNS) complements IP addressing by mapping human-readable domain names to IP addresses, simplifying the process of locating resources on the internet. In distributed systems, addressing is a critical aspect as it enables entities to locate and communicate with each other across a network, fostering connectivity and collaboration.

Communication models in computer networking dictate how data is exchanged between devices. Two fundamental communication models are often cited: connection-oriented and connectionless. In a connection-oriented model, exemplified by TCP, a reliable and ordered connection is established before data transfer, ensuring that data arrives intact and in the correct order. In contrast, a connectionless model, as seen in the User Datagram Protocol (UDP), involves sending data without prior setup, providing a more lightweight and faster approach at the cost of potential data loss. The choice between these models depends on the requirements of the distributed system, balancing factors like reliability, latency, and overhead.

The advent of the Internet has transformed computer networking into a ubiquitous and essential component of everyday life. The relevance of networking to distributed systems becomes apparent when considering the evolution of computing paradigms. Traditional monolithic applications have given way to distributed systems, where computing resources are distributed across multiple nodes or devices. Cloud computing, a cornerstone of contemporary distributed systems, relies heavily on networking infrastructure to provide on-demand access to shared computing resources. Networking technologies like Virtual Private Clouds (VPCs), Software-Defined Networking (SDN), and Content Delivery Networks (CDNs) contribute to the scalability, flexibility, and efficiency of distributed systems in the cloud.

One of the key principles in distributed systems is the concept of transparency, wherein the underlying complexities of the distributed environment are abstracted from end-users and applications. Network transparency, a subset of this principle, ensures that the distribution of resources and communication details are hidden from the applications. This allows applications to operate as if they were running on a single, non-distributed machine. Achieving network transparency involves mechanisms like Remote Procedure Call (RPC) and middleware layers that abstract the intricacies of distributed communication. Networking protocols and technologies enable this abstraction by providing a reliable and standardized foundation for communication in distributed systems.

The relevance of computer networking to distributed systems extends to the challenges and considerations inherent in distributed computing. Latency, bandwidth, and network congestion become critical factors in the performance of distributed systems. Efficient communication protocols and strategies, such as caching, compression, and load balancing, are employed to optimize data transfer and minimize delays. Network security is paramount, with encryption, authentication, and intrusion detection mechanisms safeguarding sensitive information transmitted across distributed networks. As the scale of distributed systems grows, the design of efficient and fault-tolerant communication becomes increasingly intricate, demanding a deep understanding of networking principles.

The concept of the Internet of Things (IoT) further underscores the importance of networking in distributed systems. IoT involves the interconnection of everyday devices, ranging from household appliances to industrial machinery, creating a vast network of interconnected entities. Networking protocols like MQTT (Message Queuing Telemetry Transport) and CoAP (Constrained Application Protocol) facilitate communication in IoT environments. The distributed nature of IoT systems relies heavily on networking to enable seamless communication between devices, collect data from sensors, and facilitate real-time decision-making. Networking technologies, such as 5G, play a pivotal role in providing the necessary connectivity and bandwidth to support the massive scale and diverse requirements of IoT deployments.

In conclusion, the basics of computer networking form an indispensable foundation for the design, implementation, and operation of distributed systems. Protocols, topologies, addressing, and communication models define the landscape of networking, providing the essential framework for entities in distributed systems to communicate and collaborate. The evolution of networking technologies, driven by the growth of the internet, cloud computing, and IoT, highlights the ever-increasing relevance of networking in the field of distributed computing. As distributed systems continue to shape the landscape of modern computing, a deep understanding of networking principles remains essential for architects, developers, and administrators navigating the complexities of distributed environments.

Understanding protocols, IP addressing, and subnetting.

Protocols, IP addressing, and subnetting are fundamental concepts in computer networking, collectively forming the backbone of communication within and between networks. Protocols serve as the set of rules and conventions that govern the exchange of data between devices. In the realm of networking, the Internet Protocol (IP) is a cornerstone protocol, facilitating the identification and communication between devices in a network. IP is a connectionless and packet-switched protocol, designed to handle the routing and addressing of data packets. It forms the basis of the Internet Protocol Suite, commonly known as TCP/IP, which encompasses a suite of protocols such as Transmission Control Protocol (TCP), User Datagram Protocol (UDP), and Internet Control Message Protocol (ICMP). TCP provides reliable, connection-oriented communication, while UDP offers a lightweight, connectionless alternative suitable for scenarios where low latency is prioritized over reliability.

IP addressing is a fundamental aspect of networking, providing a means to uniquely identify and locate devices within a network. IP addresses are numerical labels assigned to each device participating in a network that uses the Internet Protocol for communication. IPv4 (Internet Protocol version 4) is the most widely used IP addressing scheme and is expressed as a series of four decimal numbers separated by dots, each ranging from 0 to 255. For example, an IPv4 address might look like 192.168.1.1. IPv6 (Internet Protocol version 6) is the successor to IPv4 and addresses the limitations of IPv4 by using a longer 128-bit address space, allowing for a vastly larger number of unique addresses. IPv6 addresses are typically represented in hexadecimal format and may look like 2001:0db8:85a3:0000:0000:8a2e:0370:7334.

Subnetting is a technique employed in IP networking to divide a larger network into smaller, more manageable sub-networks or subnets. This is particularly valuable for efficient address space utilization and improved network organization. Subnetting involves borrowing bits from the host portion of an IP address to create sub-networks, allowing network administrators to allocate address space more granularly based on organizational needs. Subnet masks are used to determine which portion of an IP address represents the network and which portion represents the host. For instance, in a subnet mask of 255.255.255.0, the first 24 bits represent the network, and the remaining 8 bits represent hosts within that network. Subnetting enhances network security, optimizes traffic flow, and facilitates efficient utilization of IP addresses.

Understanding IP addressing and subnetting is crucial for network administrators and architects to design and manage networks effectively. Classless Inter-Domain Routing (CIDR) is an extension of IP addressing that allows for more flexible allocation of IP addresses by specifying the number of bits used for the network and host portions. CIDR notation, such as 192.168.1.0/24, indicates both the network address and the subnet mask, providing a concise representation of IP address assignments. This notation is widely used in routing tables and network planning.

Dynamic Host Configuration Protocol (DHCP) is another essential protocol that simplifies the management of IP addresses within a network. DHCP automates the process of assigning IP addresses to devices, eliminating the need for manual configuration. DHCP servers dynamically allocate IP addresses to devices when they join a network, ensuring efficient use of available addresses and simplifying network administration. This is particularly beneficial in large networks where manual IP address assignment would be impractical.

Furthermore, Network Address Translation (NAT) is a technique used to manage the shortage of public IP addresses. NAT allows multiple devices within a private network to share a single public IP address when communicating with external networks, such as the internet. NAT translates private IP addresses to a public address when data leaves the private network and performs the reverse translation when data returns. This method extends the usability of the limited IPv4 address space and enhances network security by concealing internal network structures.

The concept of subnetting and IP addressing is crucial when designing and implementing Virtual Local Area Networks (VLANs), which are used to segment a larger physical network into multiple logically isolated networks. VLANs provide the flexibility to group devices logically based on criteria such as department or function, facilitating improved network management, security, and efficiency. VLANs are often employed in enterprise networks to enhance scalability and security.

In conclusion, protocols, IP addressing, and subnetting are foundational elements in computer networking that enable the seamless and efficient communication of devices within and between networks. Protocols, such as the Internet Protocol Suite, establish the rules for data exchange, while IP addressing provides a unique identification mechanism for devices. Subnetting refines IP addressing, allowing for efficient address space utilization and improved network organization. DHCP automates IP address assignment, NAT addresses the scarcity of public IP addresses, and VLANs enhance network segmentation and management. Mastery of these concepts is essential for network administrators and architects to design, implement, and manage robust and scalable networks in the dynamic landscape of modern computing.

In-depth exploration of the client-server architectural pattern.

The client-server architectural pattern is a fundamental and widely employed paradigm in the design and implementation of distributed systems, orchestrating the interaction between two distinct entities: the client and the server. This model delineates the roles and responsibilities of each component, fostering a structured approach to distributed computing. At its core, the client-server pattern embodies a division of labor, where clients initiate requests for services or resources, and servers respond by providing the requested data or functionalities. This clear separation of concerns enables modularity, scalability, and ease of maintenance, forming the basis for a diverse array of applications and services.

The client, in the client-server model, represents the end-user interface or application that interacts with the system. Clients are responsible for initiating requests, processing responses, and presenting information to users in a human-readable format. Clients can take various forms, ranging from traditional desktop applications to web browsers, mobile apps, or even other servers acting as clients in more complex architectures. The client-side logic is typically focused on user interactions, input validation, and rendering the user interface, abstracting away the intricacies of data retrieval and processing, which are delegated to the server.

On the other side of the equation, the server in the client-server architecture serves as the central repository of resources, data, or processing capabilities. Servers handle incoming requests from clients, execute the necessary operations, and furnish the results or data back to the requesting clients. The server-side logic is responsible for processing requests, interacting with databases or other external resources, and encapsulating the business logic of the application. This centralized approach streamlines the management and maintenance of the application, as updates or changes can be implemented on the server without requiring modifications on individual client devices.

Communication between clients and servers in the client-server model relies on well-defined protocols, often leveraging standard communication protocols like HTTP, HTTPS, or custom protocols designed for specific applications. The use of standardized communication protocols facilitates interoperability and allows clients and servers to be implemented using different technologies or platforms. The client initiates a request, which includes information about the desired operation or resource, and the server responds accordingly. This interaction may involve simple data retrieval, complex computations, or the execution of business processes, depending on the nature of the application.

One notable advantage of the client-server architecture is its scalability. The modular separation of clients and servers allows for the independent scaling of these components based on demand. As the user base or workload increases, additional servers can be deployed to handle the growing number of client requests. This scalability is particularly advantageous in scenarios where the client workload is unpredictable or experiences significant fluctuations, as resources can be allocated dynamically to meet changing demands. Cloud computing further amplifies the scalability of client-server architectures by providing flexible and on-demand resources.

Security considerations are paramount in the client-server model, especially when dealing with sensitive data or critical operations. Authentication mechanisms, such as username-password pairs, tokens, or certificates, are commonly employed to verify the identity of clients and ensure that only authorized users access the server's resources. Encryption, through protocols like SSL/TLS, is utilized to secure the communication channel between clients and servers, preventing eavesdropping or tampering with data during transmission. Additionally, access controls and authorization mechanisms are implemented on the server to regulate which clients can perform specific operations or access particular resources.

Client-server architectures find application in a myriad of domains and industries. Web applications, a ubiquitous example, leverage the client-server model with browsers acting as clients and web servers delivering content and processing requests. Database management systems embody the client-server pattern, where client applications interact with database servers to retrieve or modify data. File servers, email servers, and content delivery networks (CDNs) all rely on the client-server architecture to distribute resources efficiently and respond to diverse client demands.

The evolution of the client-server model has seen variations and refinements, including the introduction of multi-tier architectures. Three-tier architectures, in particular, expand on the traditional client-server model by introducing an intermediary application or service layer, often referred to as the middleware or business logic layer. This three-tier structure segregates the client-side user interface, the server-side application logic, and the data storage or retrieval functionality. This separation enhances modularity, scalability, and maintainability, with each tier focused on specific aspects of the application's functionality.

Despite its numerous advantages, the client-server architecture is not without challenges. One notable concern is the potential for bottlenecking at the server, especially in scenarios where a large number of clients simultaneously request resources or services. Load balancing techniques, such as distributing incoming requests across multiple servers, help alleviate this challenge by ensuring a more even distribution of workload. Additionally, issues related to network latency and responsiveness may arise, particularly when clients are geographically distant from the server. Content delivery networks (CDNs) and caching mechanisms are often employed to mitigate these challenges, optimizing the delivery of content to clients.

In conclusion, the client-server architectural pattern stands as a cornerstone in the landscape of distributed systems, providing a structured and modular approach to designing and deploying applications. Its division of labor between clients and servers enables scalability, ease of maintenance, and centralized management of resources. Standardized communication protocols facilitate interoperability, while security mechanisms safeguard sensitive data. The adaptability of the client-server model, evident in its various implementations across web applications, databases, and distributed systems, underscores its enduring relevance in the dynamic and evolving realm of modern computing.

Role of servers and clients in distributed systems.

In distributed systems, the roles of servers and clients are fundamental, shaping the architecture, functionality, and interactions within the distributed environment. Servers and clients represent two distinct entities that collaborate to achieve shared goals, and understanding their roles is crucial for designing, implementing, and maintaining effective distributed systems.

Servers play a central role in distributed systems, serving as repositories of resources, data, or services. These resources could range from databases, files, computational power, to specific functionalities or business logic. Servers are responsible for handling incoming requests from clients, executing the necessary operations, and providing responses or delivering data back to the clients. The server-side logic encompasses the processing of requests, interaction with databases or external resources, and encapsulation of the core business logic of the distributed application. The centralized nature of servers enhances the manageability and maintenance of the system, as updates or changes can be implemented on the server without necessitating modifications on individual client devices.

The server's role extends beyond mere data storage; it includes the facilitation of communication and coordination among clients. In client-server architectures, servers act as authoritative entities, validating requests, enforcing security measures, and orchestrating the flow of information. For example, in a web application, the server receives HTTP requests from clients, processes them, and returns HTML, CSS, or other data to be rendered on the client-side. Servers may also implement caching mechanisms to optimize responses and alleviate potential bottlenecks, enhancing the overall performance of distributed systems.

Security is a critical aspect of the server's responsibilities. Servers must authenticate clients to ensure that only authorized entities access resources or services. Authentication mechanisms, such as user-name-password pairs, tokens, or certificates, are commonly employed to verify the identity of clients. Once authenticated, servers enforce access controls and authorization mechanisms to regulate which clients can perform specific operations or access particular resources. Encryption, through protocols like SSL/TLS, is utilized to secure the communication channel between clients and servers, preventing eavesdropping or tampering with data during transmission.

Furthermore, servers in distributed systems often incorporate fault tolerance mechanisms to ensure continuous operation even in the face of failures. Redundancy, replication, and distributed consensus protocols contribute to the resilience of server-side components, allowing the system to maintain functionality and data consistency despite individual server failures. The ability to detect and recover from faults, such as server crashes or network partitions, is crucial for the reliability of distributed systems.

Clients, in contrast, represent the end-user interface or application that interacts with the distributed system. Clients initiate requests for services, resources, or data from servers, process the responses, and present information to users in a human-readable format. Clients can take various forms, including traditional desktop applications, web browsers, mobile apps, or even other servers acting as clients in more complex architectures. The client-side logic focuses on user interactions, input validation, and rendering the user interface, abstracting away the intricacies of data retrieval and processing, which are delegated to the server.

The client's primary responsibility is to provide a user-friendly interface and experience. In graphical user interfaces (GUIs), clients render visual elements, collect user input, and convey relevant information to the users. In web applications, the client-side logic, often implemented using technologies like HTML, CSS, and JavaScript, enables dynamic and interactive user interfaces. Client applications must be responsive, providing timely feedback to user actions and ensuring a smooth and seamless experience.

Clients may also cache data locally to optimize performance and reduce the need for repeated requests to the server. Caching mechanisms on the client side can enhance responsiveness and reduce the load on servers, especially in scenarios where data does not change frequently. However, careful consideration must be given to cache consistency to avoid presenting outdated or inconsistent information to users.

The diversity of clients in distributed systems introduces challenges related to heterogeneity and interoperability. Clients may run on different platforms, use various technologies, or have distinct capabilities. Ensuring that clients can effectively communicate with servers and other clients is essential for the overall success of distributed systems. Standardized communication protocols, such as HTTP or custom protocols designed for specific applications, play a vital role in enabling interoperability between diverse clients and servers.

In scenarios where clients need to interact with each other directly, without involving a central server, a peer-to-peer (P2P) architecture may be employed. In P2P systems, clients act both as consumers and providers of resources, collaborating in a decentralized manner. File sharing applications and certain communication platforms are examples where clients in a P2P architecture directly exchange data or services without relying on a central server.

Security considerations for clients involve protecting user data, ensuring secure communication with servers, and implementing measures to guard against client-side attacks. Techniques such as secure coding practices, encryption of sensitive information, and adherence to security best practices help mitigate potential vulnerabilities on the client side. Moreover, clients should be resistant to tampering and unauthorized access to prevent malicious activities that may compromise the integrity of the distributed system.

The roles of clients and servers in distributed systems are not strictly confined to simple binary relationships. Modern distributed systems often involve complex architectures with multiple layers and tiers, introducing intermediary components such as load balancers, middleware, and microservices. These components contribute to the overall functionality, scalability, and resilience of the distributed system, orchestrating the interactions between clients and servers in sophisticated ways.

In conclusion, the roles of servers and clients in distributed systems are integral to the design, functionality, and success of modern computing architectures. Servers serve as central repositories of resources and execute critical operations, while clients provide user interfaces, initiate requests, and present information to end-users. The collaborative interaction between clients and servers, governed by standardized communication protocols and security measures, underpins the effectiveness and reliability of distributed systems. As technology evolves, the roles of clients and servers continue to adapt, shaping the landscape of distributed computing in response to the growing demands for efficiency, scalability, and user-centric experiences.

Characteristics and advantages of peer-to-peer architectures.

Peer-to-peer (P2P) architectures represent a decentralized paradigm in distributed systems, where interconnected nodes collaborate on a peer-level to share resources, information, or services. The characteristics of P2P architectures fundamentally distinguish them from traditional client-server models, offering unique advantages that have contributed to their widespread adoption across various domains.

One key characteristic of P2P architectures is the absence of a central server or authority. In contrast to client-server models where a central server mediates communication and resource sharing, P2P systems enable direct interaction between peers. Each node in a P2P network has equal status, serving both as a consumer and provider of resources. This decentralized nature fosters resilience and scalability, as the system's functionality is not reliant on a single point of failure, and additional peers can join the network without imposing a significant burden on existing nodes.

Scalability is a notable advantage of P2P architectures, allowing networks to grow organically with an increasing number of nodes. As new peers join, they contribute their resources to the network, enhancing its capacity and capabilities. This dynamic scalability is particularly advantageous in scenarios where the size of the user base or the demand for resources is unpredictable or subject to significant fluctuations. P2P networks, through their decentralized structure, distribute the load across multiple nodes, mitigating the risk of bottlenecks and enhancing overall system performance.

P2P architectures excel in scenarios where resource discovery and distribution are distributed tasks. Traditional client-server models may encounter challenges when dealing with large-scale file sharing or content distribution, as the central server can become a point of congestion. P2P networks, on the other hand, distribute these tasks among peers, allowing each node to contribute to both the discovery and dissemination of resources. This approach leads to efficient resource utilization, reduced reliance on central infrastructure, and improved overall network responsiveness.

Flexibility and adaptability characterize P2P architectures, making them well-suited for dynamic and diverse environments. Peers can join or leave the network without disrupting the overall functionality, contributing to the system's fault tolerance and robustness. This inherent adaptability makes P2P architectures suitable for applications where nodes may enter or exit frequently, such as collaborative file sharing, streaming, or communication platforms.

Another notable characteristic of P2P architectures is their potential for self-organization. Peers in a P2P network can autonomously discover and establish connections with other nodes based on specific protocols or algorithms. This decentralized decision-making process reduces the need for centralized control and administration, facilitating the creation of ad-hoc networks where nodes can communicate and collaborate without relying on predefined structures. Self-organizing P2P systems demonstrate a high degree of resilience to changes in network topology and exhibit emergent behavior, where global properties of the network arise from local interactions among peers.

Security considerations play a crucial role in P2P architectures, and the decentralized nature of these systems can contribute to enhanced security in certain scenarios. The absence of a central point of attack reduces the impact of potential security breaches, making it more challenging for malicious actors to compromise the entire system. Additionally, the distributed nature of P2P networks can facilitate the implementation of privacy-preserving measures, as peers may have greater control over their data and interactions within the network. However, security in P2P architectures also presents challenges, such as the potential for malicious nodes, the need for robust authentication mechanisms, and the prevention of unauthorized access.

P2P architectures are particularly well-suited for applications requiring a high degree of resilience and fault tolerance. The decentralized nature of P2P networks ensures that no single point of failure can disrupt the entire system. In scenarios where reliability is paramount, such as in communication networks or file-sharing platforms, the redundancy and self-healing capabilities of P2P architectures provide a robust foundation.

The adaptability of P2P architectures extends to their use in content delivery and distribution. Peer-to-peer file sharing, for instance, leverages the collective resources of network participants to distribute large files efficiently. Popularized by protocols like BitTorrent, this approach allows users to download and upload parts of a file simultaneously, maximizing bandwidth utilization and reducing the load on centralized servers. P2P content distribution is particularly advantageous for scenarios where traditional server-based approaches may struggle to cope with high demand or face bandwidth limitations.

Collaborative applications, such as distributed databases or shared computing environments, benefit from the decentralized nature of P2P architectures. In collaborative settings, peers can contribute computational power, storage, or specific expertise, forming a distributed computing network. This collaboration enables the pooling of resources, making it possible to solve complex problems that would be challenging for individual nodes to tackle independently. P2P distributed computing platforms, like SETI@home, exemplify the potential for harnessing collective computing power for scientific research or data analysis.

The field of blockchain technology represents a notable application of P2P architectures, particularly in the context of decentralized ledgers and cryptocurrencies. Blockchain networks operate on a P2P model, where nodes (miners or validators) maintain a shared, decentralized ledger of transactions. Consensus mechanisms, such as proof-of-work or proof-of-stake, enable nodes to agree on the state of the ledger without the need for a central authority. The transparency, security, and decentralization offered by blockchain networks align with the core principles of P2P architectures, providing a tamper-resistant and distributed framework for digital transactions.

Despite the numerous advantages, P2P architectures also face challenges and limitations. One significant challenge is the potential for free-riding, where some peers consume resources without contributing adequately to the network. In scenarios like file sharing, this can lead to imbalances where certain files are readily available while others may be challenging to obtain. Mitigating free-riding often requires the implementation of incentives or reputation systems to encourage active participation.

In conclusion, peer-to-peer architectures embody a decentralized and collaborative approach to distributed systems, offering a range of advantages such as scalability, adaptability, fault tolerance, and enhanced security. These characteristics make P2P architectures well-suited for diverse applications, from file sharing and content distribution to collaborative computing and blockchain technology. The flexibility and resilience inherent in P2P systems contribute to their continued relevance in the ever-evolving landscape of distributed computing, where decentralized, self-organizing networks play a pivotal role in addressing the challenges of modern information exchange and collaboration.

Challenges in maintaining connectivity and data consistency.
Maintaining connectivity and ensuring data consistency pose significant challenges in distributed systems, where multiple nodes or components collaborate to provide a seamless and reliable computing environment. These challenges are inherent to the complexities introduced by the distribution of resources, the potential for network failures, and the need to synchronize data across disparate entities.

One of the primary challenges in maintaining connectivity lies in the dynamic and unpredictable nature of network environments. Networks, whether local or global, are subject to various factors such as latency, bandwidth limitations, packet loss, and intermittent connectivity issues. In distributed systems, where components may be geographically dispersed, ensuring a consistent and stable network connection between nodes becomes a non-trivial task. Network partitions, where communication between certain nodes is temporarily or permanently disrupted, can occur due to factors like network failures or geographic distances. Dealing with such partitions requires robust strategies to detect, handle, and recover from network disruptions, all while preserving the integrity of ongoing operations.

The scalability of distributed systems introduces another layer of complexity in maintaining connectivity. As the number of nodes in a system grows, the potential for increased network traffic and contention rises. Scalability challenges often manifest in scenarios where communication bottlenecks occur, leading to delays, timeouts, or degraded performance. Load balancing mechanisms are essential to distribute network traffic evenly across nodes, preventing individual nodes from becoming overwhelmed and ensuring a more uniform experience for users or applications. However, devising efficient load balancing strategies that adapt to changing network conditions and dynamically allocate resources is a continual challenge in maintaining connectivity.

Data consistency, or the assurance that all nodes in a distributed system agree on the current state of shared data, is a critical aspect of maintaining the integrity and reliability of distributed applications. Achieving data consistency becomes challenging due to factors such as concurrent updates, network delays, and the lack of a centralized authority to enforce consistency across all nodes. The trade-off between consistency and performance is a well-known challenge, often described by the CAP theorem (Consistency, Availability, Partition

Tolerance). The CAP theorem posits that in the presence of a network partition (P), a distributed system must choose between maintaining Consistency (C) or ensuring Availability (A). Striking the right balance between these conflicting goals requires careful consideration of the application's requirements and the inherent trade-offs in data consistency models.

In distributed databases, the challenge of maintaining data consistency is further amplified by the need for transactional integrity across multiple nodes. Distributed transactions involve operations that span multiple databases or nodes, and ensuring the Atomicity, Consistency, Isolation, and Durability (ACID) properties becomes complex when distributed across a network. Techniques such as two-phase commit protocols are used to coordinate distributed transactions and enforce consistency, but they come with their own set of challenges, including the potential for blocking and increased vulnerability to network partitions.

Eventual consistency, an alternative to strong consistency models, acknowledges that, in distributed systems, achieving immediate consistency across all nodes may not be feasible or practical. Instead, eventual consistency allows nodes to converge to a consistent state over time, tolerating temporary inconsistencies. Implementing eventual consistency requires careful consideration of conflict resolution strategies, versioning mechanisms, and reconciliation techniques to ensure that eventual convergence does not compromise data integrity. This approach is often suitable for scenarios where strict consistency is not a strict requirement, and the emphasis is on availability and partition tolerance.

Asynchronous communication models, where nodes communicate without waiting for immediate responses, present additional challenges in maintaining data consistency. In scenarios where updates are disseminated asynchronously, ensuring that all nodes eventually converge to a consistent state becomes a complex task. This challenge is particularly evident in distributed messaging systems, where messages may be delivered out of order or delayed due to network conditions. Techniques such as vector clocks or causality tracking are employed to establish partial orders among events and enable consistent causality tracking across distributed nodes, mitigating the challenges of asynchronous communication.

Ensuring data consistency becomes more intricate in distributed systems that embrace microservices architecture, where applications are decomposed into smaller, independent services that communicate via APIs. Each microservice may have its own database or state, and maintaining consistency across the entire system requires coordinating updates and ensuring that changes in one microservice do not lead to inconsistencies in others. Strategies such as distributed transactions, event sourcing, and eventual consistency models are employed based on the specific requirements and trade-offs of each microservice.

Furthermore, the introduction of edge computing and the proliferation of Internet of Things (IoT) devices present new challenges in maintaining data consistency. Edge computing involves processing data closer to the source or end-user, and IoT devices generate vast amounts of data that may need to be synchronized with centralized databases. Ensuring consistency between edge devices and centralized systems, especially in environments with intermittent connectivity, requires innovative solutions that balance the need for real-time processing at the edge with the requirements of data consistency at the core.

Addressing challenges in maintaining connectivity and data consistency necessitates the integration of various techniques and technologies into the design of distributed systems. Consensus algorithms, such as the Paxos or Raft protocols, are employed to achieve agreement among nodes in the presence of network partitions. These algorithms coordinate the distributed nodes to ensure that they reach a consensus on the state of shared data or the order of executed operations. However, implementing consensus algorithms introduces its own set of challenges, including the potential for increased latency, vulnerability to certain failure scenarios, and the difficulty of achieving consensus in large-scale systems.

Distributed caching and replication strategies are used to enhance data availability and reduce latency by storing copies of frequently accessed data closer to the nodes that need it. However, these strategies must be carefully managed to avoid inconsistencies between cached copies and the authoritative data source. Techniques such as cache invalidation, write-through and write-behind caching, and quorum-based replication are employed to strike a balance between data consistency and performance.

The advent of distributed ledger technologies, including blockchain, introduces novel approaches to addressing challenges in maintaining data consistency, especially in scenarios where a shared and tamper-resistant ledger is required. Blockchain, which operates on a decentralized and distributed ledger model, ensures that all nodes have a consistent view of transactions by incorporating cryptographic techniques and consensus mechanisms. While blockchain presents innovative solutions, it also introduces challenges such as scalability concerns, high resource requirements, and the need for energy-intensive consensus algorithms.

In conclusion, maintaining connectivity and ensuring data consistency are paramount challenges in the design and operation of distributed systems. The dynamic and unpredictable nature of network environments, the trade-offs between consistency and performance, and the complexities introduced by distributed architectures necessitate careful consideration of strategies and techniques. From consensus algorithms and distributed transactions to eventual consistency models and innovative approaches like blockchain, addressing these challenges requires a holistic understanding of the specific requirements and constraints of each distributed system. As technology continues to evolve, so too will the methods and solutions employed to maintain connectivity and data consistency in the intricate landscape of distributed computing.

The role of middleware in abstracting communication complexities.

Middleware plays a pivotal role in the realm of distributed systems by serving as a crucial layer that abstracts and manages communication complexities between different components, services, or applications. This intermediary software layer acts as a bridge, facilitating seamless communication and interaction among disparate entities in a distributed environment. The primary objective of middleware is to shield developers and applications from the intricacies of low-level communication protocols, network details, and heterogeneity, allowing them to focus on business logic and functionality.

One fundamental aspect of the role of middleware is its capacity to provide a unified and standardized communication interface. In heterogeneous distributed systems where diverse technologies, programming languages, and platforms coexist, achieving interoperability becomes a daunting challenge. Middleware steps in to address this challenge by offering a common ground for communication. By defining standard communication protocols and data formats, middleware allows components written in different languages or running on different platforms to exchange information seamlessly. This abstraction of heterogeneity simplifies the development process, as developers can focus on the functionality of their applications without the burden of dealing with the intricacies of diverse communication infrastructures.

Furthermore, middleware excels in handling the complexities of communication protocols and message formats. In distributed systems, components may use various communication paradigms such as message passing, remote procedure calls (RPC), or publish-subscribe mechanisms. Middleware abstracts these diverse communication patterns, providing a consistent and high-level interface for developers. Whether a system employs Simple Object Access Protocol (SOAP), Representational State Transfer (REST), or custom messaging formats, middleware shields developers from the low-level details, enabling them to build applications without delving into the specifics of each communication protocol.

Middleware also plays a crucial role in addressing challenges related to scalability and adaptability. As distributed systems grow in size and complexity, the need for scalable communication becomes imperative. Middleware solutions often incorporate features such as load balancing, connection pooling, and distributed caching to optimize communication and ensure efficient resource utilization. These features help distribute the communication load across various nodes in the system, preventing bottlenecks and enhancing scalability. Additionally, middleware is designed to adapt to changes in the system's configuration or topology, dynamically adjusting communication mechanisms and protocols based on the evolving requirements of the distributed environment.

The abstraction provided by middleware extends to the management of data consistency and integrity in distributed systems. In scenarios where multiple components or services need to share and synchronize data, middleware offers solutions to maintain data consistency without burdening developers with the intricacies of distributed transactions. Middleware may employ techniques like two-phase commit protocols, event-driven architectures, or distributed caching to ensure that data remains coherent across different nodes in the system. This abstraction shields developers from the complexities of implementing consistency mechanisms manually and promotes the development of robust and reliable distributed applications.

Security is a critical concern in distributed systems, and middleware serves as a vital layer for implementing security measures. Middleware solutions often provide built-in security features such as encryption, authentication, and authorization to safeguard communication channels and data transmission. By abstracting the implementation details of security protocols, middleware simplifies the process of securing communication in distributed systems. Developers can leverage these security features without delving into the intricacies of cryptographic algorithms or authentication mechanisms, streamlining the development process and ensuring that security considerations are seamlessly integrated into the distributed application.

Middleware also contributes significantly to fault tolerance and reliability in distributed systems. In dynamic and unpredictable network environments, failures can occur at any time, ranging from network disruptions to node crashes. Middleware abstracts the complexities of fault detection, recovery, and resilience by incorporating mechanisms like automatic retries, failover strategies, and redundancy. This abstraction shields developers from the nuances of handling failures manually, ensuring that the distributed system can gracefully recover from disruptions without compromising overall reliability.

The role of middleware extends to the implementation of asynchronous communication patterns in distributed systems. Asynchronous communication, where components can send messages or requests without waiting for immediate responses, is crucial for building responsive and scalable applications. Middleware provides abstractions for implementing asynchronous communication models such as message queues, publish-subscribe patterns, and event-driven architectures. By abstracting the intricacies of managing asynchronous communication, middleware enables developers to build applications that can handle high loads, provide real-time responsiveness, and scale effectively.

Middleware solutions are also instrumental in addressing the challenges posed by the emergence of microservices architectures. In microservices environments, where applications are composed of small, independent services, communication between services becomes a critical aspect. Middleware abstracts the complexities of service discovery, load balancing, and inter-service communication, allowing developers to focus on building and deploying microservices without being bogged down by the intricacies of communication between distributed components. This abstraction fosters modularity, flexibility, and ease of maintenance in microservices architectures.

Moreover, the role of middleware is crucial in facilitating the integration of legacy systems with modern distributed architectures. Many organizations operate with existing systems that may use older technologies or communication protocols. Middleware acts as a mediator, enabling the integration of legacy systems with newer components in a distributed environment. This abstraction allows organizations to modernize their systems gradually, leveraging the capabilities of distributed architectures without the need for a complete overhaul of existing infrastructure.

In conclusion, middleware serves as a linchpin in the design and development of distributed systems by abstracting communication complexities. By providing a unified and standardized interface, handling diverse communication protocols, addressing scalability challenges, ensuring data consistency, enhancing security, and managing fault tolerance, middleware allows developers to build distributed applications without being encumbered by the intricacies of the underlying communication infrastructure. The role of middleware extends across a spectrum of distributed systems, from microservices architectures and asynchronous communication to security and integration with legacy systems, making it an indispensable component in the dynamic landscape of modern computing.

Different types of middleware: message-oriented, object-oriented, and transactional.

Middleware, a vital component in distributed systems, comes in various types, each tailored to specific communication patterns and requirements. Message-oriented middleware (MOM) stands out as a key category designed to facilitate asynchronous communication between distributed components. In MOM, communication is achieved through messages, allowing systems to decouple sender and receiver components. This decoupling is crucial for building responsive and scalable distributed applications. MOM employs mechanisms such as message queues and publish-subscribe patterns. In message queues, messages are stored until consumed by the intended receiver, providing a buffer that allows components to operate independently. In publish-subscribe models, components subscribe to specific topics, and messages are broadcast to all interested subscribers. This flexibility makes MOM particularly suitable for scenarios where components need to communicate without waiting for immediate responses, enabling efficient handling of high loads and supporting real-time responsiveness.

Another significant category is object-oriented middleware (OOM), which focuses on enabling communication and interaction between distributed objects. In object-oriented systems, components are encapsulated as objects with defined interfaces, and OOM ensures seamless communication between these objects across a distributed environment. A prominent example of OOM is the Common Object Request Broker Architecture (CORBA), a middleware standard that facilitates communication between objects written in different programming languages. CORBA uses the Object Request Broker (ORB) to manage object communication, handling tasks such as object instantiation, method invocation, and parameter passing. This abstraction of communication details allows developers to build distributed applications without concerning themselves with the intricacies of underlying communication protocols or object interactions. OOM is particularly advantageous in scenarios where distributed components need to collaborate by invoking methods on remote objects.

Transactional middleware represents a specialized category designed to address the challenges of maintaining transactional integrity in distributed systems. Transactions, sequences of operations that must be executed as a single unit, are critical for ensuring data consistency across multiple components or databases. Transactional middleware abstracts the complexities of coordinating distributed transactions, providing mechanisms to enforce the Atomicity, Consistency, Isolation, and Durability (ACID) properties. Two-phase commit protocols, a common approach in transactional middleware, ensure that all participating nodes agree to commit or abort a transaction. However, these protocols come with challenges, including the potential for blocking and increased vulnerability to network partitions. Despite these challenges, transactional middleware is essential in scenarios where maintaining data consistency and integrity is paramount, such as in banking systems, inventory management, or any application where accurate and reliable transactional processing is critical.

Each type of middleware, whether message-oriented, object-oriented, or transactional, offers a distinct set of advantages and is suited to specific use cases. Message-oriented middleware excels in scenarios where asynchronous communication and decoupling are essential, such as in event-driven architectures, messaging systems, or applications requiring real-time responsiveness. Object-oriented middleware, exemplified by CORBA, provides a foundation for building distributed applications by abstracting object interactions and supporting communication between objects regardless of their implementation language. Transactional middleware, while introducing additional complexity, is indispensable for applications where maintaining transactional integrity is non-negotiable, ensuring that distributed transactions occur reliably and consistently.

In the realm of message-oriented middleware, the publish-subscribe pattern is a notable mechanism that enhances the scalability and responsiveness of distributed systems. In this pattern, components subscribe to specific topics of interest, and messages related to those topics are broadcast to all interested subscribers. This decoupled communication model allows publishers to broadcast messages without direct knowledge of the subscribers, facilitating dynamic and flexible communication patterns. Systems that leverage publish-subscribe patterns can efficiently disseminate information to multiple subscribers simultaneously, making this pattern ideal for scenarios such as real-time data streaming, news feeds, or event-driven architectures where components need to react to specific events without direct dependencies on one another.

Object-oriented middleware, as seen in the CORBA standard, provides a framework for building distributed systems based on the principles of object-oriented programming. CORBA enables communication between objects written in different programming languages, allowing developers to encapsulate functionality within objects and expose well-defined interfaces for interaction. The Object Request Broker (ORB) in CORBA acts as an intermediary that manages object communication, handling tasks such as locating objects, invoking methods remotely, and managing parameter passing. This abstraction of communication details empowers developers to focus on designing and implementing objects, fostering modularity and encapsulation. However, challenges such as language interoperability, versioning, and the complexity of distributed object interactions need to be addressed when working with object-oriented middleware.

Transactional middleware, with its emphasis on maintaining transactional integrity, introduces a layer of complexity necessary for applications that demand reliable and consistent transaction processing. Two-phase commit protocols, a prevalent mechanism in transactional middleware, coordinate the decision-making process among distributed nodes to ensure that all participants either commit or abort a transaction. While this approach provides strong guarantees of data consistency, it also introduces challenges, such as the potential for blocking in the presence of network failures or the need for careful handling of distributed transactions involving multiple resources. Despite these challenges, transactional middleware is essential in domains like finance, e-commerce, and enterprise resource planning (ERP) systems, where ensuring the correctness of transactions is paramount.

Moreover, the convergence of these middleware types is often observed in modern distributed systems. Many middleware solutions incorporate aspects of message-oriented, object-oriented, and transactional middleware to provide comprehensive support for various communication patterns and requirements. For instance, enterprise service buses (ESBs) serve as middleware solutions that integrate different applications and services by facilitating message-based communication, supporting service-oriented architectures (SOA), and often incorporating transactional capabilities. This convergence reflects the evolving needs of distributed systems, where diverse communication patterns and transactional requirements coexist within a unified middleware framework.

In conclusion, the landscape of middleware is rich and diverse, offering solutions tailored to specific communication paradigms and requirements. Message-oriented middleware excels in scenarios requiring asynchronous communication and decoupling, object-oriented middleware abstracts object interactions in distributed systems, and transactional middleware ensures the integrity of distributed transactions. The interplay of these middleware types, often converging in modern solutions, reflects the nuanced demands of building robust and scalable distributed systems. As technology continues to advance, middleware will continue to evolve, providing essential abstractions that empower developers to navigate the complexities of distributed computing and build applications that meet the diverse needs of the modern computing landscape.

Understanding scalability challenges in distributed systems.

Scalability, a pivotal aspect of distributed systems, refers to the system's ability to handle an increasing workload by efficiently and effectively expanding resources. While scalability is a desirable trait, achieving it in distributed systems introduces numerous challenges that stem from the complex nature of distributed architectures and the dynamic characteristics of modern computing environments. One of the primary challenges is associated with the coordination and communication among distributed nodes. As the size of a distributed system grows, the volume of inter-node communication increases, leading to potential bottlenecks and congestion. This heightened communication overhead can degrade performance and hinder the system's ability to scale seamlessly. Addressing this challenge requires sophisticated strategies such as load balancing, where incoming requests are evenly distributed across nodes, ensuring optimal resource utilization and preventing certain nodes from becoming overwhelmed.

Data consistency poses another substantial challenge to scalability in distributed systems. As the number of nodes increases, maintaining consistency across distributed databases or storage systems becomes more intricate. Striking a balance between achieving high scalability and ensuring data consistency is a classic trade-off, often encapsulated by the CAP theorem (Consistency, Availability, Partition Tolerance). The CAP theorem posits that in the presence of a network partition (P), a distributed system must choose between maintaining Consistency (C) or ensuring Availability (A). Achieving both strict consistency and high availability simultaneously is challenging, and distributed systems often opt for eventual consistency models where nodes converge to a consistent state over time, acknowledging that immediate consistency may not always be feasible in highly scalable architectures.

The dynamic nature of modern computing environments introduces additional scalability challenges, particularly in the context of elasticity and adaptability. Cloud computing platforms exemplify this dynamism, allowing organizations to scale their infrastructure based on demand. However, achieving seamless scalability in the cloud necessitates overcoming challenges related to resource provisioning, auto-scaling policies, and effective utilization of cloud-native services. Ensuring that a distributed system can dynamically scale up or down in response to varying workloads requires the integration of auto-scaling mechanisms, monitoring tools, and adaptive algorithms that can adjust resource allocations based on real-time demand patterns.

Distributed systems often grapple with the challenge of maintaining performance consistency under varying workloads. In scenarios where the system experiences sudden spikes in demand, commonly known as flash crowds or distributed denial of service (DDoS) attacks, ensuring that the system can scale rapidly and handle increased loads without degradation in performance becomes crucial. Implementing effective load shedding mechanisms, where non-critical tasks or requests are temporarily delayed or dropped during peak loads, is a strategy to maintain overall system stability and prevent cascading failures.

The architecture of distributed systems also plays a pivotal role in scalability challenges. Traditional monolithic architectures, where all components are tightly integrated into a single application, may face difficulties in scaling due to their inherent complexity and interdependence. The shift towards microservices architectures, where applications are decomposed into smaller, independent services, offers a more scalable approach. Microservices enable organizations to scale individual components independently, allowing for greater flexibility and responsiveness to varying workloads. However, adopting microservices introduces challenges related to service discovery, communication between services, and the need for robust orchestration and monitoring tools to manage the complexity introduced by distributed services.

Ensuring the scalability of distributed systems requires thoughtful consideration of data storage and retrieval mechanisms. In scenarios where the system relies on traditional relational databases, scaling can become challenging due to the limitations of vertical scaling, where a single database server's resources are augmented. Horizontal scaling, achieved by adding more database nodes, is often preferred for improved scalability. However, achieving horizontal scaling in distributed databases introduces complexities related to data partitioning, sharding, and the need for distributed query processing. NoSQL databases, designed to handle large volumes of unstructured or semi-structured data, often provide more natural support for horizontal scaling, making them suitable for highly scalable distributed systems.

The geographic distribution of nodes in a distributed system introduces challenges related to latency and network communication. In scenarios where nodes are spread across different regions or data centers, the latency introduced by communication over long distances can impact the overall system performance. Content delivery networks (CDNs) and edge computing architectures are employed to mitigate these challenges by distributing content and processing closer to end-users, reducing latency and enhancing the scalability of applications that require low response times.

Security considerations pose a significant challenge in the context of scalable distributed systems. As the number of nodes increases, the attack surface expands, making the system more susceptible to various security threats. Ensuring secure communication, access control, and protection against malicious activities become paramount. Scalable systems must incorporate robust security measures such as encryption, authentication, and authorization mechanisms. However, implementing security at scale requires careful consideration of factors such as key management, secure communication protocols, and the potential impact of security measures on overall system performance.

Scalability challenges also manifest in the context of stateful versus stateless architectures. Stateless architectures, where each request from a client contains all the information necessary for processing, are generally more scalable as they don't rely on maintaining session state between requests. Stateful architectures, on the other hand, require maintaining session information, introducing challenges related to load balancing and fault tolerance. Achieving scalability in stateful architectures often involves strategies such as session affinity, where requests from the same client are directed to the same server, or the use of distributed caching to store and retrieve session state efficiently.

The advent of emerging technologies, such as the Internet of Things (IoT) and edge computing, introduces scalability challenges unique to distributed systems operating in these environments. IoT devices generate vast amounts of data that need to be processed and managed, necessitating scalable solutions for data storage, processing, and communication. Edge computing, where processing occurs closer to the data source, demands scalable architectures that can efficiently distribute computation across edge nodes while maintaining coordination with central systems. Balancing the scalability requirements of IoT and edge computing with the constraints of resource-constrained devices poses intricate challenges in designing scalable and efficient distributed systems.

In conclusion, scalability challenges in distributed systems arise from the intricate interplay of factors such as communication overhead, data consistency, dynamic environments, performance consistency, architectural choices, storage mechanisms, network latency, security concerns, statefulness, and the evolving landscape of emerging technologies. Addressing these challenges requires a holistic and adaptive approach, leveraging strategies such as load balancing, auto-scaling, microservices architectures, horizontal scaling, content delivery networks, secure communication protocols, and innovative solutions tailored to the specific requirements of the distributed system. As technology continues to evolve, scalability in distributed systems remains a dynamic area of research and implementation, where organizations strive to strike a balance between accommodating growing workloads and maintaining optimal performance, responsiveness, and reliability.

Techniques for load balancing to distribute work effectively.

Load balancing, a critical aspect of distributed systems, encompasses a variety of techniques aimed at distributing computational workloads efficiently among multiple nodes to optimize resource utilization, enhance system performance, and ensure responsiveness. One prevalent technique in load balancing is the use of a load balancer, a specialized component or service that acts as an intermediary between clients and a pool of backend servers. Load balancers employ algorithms to make dynamic decisions on how to distribute incoming requests across the available servers based on factors such as server health, current load, and response times. This approach, known as static or dynamic load balancing, enables the system to adapt to varying workloads, preventing individual servers from becoming overwhelmed and ensuring that the overall system scales effectively.

An essential strategy for load balancing is the Round Robin algorithm, a simple and widely used method that evenly distributes incoming requests across a pool of servers in a circular fashion. Each server in the pool receives requests in turn, and once the last server is reached, the cycle repeats. While Round Robin is straightforward and easy to implement, it may not account for variations in server capacities or workloads, leading to potential imbalances. To address this limitation, Weighted Round Robin introduces the concept of assigning weights to servers, allowing the load balancer to consider the varying capacities of individual servers when distributing requests. This ensures a more nuanced distribution of workloads based on the specified weights, catering to the differences in processing power or resource availability.

Dynamic algorithms, such as Least Connections or Least Response Time, offer more intelligent load balancing by considering the current state of each server in the pool. Least Connections allocates incoming requests to the server with the fewest active connections, aiming to evenly distribute the load based on the actual workload each server is handling. Similarly, Least Response Time directs requests to the server with the lowest response time, prioritizing servers that can process requests more quickly. These dynamic algorithms enhance system efficiency by adapting to real-time conditions, allowing the load balancer to direct traffic to the servers that can handle it most effectively at any given moment.

Another notable approach is the Weighted Least Connections algorithm, an extension of Least Connections that incorporates server weights to account for differences in capacity. By combining the principles of Least Connections with weighted assignments, this algorithm ensures a more balanced distribution of workloads across servers, considering both the current load and the specified weights. Weighted Least Connections provides a versatile solution for load balancing in scenarios where servers have distinct capacities or processing capabilities.

Load balancing techniques also extend to more sophisticated algorithms, such as the Least Time algorithm, which dynamically calculates the expected processing time for each server and directs requests to the server with the lowest anticipated completion time. This predictive approach leverages historical performance metrics to make informed load balancing decisions, optimizing resource allocation and minimizing response times. While effective, algorithms like Least Time may require more computational overhead to continuously analyze and predict server performance.

In addition to server-centric approaches, client-centric load balancing techniques aim to optimize the distribution of requests by considering client-related factors. One such technique is the IP Hash method, where the load balancer uses a hash function based on client IP addresses to consistently map clients to specific servers. This ensures that requests from the same client are consistently directed to the same server, promoting session persistence and facilitating caching strategies. While IP Hash offers benefits in scenarios where maintaining state across requests is crucial, it may pose challenges when handling dynamic or changing client IP addresses.

Content-based load balancing focuses on distributing workloads based on specific characteristics of the incoming requests. Application-layer content-based routing allows load balancers to inspect the content of requests, such as URL paths or headers, and make routing decisions accordingly. This technique is particularly useful in scenarios where different parts of an application have varying processing requirements or rely on specialized backend servers. By intelligently routing requests based on content, content-based load balancing enhances resource utilization and ensures that each type of workload is directed to the most suitable backend servers.

Load balancing strategies also extend to more adaptive and learning-based approaches, such as machine learning algorithms. These algorithms leverage historical data on server performance, request patterns, and system behavior to predict optimal load balancing decisions. Reinforcement learning models, for instance, can continuously adapt and refine load balancing strategies based on real-time feedback and evolving system conditions. While machine learning-based approaches offer the potential for highly adaptive and optimized load balancing, they require robust training datasets, continuous monitoring, and may introduce complexities in terms of model interpretation and maintenance.

Global Server Load Balancing (GSLB) represents a specialized form of load balancing designed to optimize the distribution of workloads across geographically distributed servers or data centers. GSLB takes into account factors such as server proximity to clients, server health, and the overall system load to direct requests to the most suitable server or data center. This is particularly crucial for organizations operating across multiple regions, where minimizing latency and optimizing global availability are essential. GSLB ensures that clients are directed to the nearest and most responsive servers, contributing to improved user experience and efficient resource utilization.

Load balancing techniques are not limited to traditional web-based applications but extend to various protocols and communication patterns. For instance, load balancing in messaging systems, often used in enterprise environments or distributed architectures, involves distributing messages among multiple message brokers or queues. Techniques such as message partitioning, where messages are divided based on specific criteria, and dynamic routing based on message content contribute to efficient load balancing in messaging systems. This ensures that message processing is distributed effectively across the available resources, preventing bottlenecks and enhancing the scalability of messaging architectures.

While load balancing primarily focuses on distributing incoming requests, effective load balancing also necessitates robust health checks and monitoring mechanisms. Health checks involve periodically assessing the status and performance of backend servers to identify any potential issues or failures. Load balancers use this information to make informed decisions about directing traffic away from unhealthy servers, preventing them from impacting the overall system performance. Proactive health checks and monitoring contribute to the reliability and stability of load balancing strategies, ensuring that clients are consistently directed to healthy and responsive servers.

In conclusion, load balancing techniques represent a diverse and evolving set of strategies designed to distribute workloads effectively across distributed systems. From traditional algorithms like Round Robin and Least Connections to more advanced approaches such as machine learning-based models and content-based routing, load balancing plays a pivotal role in optimizing resource utilization, enhancing system performance, and ensuring the responsiveness of modern distributed applications. As organizations continue to embrace distributed architectures and face evolving challenges in scalability and resource management, load balancing remains a critical component for achieving optimal performance and maintaining a seamless user experience.

Chapter 3: Concurrency and Parallelism in Operating Environments

Defining concurrency and its relevance in distributed environments.

Concurrency, in the realm of computing, refers to the ability of a system to execute multiple tasks or processes simultaneously. It is a fundamental concept that enables overlapping or interleaved execution of operations, allowing a system to make progress on multiple tasks concurrently rather than sequentially. Concurrency is crucial in addressing the challenges posed by the increasing demand for performance, responsiveness, and efficiency in modern computing environments. In distributed systems, where computing resources are spread across multiple nodes, the significance of concurrency becomes even more pronounced. The distributed nature of these systems introduces complexities related to communication, synchronization, and coordination, making concurrency an essential aspect of designing and implementing effective distributed applications.

In a distributed environment, concurrency plays a pivotal role in improving overall system efficiency and responsiveness. The ability to perform multiple tasks concurrently allows distributed systems to better utilize available resources, minimizing idle time and ensuring optimal throughput. This is particularly vital in scenarios where a distributed application must handle a large number of concurrent requests or processes. By executing tasks concurrently, a distributed system can harness the processing power of multiple nodes, distributing the workload and preventing bottlenecks that could arise in a strictly sequential execution model.

Concurrency in distributed environments also addresses the challenges posed by latency and communication overhead. As tasks are executed concurrently on different nodes, a distributed system can leverage parallelism to reduce the time it takes to complete a set of operations. This is especially beneficial in scenarios where communication between nodes is involved, as concurrent execution allows overlapping communication and computation, mitigating the impact of network latency and enhancing the overall responsiveness of the distributed application.

The concept of concurrency extends beyond the traditional notion of parallelism and embraces asynchronous communication and non-blocking operations. In distributed systems, where components may be geographically dispersed and subject to variable latencies, asynchronous concurrency becomes particularly relevant. Asynchronous programming models allow tasks to proceed independently, enabling a distributed system to initiate multiple operations and continue processing without waiting for each operation to complete. This approach enhances responsiveness by minimizing the impact of latency, enabling a system to efficiently handle a diverse set of tasks with varying processing times.

Concurrency is closely tied to the concept of multithreading, where a program or application is divided into multiple threads of execution that can run concurrently. In distributed environments, multithreading enables a node to execute multiple threads simultaneously, each handling a distinct task or set of tasks. This parallel execution model is advantageous in scenarios where a distributed application must handle a diverse range of activities concurrently, such as processing user requests, handling background tasks, or managing communication with other nodes. Multithreading in distributed systems requires careful consideration of synchronization mechanisms to ensure data consistency and avoid conflicts that may arise when multiple threads access shared resources.

The concept of distributed concurrency also encompasses the notion of distributed transactions, where a set of operations across multiple nodes must be executed atomically. In distributed databases or transactional systems, ensuring the atomicity, consistency, isolation, and durability (ACID) properties of transactions across multiple nodes is a challenging yet critical aspect of concurrency control. Distributed transaction management systems implement protocols and algorithms to coordinate transactions across nodes, ensuring that transactions are executed in a manner that preserves data consistency and integrity in the face of failures or concurrent access.

Concurrency control mechanisms in distributed systems must address the challenges posed by potential conflicts when multiple nodes attempt to access or modify shared resources concurrently. Techniques such as locking, optimistic concurrency control, and distributed consensus protocols play a crucial role in managing concurrent access to data and ensuring that transactions proceed in a coordinated and consistent manner across distributed nodes. These mechanisms are essential for preventing data inconsistencies, race conditions, and conflicts that may arise when multiple nodes attempt to update shared data concurrently.

The relevance of concurrency in distributed environments is further accentuated by the rise of microservices architectures and containerization. Microservices, which decompose applications into small, independent services, often operate concurrently to handle various functionalities. Concurrent execution of microservices allows for modular and scalable architectures, where each service can independently process requests and communicate with other services concurrently. Containerization technologies, such as Docker and Kubernetes, facilitate the deployment of distributed applications composed of multiple containers running concurrently. Managing the concurrent execution of containers enables efficient resource utilization and scalability in distributed systems.

Concurrency in distributed systems also intersects with fault tolerance and resilience. The ability to execute tasks concurrently contributes to the fault tolerance of a system by allowing it to continue operating even in the presence of failures. Redundancy and replication of tasks across multiple nodes, coupled with mechanisms for detecting and recovering from failures, enhance the resilience of distributed applications. Concurrency enables the distribution of tasks and responsibilities across multiple nodes, reducing the impact of individual node failures and ensuring that the system can adapt to changing conditions dynamically.

Moreover, the concept of event-driven concurrency is prevalent in distributed systems, especially in the context of reactive programming and real-time processing. Event-driven models leverage asynchronous and non-blocking concurrency to respond to events or messages in real time. This is particularly relevant in distributed systems handling streaming data, user interactions, or sensor data. Event-driven concurrency allows a distributed system to efficiently process incoming events concurrently, ensuring timely and responsive reactions to dynamic changes in the environment.

Concurrency in distributed systems also aligns with the principles of scalability. The ability to scale a distributed system horizontally, by adding more nodes, relies on effective concurrency management. Scalable distributed systems distribute tasks across multiple nodes, allowing them to handle increasing workloads by executing tasks concurrently. Techniques such as load balancing, which distributes incoming requests among available nodes, and sharding, which partitions data across multiple nodes, leverage concurrency to achieve scalability and ensure that the system can grow to meet evolving demands.

In conclusion, concurrency is a foundational concept with profound relevance in distributed environments. Its role extends beyond parallelism to encompass asynchronous communication, distributed transactions, fault tolerance, scalability, and responsiveness in modern distributed systems. The ability to execute tasks concurrently empowers distributed applications to harness the collective processing power of multiple nodes, efficiently handle diverse workloads, and adapt to dynamic conditions. As the landscape of distributed computing continues to evolve, concurrency remains a key enabler for building robust, scalable, and responsive distributed systems that meet the complex demands of contemporary computing scenarios.

Challenges and benefits of managing concurrent processes.

Managing concurrent processes presents both challenges and benefits that are intrinsic to the complex nature of parallel execution in computing environments. One of the primary challenges lies in the potential for race conditions, where multiple processes attempt to access shared resources simultaneously, leading to unpredictable and erroneous behavior. Ensuring proper synchronization mechanisms, such as locks or semaphores, becomes crucial to prevent race conditions and maintain the consistency of shared data. However, the implementation of synchronization introduces its own set of challenges, including the risk of deadlocks, where processes are unable to proceed due to cyclic dependencies on resources. Striking a balance between preventing race conditions and avoiding deadlocks requires careful design and consideration of the specific requirements of concurrent processes.

Concurrency also introduces the challenge of coordinating communication and data sharing between processes. In a distributed environment, where processes may run on separate nodes, efficient and reliable communication becomes paramount. Synchronization mechanisms must extend beyond local inter-process communication to address the complexities of distributed systems. The overhead of inter-process communication, especially in scenarios involving remote processes, introduces latency and potential bottlenecks that impact overall system performance. Developing effective communication strategies, such as message passing or shared memory models, and handling the intricacies of network communication represent ongoing challenges in managing concurrent processes in distributed environments.

Another notable challenge is managing resource contention, where multiple processes compete for limited resources such as CPU time, memory, or I/O operations. In the absence of effective resource management, processes may experience delays or starvation, hindering overall system performance. Techniques like priority scheduling and resource allocation algorithms aim to address these challenges by prioritizing processes based on their importance or allocating resources judiciously. However, the trade-offs involved in resource management, such as the potential for priority inversion or resource underutilization, add complexity to the task of ensuring fair and efficient utilization of system resources in concurrent environments.

Concurrency introduces intricacies in error handling and debugging, making it challenging to identify and resolve issues that arise during parallel execution. Traditional debugging tools may struggle to provide insights into the dynamic interactions between concurrent processes, making it difficult to pinpoint the root cause of errors or unexpected behavior. Techniques such as logging, tracing, and the use of specialized debugging tools designed for concurrent systems become essential for effective debugging. Additionally, the non-deterministic nature of concurrent execution, where the order of process execution may vary, complicates the reproducibility of issues and requires sophisticated debugging strategies.

Despite these challenges, managing concurrent processes offers a range of benefits that are instrumental in improving the performance, responsiveness, and efficiency of computing systems. One of the primary advantages is the potential for increased throughput and reduced execution time. By allowing multiple processes to execute concurrently, a system can exploit parallelism and harness the collective computational power of multiple cores or nodes. This is particularly beneficial in scenarios where tasks can be divided into independent subtasks that can be executed simultaneously, leading to overall performance gains.

Concurrency also contributes to enhanced responsiveness in systems that involve user interactions or real-time processing. By allowing processes to run concurrently, a system can remain responsive to user inputs or external events, ensuring timely reactions to dynamic changes. This responsiveness is crucial in various applications, such as interactive software, web servers, and systems handling streaming data, where immediate reactions to events are essential for providing a seamless user experience.

The ability to manage concurrent processes facilitates the development of scalable systems. Scalability, the capacity to handle increasing workloads by adding more resources, is a critical consideration in modern computing environments. Concurrent execution enables systems to scale horizontally by distributing tasks across multiple nodes or cores, preventing bottlenecks and accommodating growing workloads. Techniques such as load balancing, parallel algorithms, and distributed computing leverage concurrency to achieve scalability and ensure that a system can adapt to changing demands efficiently.

Concurrency supports the development of responsive and interactive user interfaces. In graphical user interfaces (GUIs), for instance, concurrent processes enable the simultaneous execution of tasks such as user input processing, rendering graphics, and handling background computations. This concurrency enhances the overall user experience by preventing the GUI from becoming unresponsive during resource-intensive operations. The responsiveness of user interfaces is crucial in applications ranging from desktop software to web browsers and mobile apps, where users expect smooth and interactive interactions.

Managing concurrent processes is essential for building resilient and fault-tolerant systems. By distributing tasks across multiple processes or nodes, a system can continue operating even in the presence of failures or errors in specific components. Redundancy and replication of processes contribute to fault tolerance, ensuring that the failure of one process does not lead to the overall failure of the system. This resilience is critical in distributed systems, cloud computing environments, and mission-critical applications where system reliability and continuous operation are paramount.

Concurrency facilitates the development of modular and maintainable software architectures. The decomposition of tasks into independent concurrent processes allows developers to create modular components that can be developed, tested, and maintained independently. This modularity enhances code readability, maintainability, and the ease of incorporating changes or updates. Concurrent programming models, such as actor-based or message-passing models, promote loose coupling between components, enabling more straightforward scalability and adaptability to evolving system requirements.

Moreover, managing concurrent processes is fundamental in harnessing the potential of parallel hardware architectures, such as multi-core processors and GPUs. Concurrency enables the effective utilization of parallel resources, allowing developers to design algorithms and applications that can exploit the parallel processing capabilities of modern hardware. Parallelism in computing architectures is a key factor in achieving high performance and computational efficiency, making concurrency a cornerstone in the development of applications for scientific computing, simulations, and data-intensive tasks.

In conclusion, managing concurrent processes involves navigating a landscape of challenges and benefits inherent in the complex nature of parallel execution. The challenges, including race conditions, communication complexities, resource contention, debugging intricacies, and the non-deterministic nature of concurrent systems, demand careful consideration and sophisticated strategies. However, the benefits, such as increased throughput, responsiveness, scalability, fault tolerance, modular software architectures, and efficient utilization of parallel hardware, underscore the importance of concurrency in modern computing. Effectively managing concurrent processes is not only a technical requirement but also a key enabler for building systems that meet the performance, responsiveness, and scalability demands of contemporary computing scenarios.

Understanding parallel processing and its significance.

Parallel processing, a paradigm in computing where multiple tasks or processes are executed simultaneously, represents a fundamental approach to harnessing the computational power of modern systems. At its core, parallel processing aims to divide a complex problem into smaller, manageable tasks that can be solved concurrently, thereby improving overall system performance, efficiency, and responsiveness. The significance of parallel processing is deeply rooted in its ability to address the ever-growing demand for computational power driven by the complexity of modern applications, the explosion of data, and the evolution of hardware architectures.

The fundamental premise of parallel processing is to exploit the parallelism inherent in many computational problems. Traditional, sequential computing models, where a single processor executes instructions one after the other, face limitations in terms of speed and efficiency as computational demands escalate. Parallel processing, on the other hand, enables the simultaneous execution of multiple instructions or tasks, distributing the workload across multiple processors or cores. This concurrent execution paradigm allows systems to perform computations more rapidly by capitalizing on the parallel nature of many real-world problems.

One of the primary motivations for employing parallel processing is to enhance computational speed and throughput. By dividing a computational task into smaller subtasks and executing them simultaneously, parallel processing can achieve significant time savings compared to sequential processing. This is particularly crucial in scenarios where computations are time-sensitive, such as scientific simulations, data analysis, and real-time processing. The ability to parallelize computations enables systems to handle larger datasets and perform complex calculations at a pace that would be impractical or unfeasible with sequential processing.

Parallel processing plays a pivotal role in addressing the challenges posed by the increasing complexity of algorithms and computations. As algorithms become more sophisticated and data-intensive, the demand for computational power escalates. Parallelizing algorithms allows them to be decomposed into parallelizable components, which can be executed concurrently. This approach is particularly evident in fields like artificial intelligence, machine learning, and scientific computing, where parallel processing accelerates tasks such as training complex models, analyzing vast datasets, and simulating intricate systems.

The significance of parallel processing extends to the realm of hardware architectures, where multi-core processors and parallel computing systems have become ubiquitous. Multi-core processors incorporate multiple processing units on a single chip, allowing concurrent execution of tasks. Parallel computing systems, ranging from clusters of interconnected computers to specialized parallel architectures, provide scalable solutions for tackling computationally intensive problems. The adoption of parallel hardware architectures aligns with the parallelization of software and algorithms, unlocking the full potential of parallel processing in achieving high-performance computing.

Parallel processing is integral to overcoming the limitations imposed by the von Neumann architecture, the traditional model of sequential computation. In von Neumann architecture, a single processing unit fetches and executes instructions sequentially, creating a bottleneck as computational demands escalate. Parallel processing, by distributing tasks across multiple processing units, mitigates this bottleneck, leading to improved scalability and performance. This shift towards parallel architectures is exemplified by the emergence of Graphics Processing Units (GPUs), originally designed for rendering graphics but repurposed for parallel computing due to their highly parallel nature. GPUs excel at performing parallel computations and have become essential in accelerating tasks such as scientific simulations, image processing, and machine learning.

Parallel processing is particularly relevant in scientific computing and simulations, where complex models and simulations demand substantial computational resources. Numerical simulations, weather forecasting, fluid dynamics, and molecular dynamics simulations are examples of applications that benefit significantly from parallel processing. By parallelizing the calculations involved in these simulations, researchers can achieve faster results, explore larger parameter spaces, and conduct more realistic and detailed simulations, ultimately advancing scientific understanding and discovery.

The advent of big data has further underscored the importance of parallel processing in handling and analyzing vast datasets efficiently. In scenarios where datasets are too large to fit into the memory of a single processor, parallel processing provides a scalable solution. MapReduce, a programming model for processing and generating large datasets, is a notable example of parallel processing applied to big data. Distributed frameworks like Apache Hadoop and Apache Spark implement parallel processing to distribute the processing of large datasets across clusters of computers, facilitating the efficient analysis of massive volumes of data.

Parallel processing is instrumental in the domain of real-time systems and applications that demand low-latency responses. In real-time computing, where tasks must be completed within stringent time constraints, parallel processing enables the simultaneous execution of multiple tasks, ensuring timely responses. Industries such as finance, telecommunications, and autonomous systems leverage parallel processing to handle real-time data streams, process transactions, and make split-second decisions. The significance of parallel processing in real-time applications extends to fields like robotics and autonomous vehicles, where rapid and concurrent processing of sensor data is essential for real-time decision-making.

The adoption of parallel processing has become a cornerstone in the evolution of high-performance computing (HPC). HPC environments, prevalent in scientific research, engineering simulations, and computational modeling, rely on parallel processing to achieve the computational power necessary for tackling complex problems. Parallel algorithms, parallel architectures, and parallel programming models are foundational elements in the design of HPC systems, enabling researchers and scientists to perform simulations, analyses, and computations at scales previously unattainable with sequential computing.

Parallel processing is closely intertwined with the development of parallel algorithms, which are designed to efficiently distribute tasks across multiple processing units. Algorithmic parallelization requires a fundamental shift in the design and structure of algorithms to enable concurrent execution. Parallel algorithms range from task parallelism, where independent tasks are executed concurrently, to data parallelism, where the same operation is performed on multiple data elements simultaneously. Parallel algorithms are a key enabler for realizing the potential of parallel processing, ensuring that computations can be effectively distributed and coordinated across multiple processing units.

The significance of parallel processing in the context of parallel algorithms extends to the concept of parallelism at different levels, including instruction-level parallelism (ILP), thread-level parallelism (TLP), and data-level parallelism (DLP). ILP involves the simultaneous execution of multiple instructions within a single processor, enhancing the execution speed of individual tasks. TLP focuses on concurrent execution of threads or processes, exploiting multiple processors or cores to handle distinct tasks concurrently. DLP, often associated with SIMD (Single Instruction, Multiple Data) architectures, involves the simultaneous processing of multiple data elements using the same instruction. These levels of parallelism collectively contribute to the overarching significance of parallel processing in achieving high computational efficiency and performance.

In conclusion, parallel processing stands as a foundational paradigm in computing, offering a powerful approach to meet the escalating demands for computational power, efficiency, and speed. The significance of parallel processing is evident across diverse domains, including scientific computing, big data analytics, real-time systems, high-performance computing, and the evolution of hardware architectures. By harnessing the potential of parallelism, parallel processing enables the concurrent execution of tasks, the efficient utilization of multi-core processors, and the scalability necessary for tackling complex computational challenges. As the landscape of computing continues to evolve, the role of parallel processing remains central to driving advancements in performance, enabling the development of applications that push the boundaries of computational capabilities.

Techniques for parallelizing tasks in distributed systems.

Parallelizing tasks in distributed systems is a crucial aspect of achieving efficient utilization of resources and optimizing overall system performance. Various techniques and strategies are employed to distribute and execute tasks concurrently across multiple nodes in a distributed environment. One fundamental approach is task parallelism, where a computational problem is decomposed into independent tasks that can be executed concurrently. This technique is particularly effective when the tasks are self-contained and do not depend on each other's results. Task parallelism facilitates load balancing, enabling the system to distribute tasks evenly among available nodes to maximize resource utilization. As each node independently processes its assigned task, the overall execution time is reduced, contributing to improved system throughput.

Another prevalent technique for parallelizing tasks in distributed systems is data parallelism, where the same operation is performed on multiple data elements concurrently. This approach is well-suited for tasks that involve processing large datasets or performing similar computations on different portions of the data. Data parallelism often leverages parallel programming models like MapReduce, which divides a task into map and reduce phases. The map phase processes data in parallel across multiple nodes, and the results are then combined during the reduce phase. Data parallelism is widely employed in big data processing frameworks, enabling the distributed analysis of large datasets across clusters of interconnected nodes.

In the context of parallelizing tasks in distributed systems, pipeline parallelism is a technique that involves breaking down a task into a sequence of stages, each handled by a different node. Each node performs its designated stage of the task, and the results are passed to the next stage in a pipelined fashion. This approach is particularly beneficial for tasks with a well-defined sequence of operations, as it enables continuous processing and minimizes idle time. Pipeline parallelism is commonly used in scenarios such as stream processing, where data is continuously flowing through a series of processing stages, and each stage is executed concurrently by different nodes.

Concurrency control mechanisms are essential when parallelizing tasks that involve shared resources or data. Lock-based synchronization is a common technique used to manage access to shared resources. Nodes acquire locks before accessing shared resources, ensuring that only one node can modify the resource at a time. While effective, lock-based synchronization can introduce contention and potential bottlenecks, especially in scenarios with frequent updates to shared resources. To mitigate these issues, optimistic concurrency control techniques, such as versioning or timestamp-based methods, are employed. Optimistic concurrency control allows multiple nodes to operate on shared resources concurrently, and conflicts are resolved during the final stages of the computation.

In distributed systems, parallelizing tasks often involves dealing with the challenges of coordinating communication between nodes. Message-passing is a fundamental communication paradigm for parallel and distributed computing. In this approach, nodes communicate by exchanging messages, allowing them to share information and synchronize their activities. The Message Passing Interface (MPI) is a widely used standard for implementing message-passing communication in distributed systems. MPI enables nodes to send and receive messages, facilitating the coordination of parallel tasks. Another communication model, Remote Procedure Call (RPC), allows nodes to invoke procedures or functions on remote nodes as if they were local. RPC mechanisms simplify the communication between distributed components, contributing to the effective parallelization of tasks.

Distributed frameworks and libraries provide abstractions and tools to simplify the parallelization of tasks in distributed systems. Apache Hadoop, a popular distributed processing framework, utilizes the MapReduce programming model for parallelizing large-scale data processing tasks. Hadoop abstracts the complexity of parallel execution by automatically handling task distribution, fault tolerance, and data shuffling. Similarly, Apache Spark, built on top of the Hadoop Distributed File System (HDFS), introduces Resilient Distributed Datasets (RDDs) to provide a high-level abstraction for parallel data processing. These frameworks hide the intricacies of distributed computing, allowing developers to focus on defining the computation logic rather than managing the low-level details of task parallelism.

Parallelizing iterative algorithms, commonly used in machine learning and numerical simulations, presents a unique set of challenges. These algorithms involve repeatedly applying the same operation to a dataset until a convergence criterion is met. In distributed systems, efficiently parallelizing iterative algorithms requires careful consideration of data distribution, communication overhead, and load balancing. Techniques like bulk synchronous parallel (BSP) models aim to synchronize nodes at predefined intervals during iterations, managing the exchange of intermediate results. Furthermore, techniques such as data partitioning and dynamic load balancing become crucial for distributing the workload evenly and ensuring that nodes remain actively engaged in the parallel computation.

Partitioning data across nodes is a key strategy for parallelizing tasks in distributed systems. Data partitioning techniques involve dividing a dataset into subsets that can be processed independently by different nodes. Hash-based partitioning and range-based partitioning are common approaches used to distribute data evenly across nodes. Hash-based partitioning assigns data based on a hash function, ensuring a uniform distribution, while range-based partitioning distributes data according to specified ranges. By partitioning data effectively, the system can parallelize the processing of subsets, enabling concurrent execution and optimal resource utilization.

Load balancing is a critical consideration when parallelizing tasks in distributed systems, ensuring that the computational workload is evenly distributed among nodes. Dynamic load balancing techniques adapt to changing conditions during the execution of parallel tasks. These techniques involve monitoring the workload on each node and redistributing tasks to maintain a balanced system. Adaptive load balancing algorithms consider factors such as computational resources, communication delays, and node availability to make dynamic decisions on task allocation. Effective load balancing enhances the scalability and responsiveness of distributed systems, preventing situations where some nodes are underutilized while others are overloaded.

Parallelizing tasks in the context of machine learning introduces the concept of model parallelism and data parallelism. Model parallelism involves distributing the components of a machine learning model across different nodes, allowing each node to focus on a subset of the model's parameters. This approach is suitable for large models that do not fit into the memory of a single node. On the other hand, data parallelism involves distributing portions of the dataset to different nodes, allowing each node to train on its subset of data. Techniques such as synchronous and asynchronous gradient descent are used to coordinate the updates to the model's parameters across nodes in data parallelism, enabling the parallel training of machine learning models in distributed environments.

In the context of parallelizing graph algorithms, which are prevalent in social network analysis, recommendation systems, and network analysis, techniques such as vertex-centric and edge-centric parallelization are employed. Vertex-centric parallelization focuses on parallelizing the computation for individual vertices, allowing nodes to process their local neighborhood concurrently. Edge-centric parallelization, on the other hand, distributes the computation based on edges, enabling nodes to perform operations on sets of connected edges concurrently. These techniques are instrumental in addressing the challenges posed by the inherent structure of graph data and optimizing the parallel execution of graph algorithms in distributed systems.

Asynchronous parallelism introduces a non-blocking approach to parallelizing tasks in distributed systems, allowing nodes to operate independently without waiting for the completion of each other's tasks. Asynchronous parallelism is particularly relevant in scenarios where tasks have varying execution times or where the availability of nodes fluctuates. This approach enables nodes to continue processing new tasks without being blocked by the completion of slower tasks. However, managing dependencies and ensuring consistency in the presence of asynchrony requires careful coordination and synchronization mechanisms to prevent race conditions and ensure the correctness of the parallel computation.

In conclusion, parallelizing tasks in distributed systems involves a diverse set of techniques and strategies tailored to the characteristics of the computational problem, the nature of the data, and the specific requirements of the distributed environment. Task parallelism, data parallelism, pipeline parallelism, and parallelism in communication are foundational concepts that guide the effective distribution and execution of tasks. Concurrency control mechanisms, communication models, and distributed frameworks further facilitate the coordination and synchronization of parallel tasks. Load balancing, partitioning strategies, and adaptive algorithms contribute to optimal resource utilization and system scalability. The continuous evolution of distributed computing models and the increasing demand for parallel processing capabilities underscore the importance of these techniques in achieving efficient and scalable distributed systems.

Exploring synchronization challenges in distributed systems.

Synchronization challenges in distributed systems are inherent complexities that arise from the coordination of activities across multiple nodes to ensure consistency, correctness, and reliable operation. One fundamental challenge is managing concurrent access to shared resources, such as databases or files, by multiple nodes. In a distributed environment, where nodes operate independently, conflicts may arise when multiple nodes attempt to modify shared resources simultaneously. Ensuring proper synchronization mechanisms becomes crucial to prevent data inconsistencies and maintain the integrity of shared data. Traditional techniques, such as locks and semaphores, are employed to coordinate access to shared resources, but they introduce challenges related to deadlock avoidance, contention, and the potential for performance bottlenecks.

The issue of clock synchronization poses another significant challenge in distributed systems. Nodes in a distributed environment may have independent clocks that drift over time due to variations in hardware or network delays. This clock skew can lead to challenges in ordering events and timestamps, impacting the correctness of distributed algorithms, consistency in data replication, and the ordering of operations. Clock synchronization protocols, such as the Network Time Protocol (NTP) or the Precision Time Protocol (PTP), aim to address these challenges by aligning clocks across nodes. However, achieving precise synchronization in the face of network delays and varying clock drifts remains a persistent challenge, impacting the reliability of distributed systems.

Consistency models present a nuanced synchronization challenge, particularly in distributed databases and systems where maintaining a coherent view of shared data is essential. Different consistency models, such as eventual consistency, strong consistency, and causal consistency, offer varying trade-offs between performance and reliability. Achieving a balance between ensuring consistency and allowing for concurrent updates poses challenges, especially in scenarios where nodes are geographically dispersed, communication latencies vary, and the system must operate under partitioned network conditions. Implementing distributed consistency models requires careful consideration of the application's requirements and the trade-offs involved in terms of availability, partition tolerance, and system performance.

Concurrency control mechanisms are central to addressing synchronization challenges in distributed databases. Traditional databases often use techniques like two-phase locking or multi-version concurrency control to manage concurrent access to data. In distributed databases, the challenges intensify as nodes may operate independently and require coordination to maintain consistency. Optimistic concurrency control mechanisms, such as Timestamp Ordering Protocol (TO), validate transactions at the end of their execution, reducing contention and potentially improving performance. However, resolving conflicts in optimistic concurrency control introduces challenges related to detecting and handling conflicting updates, especially in scenarios with high contention.

Distributed systems grapple with challenges related to maintaining consensus among nodes, a critical aspect for ensuring consistency and decision-making. The Consensus problem, famously illustrated by the Byzantine Generals' Problem, involves reaching an agreement among distributed nodes, even in the presence of faulty or malicious nodes. Consensus protocols, such as the Paxos algorithm and the Raft consensus algorithm, aim to address this challenge by providing a means for distributed nodes to agree on a common value or decision. Achieving consensus introduces challenges related to fault tolerance, as the system must cope with the potential failure of nodes, network partitions, and Byzantine faults. Striking a balance between achieving consensus and maintaining system responsiveness and availability is an ongoing challenge in distributed systems design.

Distributed transactions introduce synchronization challenges when ensuring the Atomicity, Consistency, Isolation, and Durability (ACID) properties across multiple nodes. Coordinating distributed transactions involves managing the two-phase commit protocol, where a coordinator node ensures that all participating nodes either commit or abort the transaction. However, challenges arise in scenarios where nodes may fail or become unavailable during the transaction, leading to potential inconsistencies. Implementing distributed transaction managers and recovery protocols becomes crucial to overcoming these challenges and ensuring that distributed transactions maintain ACID properties even in the face of failures.

The challenge of achieving fault tolerance in distributed systems adds another layer to synchronization complexities. Fault tolerance involves the system's ability to continue operating despite the failure of one or more nodes. Replication of data across multiple nodes is a common approach to enhance fault tolerance, but it introduces challenges related to maintaining consistency among replicas. Techniques such as quorum-based replication or consensus algorithms play a crucial role in achieving fault tolerance by ensuring that a majority of replicas agree on the state of shared data. However, balancing the trade-offs between fault tolerance, system responsiveness, and consistency remains a challenge, especially in scenarios where nodes may experience transient failures or network partitions.

Inconsistent views of the system state, known as the "split-brain" problem, present synchronization challenges in distributed systems, particularly in scenarios with network partitions. When network partitions occur, nodes may operate independently, leading to potential inconsistencies in the state of shared data. Techniques like quorum systems or leader election protocols aim to prevent the split-brain problem by ensuring that a majority of nodes agree on the system's state. However, determining an appropriate quorum size, handling transient partitions, and minimizing the impact on system performance introduce challenges in mitigating the split-brain problem effectively.

Communication delays and latency introduce synchronization challenges in scenarios where nodes must exchange messages or coordinate activities. In distributed systems, nodes may be geographically dispersed, leading to varying communication latencies. Achieving tight synchronization in the presence of latency introduces challenges related to the ordering of events, coordination of distributed algorithms, and maintaining the responsiveness of the system. Techniques like vector clocks or Lamport timestamps aim to address these challenges by providing a means to order events across distributed nodes. However, achieving precise synchronization in the face of dynamic network conditions and varying latencies remains an ongoing challenge in distributed system design.

Distributed systems often rely on leader election protocols to designate a primary node responsible for coordinating activities and maintaining consistency. Leader election introduces synchronization challenges, especially during the election process and when handling scenarios where the leader node may fail or become unavailable. Techniques like the Paxos algorithm or the Raft consensus algorithm provide solutions for leader election, but challenges persist in scenarios with frequent leadership changes, potential network partitions, and the need for rapid recovery.

The challenge of load balancing in distributed systems adds to the synchronization complexities, particularly when nodes have varying workloads or when the system experiences dynamic changes in demand. Load balancing involves distributing tasks evenly among nodes to maximize resource utilization and prevent performance bottlenecks. Achieving effective load balancing introduces challenges related to dynamic workload changes, the detection of under-utilized or overloaded nodes, and adapting to variations in system conditions. Techniques such as dynamic load balancing algorithms, distributed load balancers, and adaptive task allocation strategies aim to address these challenges and ensure that the system remains responsive and scalable.

Ensuring security in distributed systems presents synchronization challenges related to the coordination of secure communication, access control, and the prevention of unauthorized access. Secure communication between distributed nodes requires the establishment of secure channels, encryption, and authentication mechanisms. Synchronization challenges arise when managing access control policies across distributed nodes, especially in scenarios where nodes may have different levels of trust or operate in different security domains. Techniques such as distributed key management, secure channels, and cryptographic protocols aim to address these challenges and ensure the confidentiality, integrity, and authenticity of communication in distributed systems.

In conclusion, synchronization challenges in distributed systems encapsulate a spectrum of complexities arising from the coordination of activities across multiple nodes. Managing concurrent access to shared resources, addressing clock synchronization issues, navigating consistency models, implementing fault tolerance, and handling communication delays are fundamental aspects that demand careful consideration in distributed system design. The continuous evolution of distributed systems architecture, the emergence of new consensus algorithms, and the quest for achieving optimal trade-offs between consistency, availability, and partition tolerance underscore the ongoing nature of synchronization challenges in the dynamic landscape of distributed computing. Addressing these challenges requires a holistic approach that integrates synchronization mechanisms, fault-tolerant protocols, and adaptive strategies to ensure the reliable and efficient operation of distributed systems in diverse and dynamic environments.

Overview of synchronization mechanisms: locks, sema-phores, and barriers.

Synchronization mechanisms play a pivotal role in concurrent and distributed computing, ensuring that multiple threads or processes coordinate their activities to maintain consistency and prevent data corruption. One of the fundamental mechanisms used for synchronization is locks. Locks provide a way to control access to shared resources by allowing only one thread or process to acquire the lock at a time. When a thread holds a lock, it gains exclusive access to the critical section of code or shared resource, preventing other threads from entering that section concurrently. Locks come in various types, including binary locks (mutexes) and read-write locks. Binary locks are simple and allow either one or zero threads to access the critical section, while read-write locks enable multiple threads to read concurrently but ensure exclusive access during write operations. However, using locks can introduce challenges such as deadlocks, where threads are waiting indefinitely for each other to release locks, and contention, where multiple threads compete for the same lock, potentially degrading performance.

Semaphores represent another synchronization mechanism used to control access to shared resources but offer a more versatile approach than locks. A semaphore maintains a count that determines how many threads can access a particular resource simultaneously. A binary semaphore, similar to a lock, allows or denies access to a critical section. However, semaphores can be generalized to manage multiple resources by having a count greater than one. Threads can acquire or release semaphore permits, and the semaphore's count reflects the availability of permits for access. Semaphores are valuable for managing resources with finite capacity, implementing producer-consumer scenarios, and orchestrating access to shared pools of resources. While semaphores provide flexibility, they also require careful management to prevent issues like deadlock and ensure proper coordination among threads.

Barriers represent a synchronization mechanism designed for scenarios where a group of threads must synchronize their execution at a specific point in the program. A barrier ensures that all participating threads reach a designated synchronization point before any of them can proceed further. This is particularly useful in parallel algorithms or scenarios where multiple threads need to collaborate to achieve a specific task. Threads reach the barrier and then wait until all other threads arrive. Once the required number of threads has gathered at the barrier, they are collectively allowed to proceed. Barriers are commonly used in parallel computing, parallel algorithms, and scenarios where tasks are divided among multiple threads, requiring synchronization points to coordinate their progress. However, improper usage or mismanagement of barriers can lead to issues like deadlocks or unintended synchronization delays.

Lock-free and wait-free synchronization mechanisms represent advanced strategies aimed at minimizing contention and maximizing parallelism in concurrent systems. These mechanisms aim to enable progress in the presence of contention, avoiding scenarios where threads are blocked indefinitely. Lock-free algorithms ensure that at least one thread makes progress in a finite number of steps, while wait-free algorithms guarantee that every thread makes progress in a bounded number of steps. These mechanisms often rely on techniques like compare-and-swap (CAS) operations, atomic operations, and low-level hardware support to achieve non-blocking progress. While lock-free and wait-free synchronization mechanisms can offer improved scalability and responsiveness, they require careful design and understanding of low-level concurrency primitives.

Transactional memory represents a modern synchronization mechanism that simplifies the management of shared resources and critical sections. It provides a high-level abstraction where a sequence of operations can be executed atomically, as if in a single, indivisible transaction. In the context of multi-threaded programming, transactional memory allows threads to perform a series of operations on shared data without explicitly using locks or other low-level synchronization primitives. If conflicts arise between transactions, the system automatically manages rollbacks and retries to maintain consistency. Transactional memory aims to provide the ease of programming found in high-level, atomic transactions while offering improved performance and reduced contention compared to traditional lock-based approaches. However, achieving efficient and scalable transactional memory systems involves addressing challenges related to conflict resolution, overhead, and ensuring appropriate hardware and software support.

In conclusion, synchronization mechanisms, including locks, semaphores, and barriers, are essential tools in concurrent and distributed computing to manage shared resources, coordinate threads, and ensure the correctness of parallel execution. Locks provide exclusive access to critical sections but may lead to contention and deadlocks. Semaphores offer more flexibility by managing permits for resource access but require careful management. Barriers synchronize threads at specific points, facilitating collaboration. Lock-free and wait-free mechanisms minimize contention and aim for non-blocking progress. Transactional memory simplifies synchronization by providing high-level abstractions for atomic transactions. Each mechanism has its strengths and trade-offs, and their appropriate usage depends on the specific requirements and characteristics of the concurrent or distributed system at hand.

Overview of different distributed computing models: shared-memory vs. message-passing.

Distributed computing models are fundamental paradigms that shape the way computational tasks are organized and executed across multiple interconnected nodes. Two primary models, shared-memory and message-passing, represent distinct approaches to handling data and communication in distributed systems.

In the shared-memory model, multiple nodes access a common, shared address space, enabling them to communicate by reading and writing to shared variables. This model simplifies communication among nodes, as they can directly exchange information through shared data structures. Shared-memory systems often employ parallel programming techniques, such as threads or processes, to leverage multiple processors or cores within a node. This model facilitates the development of multithreaded applications, where threads can access shared data and synchronize their activities using synchronization primitives like locks or semaphores. Shared-memory architectures provide a high level of abstraction, making it easier for developers to reason about concurrent execution and share information among threads. However, challenges such as managing concurrent access to shared data, avoiding data inconsistencies, and ensuring proper synchronization arise, especially in large-scale distributed systems.

Conversely, the message-passing model adopts a decentralized approach to communication, where nodes exchange messages to coordinate their activities. Each node maintains its private memory space, and communication occurs explicitly through message passing. This model is often associated with distributed systems that span across networked nodes, allowing them to communicate and coordinate without a shared address space. Message-passing models are particularly prevalent in distributed computing environments where nodes are geographically dispersed or operate independently. Message-passing systems often use communication libraries or frameworks, such as MPI (Message Passing Interface) or actors in the case of actor-based models, to facilitate message exchange. While message-passing models mitigate challenges related to shared-memory access and data consistency, they introduce complexities in managing communication patterns, handling message queues, and ensuring proper coordination between distributed nodes.

Shared-memory and message-passing models represent two ends of the spectrum in distributed computing, and the choice between them depends on factors such as the nature of the application, system architecture, and scalability requirements. Shared-memory architectures are well-suited for tightly coupled systems where nodes have fast and efficient access to shared data, as seen in multiprocessor machines or symmetric multiprocessing (SMP) systems. This model is often employed in scenarios where nodes are within close proximity and can communicate rapidly through shared memory, leading to efficient coordination and reduced latency. However, shared-memory models face challenges in scaling to large distributed systems due to the inherent complexities of managing shared state across geographically dispersed nodes.

On the other hand, the message-passing model shines in scenarios where nodes are distributed across a network and may have limited or no shared memory. This model is highly scalable and adaptable to diverse network topologies, making it suitable for large-scale distributed systems, cloud computing environments, or grid computing scenarios. Message-passing models inherently handle communication in a more decentralized manner, allowing nodes to communicate asynchronously through messages. While this decentralization facilitates scalability, it also introduces challenges such as dealing with network latency, ensuring reliability in message delivery, and managing complex communication patterns.

Hybrid models often combine elements of both shared-memory and message-passing paradigms to leverage the advantages of each. For example, in distributed computing frameworks like Apache Spark, a shared-memory abstraction is employed through Resilient Distributed Datasets (RDDs), allowing nodes to share and process data in-memory. However, communication between nodes is achieved through message passing, enabling the system to scale efficiently across a distributed environment. Such hybrid approaches aim to strike a balance between the simplicity of shared-memory models and the scalability of message-passing models.

The choice between shared-memory and message-passing models also extends to the programming models and languages used in distributed computing. Languages like Java and C++ offer threading and shared-memory constructs, making them well-suited for shared-memory architectures. On the other hand, languages like Erlang or frameworks like Akka in Scala are designed with actor-based models, emphasizing message-passing concurrency and fault-tolerant communication patterns.

In conclusion, the selection between shared-memory and message-passing models in distributed computing depends on the specific requirements of the application, the nature of the distributed system, and considerations of scalability and communication patterns. Shared-memory models excel in tightly coupled environments where nodes have fast access to shared data, while message-passing models shine in scenarios where nodes are distributed and communication occurs over a network. The evolution of hybrid models reflects an ongoing effort to harness the strengths of both paradigms, providing a versatile approach to designing distributed systems that can adapt to diverse computational requirements. As the landscape of distributed computing continues to evolve, understanding the trade-offs and nuances of these models becomes essential for effective system design and development.

Examining the advantages and limitations of each model.

The shared-memory and message-passing models in distributed computing each come with their set of advantages and limitations, influencing their suitability for different applications and system architectures.

The shared-memory model offers simplicity and ease of programming, making it an attractive choice for scenarios where nodes have fast and efficient access to a common memory space. This model enables straightforward communication among nodes through shared variables, providing a familiar programming paradigm for developers accustomed to multithreaded programming. The inherent simplicity of the shared-memory model makes it well-suited for parallel computing tasks on multiprocessor machines or symmetric multiprocessing (SMP) systems, where communication is achieved through shared data structures. Moreover, shared-memory systems often employ familiar synchronization primitives like locks or semaphores, facilitating coordination among threads. This simplicity accelerates development and debugging processes, making shared-memory architectures an ideal choice for applications with moderate scalability requirements and well-defined data sharing patterns.

However, the shared-memory model faces limitations when scaling to large distributed systems or when nodes are geographically dispersed. Managing concurrent access to shared data introduces challenges such as race conditions, deadlocks, and contention, requiring careful synchronization mechanisms to avoid data inconsistencies. The need for synchronization becomes more pronounced as the number of nodes increases, leading to potential performance bottlenecks. Additionally, the requirement for a shared address space poses challenges in scenarios where nodes operate independently, potentially separated by networks with varying latencies. The scalability limitations of the shared-memory model necessitate careful consideration of system architecture and data sharing patterns, making it less suitable for highly distributed or cloud computing environments.

In contrast, the message-passing model excels in scenarios where nodes are distributed across a network and may have limited or no shared memory. This model offers scalability and flexibility, allowing nodes to communicate through explicit message passing without the need for a shared address space. The decentralization inherent in the message-passing model makes it well-suited for large-scale distributed systems, cloud computing environments, and grid computing scenarios, where nodes may span across different geographic locations. Message-passing models are designed to handle communication asynchronously, accommodating varying network latencies and providing a foundation for scalable and resilient architectures. This decentralization also enables fault tolerance and robustness, as nodes can continue to operate independently even if some nodes experience failures.

However, the message-passing model introduces its own set of challenges. Managing communication patterns becomes more complex, requiring careful consideration of message queues, routing, and addressing. The decentralized nature of message-passing systems can lead to intricate communication patterns, especially in applications with dynamic workloads or where nodes join and leave the system dynamically. Asynchronous communication can also make it challenging to reason about the order of events and ensure that nodes are synchronized at critical points in the computation. Ensuring reliability in message delivery, handling message queues efficiently, and managing the complexity of communication patterns demand additional design considerations. Despite these challenges, the message-passing model remains a powerful paradigm for achieving scalability and adaptability in highly distributed and dynamic environments.

Hybrid models seek to leverage the advantages of both shared-memory and message-passing paradigms. For instance, frameworks like Apache Spark combine shared-memory abstractions (Resilient Distributed Datasets - RDDs) with message passing to achieve scalability and fault tolerance. This hybrid approach aims to strike a balance, providing simplicity for data sharing within a node and scalability for communication across nodes. Hybrid models offer flexibility and adaptability, allowing developers to choose the most appropriate paradigm for different aspects of their applications.

In terms of programming models and languages, shared-memory models find their natural fit in languages like Java and C++, which offer threading and shared-memory constructs. These languages simplify the development of parallel applications, providing abstractions for shared data and synchronization primitives. On the other hand, languages like Erlang, designed for actor-based models, and frameworks like Akka in Scala, emphasize message-passing concurrency. These languages and frameworks are well-suited for distributed environments, where nodes communicate through message passing, and fault tolerance is a critical consideration.

In conclusion, the shared-memory and message-passing models in distributed computing each bring distinct advantages and limitations to the table. The shared-memory model offers simplicity, ease of programming, and efficiency for certain types of applications, but faces challenges in scaling to large distributed systems. The message-passing model excels in scalability, adaptability to distributed environments, and fault tolerance, but introduces complexities in managing communication patterns. Hybrid models aim to combine the strengths of both paradigms, offering a versatile approach to designing distributed systems. The choice between these models depends on factors such as the nature of the application, system architecture, scalability requirements, and communication patterns. As distributed computing continues to evolve, understanding the trade-offs and nuances of each model becomes essential for making informed decisions in system design and development.

Real-world examples of distributed systems effectively utilizing concurrency and parallelism.

Distributed systems effectively utilize concurrency and parallelism to tackle complex computational tasks across multiple nodes, enabling enhanced performance, scalability, and responsiveness. Several real-world examples illustrate the successful application of these principles, showcasing the impact of distributed computing in diverse domains.

In the realm of internet services, content delivery networks (CDNs) exemplify the efficient use of concurrency and parallelism. CDNs distribute content across geographically dispersed servers to minimize latency and improve the user experience. When a user requests a resource, such as a webpage or media file, the CDN employs parallelism to serve the content from the nearest server. Concurrent requests from multiple users are processed simultaneously, reducing load times and optimizing bandwidth usage. This distributed approach not only enhances content delivery speed but also ensures reliable and scalable performance, demonstrating how parallelism and concurrency contribute to a seamless user experience on a global scale.

Cloud computing platforms, such as Amazon Web Services (AWS), Microsoft Azure, and Google Cloud, leverage distributed systems to deliver a wide array of services. In these environments, concurrency and parallelism are fundamental to achieving efficient resource utilization and meeting the demands of diverse workloads. For instance, cloud providers use parallel processing to execute tasks concurrently on multiple virtual machines (VMs) or containers. This enables users to scale their applications horizontally by distributing workloads across numerous instances, ensuring optimal performance and responsiveness. The orchestration of parallel execution across a distributed infrastructure allows cloud computing platforms to cater to the dynamic needs of users, from running large-scale data analytics to hosting web applications.

Distributed databases, exemplified by systems like Apache Cassandra or Google Spanner, showcase the benefits of concurrency and parallelism in managing and retrieving data across multiple nodes. These databases employ sharding and replication strategies to distribute data, allowing parallel processing of queries and transactions. In a distributed database, concurrent read and write operations can be executed simultaneously on different nodes, enhancing throughput and reducing latency. The parallelization of queries across distributed nodes enables efficient data retrieval and analysis, making distributed databases suitable for handling vast amounts of information in applications ranging from e-commerce platforms to real-time analytics systems.

High-performance computing (HPC) clusters represent another domain where concurrency and parallelism play a pivotal role. In scientific research, simulations, and data-intensive computations, HPC clusters distribute tasks across numerous nodes to achieve faster results. For example, in weather forecasting, complex numerical simulations are parallelized and distributed across multiple processors or nodes to expedite the computation of atmospheric models. This parallel processing approach enables meteorologists to generate timely and accurate predictions, demonstrating the practical impact of concurrency and parallelism in scientific endeavors.

In the context of social media platforms, distributed systems efficiently handle massive amounts of data and user interactions. Platforms like Facebook or Twitter employ distributed architectures to manage user profiles, posts, and real-time interactions. Concurrency allows multiple users to engage with the platform simultaneously, with parallel processing facilitating the retrieval and display of personalized content. The ability to handle a large number of concurrent users and process real-time interactions exemplifies how distributed systems enhance the scalability and responsiveness of social media platforms.

Online retail and e-commerce platforms heavily rely on distributed systems to manage inventory, process transactions, and deliver a seamless shopping experience. During peak shopping periods, such as Black Friday or Cyber Monday, these platforms experience a surge in user activity. Through the effective use of concurrency and parallelism, distributed systems ensure that multiple users can browse, add items to their carts, and complete transactions simultaneously. The parallel processing of transactions across distributed servers prevents bottlenecks and maintains responsiveness, showcasing how these principles contribute to the success of online retail in handling large-scale operations.

Autonomous vehicles and smart transportation systems provide an intriguing example of distributed systems utilizing concurrency and parallelism. In a network of interconnected vehicles and infrastructure, concurrent processing enables real-time communication and decision-making. Each autonomous vehicle processes sensor data concurrently, assessing its surroundings and making split-second decisions based on parallel algorithms. Moreover, vehicles communicate with each other and with traffic management systems in a distributed manner, facilitating collaborative efforts to optimize traffic flow, enhance safety, and minimize congestion. The parallel processing capabilities of distributed systems are essential for achieving the responsiveness required in dynamic and safety-critical environments.

The domain of financial services, including high-frequency trading and algorithmic trading platforms, relies on distributed systems to execute transactions swiftly and efficiently. In high-frequency trading, where milliseconds can make a significant difference, concurrency enables multiple trades to be processed simultaneously. Parallelism is harnessed to execute complex algorithms across distributed servers, analyzing market data, making trading decisions, and executing orders in real time. This concurrency and parallelism in distributed systems contribute to the competitiveness and success of financial institutions in rapidly evolving markets.

Healthcare systems leverage distributed computing to manage patient data, medical records, and facilitate collaborative research. Concurrency and parallelism play a crucial role in processing and analyzing vast datasets, such as genomic information, in a timely manner. Distributed systems enable healthcare professionals to access and update patient records concurrently, improving the efficiency of medical workflows. Additionally, parallel processing supports complex simulations and data analytics in medical research, accelerating discoveries and advancements in fields like drug discovery and personalized medicine.

In summary, the real-world examples of distributed systems effectively utilizing concurrency and parallelism span a wide range of industries and applications. From content delivery networks and cloud computing platforms to distributed databases, scientific research, social media, online retail, autonomous vehicles, financial services, and healthcare, the principles of concurrency and parallelism contribute to enhanced performance, scalability, and responsiveness. These examples highlight the transformative impact of distributed computing in addressing the challenges of today's dynamic and data-intensive applications across diverse domains.

Challenges faced and lessons learned in implementing concurrent and parallel solutions.

Implementing concurrent and parallel solutions in software development introduces a spectrum of challenges and offers valuable lessons that span various domains and applications. One of the primary challenges lies in managing shared resources and avoiding race conditions. Concurrent programs, where multiple threads or processes access shared data simultaneously, are susceptible to race conditions that can lead to unpredictable behavior and data inconsistencies. Developing effective synchronization mechanisms, such as locks or semaphores, becomes crucial to mitigate these challenges. However, the lesson learned is that overusing locks can introduce contention, potentially undermining the benefits of parallelism. Striking the right balance between ensuring data consistency and allowing for parallel execution is an ongoing challenge in concurrent programming.

A key challenge in parallel computing is load balancing, particularly in scenarios where tasks have varying computational complexity. Uneven distribution of workloads among parallel threads or processors can result in some units idling while others remain heavily loaded. Implementing dynamic load balancing mechanisms, where tasks are dynamically distributed based on the current system state, can address this challenge. The lesson learned is that load balancing strategies need to be adaptive and responsive to dynamic changes in the system, ensuring optimal resource utilization and preventing performance bottlenecks.

Deadlocks represent a critical challenge in concurrent systems, where two or more threads or processes are blocked, waiting for each other to release resources. Designing and implementing deadlock avoidance or detection mechanisms is essential to ensure the robustness of concurrent solutions. However, the lesson learned is that overemphasizing deadlock prevention can lead to performance degradation. Striking a balance between preventing deadlocks and allowing for efficient resource utilization is crucial, emphasizing the need for a nuanced approach in concurrent system design.

Another challenge in concurrent and parallel programming is managing the granularity of tasks. Dividing tasks into smaller subtasks for parallel execution can enhance performance, but excessively fine granularity can introduce overhead due to communication and synchronization. Conversely, coarse-grained tasks may underutilize available resources. The lesson learned is that task granularity should be carefully tailored to the characteristics of the application and the underlying hardware architecture, optimizing the trade-off between parallel efficiency and overhead.

Scalability challenges arise when implementing concurrent and parallel solutions across distributed systems. Coordinating tasks among nodes, handling communication overhead, and ensuring data consistency become more complex as the number of nodes increases. Lessons learned include the importance of designing scalable architectures that can adapt to varying workloads and efficiently distribute tasks across nodes. Additionally, understanding the trade-offs between consistency and availability in distributed systems becomes crucial for achieving scalable and resilient solutions.

Concurrency bugs, such as race conditions, deadlocks, and data inconsistencies, pose significant challenges in debugging and maintaining concurrent code. Traditional debugging tools may not effectively identify these issues, and reproducing concurrency-related bugs can be challenging due to their nondeterministic nature. Lessons learned include the necessity of employing specialized debugging tools and adopting testing strategies that focus on uncovering concurrency bugs. Emphasizing thorough testing, code reviews, and static analysis helps identify potential issues early in the development process.

In parallel computing, achieving efficient communication between threads or processes is a key challenge. Synchronization mechanisms, message passing, and shared-memory constructs all introduce communication overhead. Balancing the need for communication with the goal of maximizing parallelism requires careful consideration. The lesson learned is that minimizing communication overhead involves optimizing the design of communication patterns, selecting appropriate communication mechanisms, and understanding the impact of communication on overall system performance.

Adapting existing sequential algorithms for parallel execution can be challenging, especially when the algorithms have inherent dependencies that limit parallelism. Identifying opportunities for parallelization and restructuring algorithms to exploit parallel execution require a deep understanding of the application domain. The lesson learned is that parallelizing algorithms often involves trade-offs, and not all algorithms can be parallelized efficiently. Selecting the right algorithms and data structures that align with the principles of parallel computing is crucial for achieving optimal performance.

In distributed systems, achieving consistency across nodes poses challenges due to factors like network delays, message ordering, and node failures. Consistency models, such as eventual consistency or strong consistency, introduce trade-offs between performance and reliability. The lesson learned is that selecting an appropriate consistency model depends on the specific requirements of the application. Striking a balance between consistency and availability is crucial, and distributed systems architects must carefully consider the implications of their consistency choices on the overall system behavior.

Concurrency and parallelism introduce challenges in terms of debugging, profiling, and performance analysis. Traditional debugging tools may not effectively handle concurrent scenarios, making it challenging to identify and diagnose issues. Profiling parallel code to understand resource utilization and bottlenecks requires specialized tools and techniques. The lesson learned is the importance of investing in tools and methodologies that support effective debugging and profiling of concurrent and parallel code. Integrating instrumentation, logging, and monitoring mechanisms becomes essential for gaining insights into the runtime behavior of parallel systems.

In the context of multi-core processors and hardware parallelism, cache coherence becomes a critical consideration. In shared-memory systems, multiple cores may cache data independently, leading to inconsistencies when different cores modify the same data. Ensuring cache coherence and minimizing cache-related bottlenecks require careful consideration of data access patterns and synchronization mechanisms. The lesson learned is that efficient cache utilization is crucial for achieving optimal parallel performance, and developers must be mindful of cache-related considerations during system design and implementation.

A critical challenge in distributed systems is handling failures gracefully. Node failures, network partitions, and transient errors can occur in complex distributed environments. Designing fault-tolerant systems that can recover from failures without compromising data consistency is a significant challenge. Lessons learned include the importance of implementing mechanisms such as replication, consensus algorithms, and automatic recovery processes. Additionally, embracing the principles of reactive programming and designing systems that can gracefully degrade functionality in the face of failures contributes to robust distributed solutions.

The complexity of coordinating tasks in distributed systems introduces challenges in achieving linear scalability. As the number of nodes increases, coordinating activities and maintaining consistency become more intricate. Lessons learned involve designing distributed systems that can scale horizontally while effectively managing coordination overhead. Techniques such as sharding, partitioning, and load balancing contribute to achieving linear scalability in distributed architectures.

Ensuring data consistency across distributed systems without sacrificing performance introduces the challenge of choosing appropriate consistency models. The trade-off between strong consistency and eventual consistency requires careful consideration of the application's requirements. Lessons learned emphasize the need for aligning the consistency model with the specific use case, understanding the implications of eventual consistency on application behavior, and implementing mechanisms to handle eventual consistency gracefully.

In conclusion, implementing concurrent and parallel solutions in software development presents a myriad of challenges across various dimensions, including resource management, load balancing, deadlock prevention, task granularity, scalability, debugging, communication, algorithm parallelization, consistency, fault tolerance, cache coherence, and handling failures. The lessons learned from these challenges underscore the importance of adopting a nuanced and context-specific approach to concurrency and parallelism. Successful implementation involves a continuous process of refinement, learning from experiences, and applying principles that align with the characteristics of the application and the underlying hardware architecture. As software development continues to evolve, the ongoing exploration of concurrency and parallelism remains integral to addressing the complexities of modern computing environments and achieving optimal performance across diverse applications and domains.

Chapter 4: Communication Protocols: Building Bridges in Distributed Systems

Understanding the crucial role of communication protocols in distributed systems.

The role of communication protocols in distributed systems is paramount, serving as the linchpin for effective coordination and interaction among nodes across a network. At the core of this role lies the need for a standardized set of rules and conventions that govern the exchange of information between distributed components, ensuring seamless communication in an environment where nodes may vary in hardware, software, and geographic location. Communication protocols define the format, structure, and semantics of messages shared between nodes, enabling interoperability and facilitating the creation of robust, scalable, and reliable distributed systems.

One of the primary functions of communication protocols is to establish a common ground for nodes with different architectures and functionalities to understand each other's messages. Standardization ensures that irrespective of the underlying hardware or software variations, nodes can interpret and process messages correctly. This aspect becomes particularly crucial in large-scale distributed systems, where heterogeneity is inevitable, and nodes may run on diverse platforms. Communication protocols, by defining the structure of messages and the rules for their interpretation, foster a shared language that enables effective communication and cooperation among nodes.

Ensuring the integrity and reliability of data exchanged between nodes is another critical facet of communication protocols. In the dynamic and often unpredictable world of distributed systems, messages may traverse through various network conditions, including latency, packet loss, and potential disruptions. Communication protocols incorporate mechanisms for error detection, correction, and prevention, safeguarding the accuracy and consistency of the information being shared. Techniques such as checksums, acknowledgment mechanisms, and retransmission strategies contribute to the robustness of communication protocols, allowing distributed systems to maintain data integrity even in the face of network challenges.

Scalability, a fundamental requirement in many distributed systems, relies heavily on the efficiency of communication protocols. As the number of nodes increases, the overhead of communication becomes a critical consideration. Well-designed protocols optimize the use of network resources, minimizing unnecessary data transfer and reducing latency. The definition of efficient communication patterns, the use of compression techniques, and the implementation of asynchronous communication mechanisms are strategies employed by communication protocols to enhance scalability. By efficiently managing the flow of information, communication protocols contribute to the ability of distributed systems to scale horizontally, accommodating increasing workloads and adapting to changes in the system's size and complexity.

Consistency and coordination across distributed nodes are essential for maintaining the overall integrity of a system. Communication protocols play a crucial role in achieving consistency by defining mechanisms for synchronization and coordination. Consensus protocols, such as the Paxos or Raft algorithms, enable nodes to reach an agreement on the state of a distributed system, ensuring that all nodes have a consistent view of the data. Coordination protocols, like Two-Phase Commit or Three-Phase Commit, enable nodes to collaborate in executing distributed transactions while ensuring atomicity and consistency. The ability of communication protocols to orchestrate coordination and consensus processes is fundamental to achieving a coherent and reliable distributed system.

In the realm of security, communication protocols become instrumental in safeguarding sensitive information and ensuring the privacy and integrity of data. Distributed systems often operate in environments where security threats are pervasive, and communication occurs over open networks. Encryption protocols, such as TLS (Transport Layer Security) or SSL (Secure Sockets Layer), provide a secure channel for communication, preventing eavesdropping and unauthorized access. Authentication mechanisms embedded in communication protocols verify the identity of communicating nodes, mitigating the risk of malicious entities infiltrating the system. By incorporating these security features, communication protocols contribute to building trust and resilience in distributed systems, making them suitable for applications that handle confidential or sensitive data.

The dynamic nature of distributed systems, where nodes may join or leave the network at any time, introduces the challenge of managing network topology changes. Communication protocols must adapt to these changes seamlessly, ensuring continuous communication and coordination among nodes. Membership protocols, such as SWIM (Scalable Weakly-consistent Infection-style Process Group Membership Protocol) or Gossip protocols, dynamically maintain an up-to-date view of the network, allowing nodes to discover and communicate with each other. By incorporating mechanisms for node discovery, failure detection, and reconfiguration, communication protocols enable distributed systems to remain resilient and responsive to changes in the network environment.

In scenarios where real-time responsiveness is critical, such as in distributed gaming or video conferencing, communication protocols play a pivotal role in minimizing latency. Protocols designed for low-latency communication, such as WebSockets or the Real-Time Transport Protocol (RTP), optimize data transmission to ensure timely delivery of messages. The ability to provide low-latency communication is essential for applications where immediate responsiveness is a priority, highlighting the versatility of communication protocols in adapting to diverse requirements across different distributed system domains.

Communication protocols also contribute to fault tolerance and recovery in distributed systems. In environments where node failures are inevitable, protocols for distributed consensus and replication, such as the Raft consensus algorithm or the CAP theorem, guide the system in maintaining availability and consistency. By defining how nodes should react to failures, recover from crashes, and synchronize their state, communication protocols enable distributed systems to withstand faults and continue functioning even when individual nodes experience disruptions. These fault-tolerance mechanisms are integral to the resilience of distributed systems in dynamic and unpredictable conditions.

The evolution of communication protocols reflects ongoing efforts to address the evolving needs and challenges of distributed systems. For instance, emerging protocols like gRPC (gRPC Remote Procedure Calls) or GraphQL focus on optimizing communication between services in microservices architectures. These protocols emphasize efficiency, flexibility, and ease of use, reflecting the demand for streamlined communication patterns in modern distributed systems.

The standardization of communication protocols is not only limited to the lower layers of the networking stack but extends to higher-level abstractions in distributed systems. Protocols like

HTTP (Hypertext Transfer Protocol) or MQTT (Message Queuing Telemetry Transport) define how applications communicate over the internet, enabling interoperability and enabling the development of diverse distributed applications. In the context of the Internet of Things (IoT), protocols like CoAP (Constrained Application Protocol) cater to resource-constrained devices, showcasing the adaptability of communication protocols to different domains and constraints.

Interoperability is a key advantage facilitated by communication protocols, allowing diverse systems to collaborate and share information seamlessly. By adhering to a common set of communication standards, distributed systems can integrate components developed using different technologies and ensure their smooth interaction. Standardized protocols enable the creation of interoperable ecosystems, fostering collaboration across different vendors, platforms, and technologies. For example, the use of REST (Representational State Transfer) as a communication style in web services promotes interoperability, allowing systems built on different technologies to communicate over the internet.

Despite their crucial role, communication protocols are not without challenges. The choice of an appropriate protocol depends on various factors, including the nature of the application, system requirements, and performance considerations. The design of efficient and effective communication protocols involves trade-offs between factors such as simplicity, extensibility, and the overhead associated with message encoding and decoding. Moreover, the deployment and maintenance of communication protocols in distributed systems require continuous monitoring, adaptation, and consideration of evolving security threats and performance improvements.

In conclusion, the crucial role of communication protocols in distributed systems encompasses a diverse range of functions, from standardizing message formats to ensuring data integrity, scalability, coordination, security, and fault tolerance. These protocols serve as the backbone of effective communication, enabling nodes to collaborate seamlessly in the complex and dynamic environment of distributed systems. As technology continues to advance, the evolution of communication protocols remains integral to the continued development of robust, efficient, and interoperable distributed systems across various domains and applications.

Overview of common communication protocols: TCP/IP, HTTP, and more.

Communication protocols play a pivotal role in facilitating the exchange of information between devices and systems, ensuring seamless connectivity in the vast digital landscape. Among the most fundamental protocols is the Transmission Control Protocol/Internet Protocol (TCP/IP), a foundational suite that underlies the functioning of the internet. TCP/IP consists of two main components: the Transmission Control Protocol (TCP) and the Internet Protocol (IP). TCP governs the reliable and ordered delivery of data, breaking it into packets, while IP manages the addressing and routing of these packets across networks. Together, they provide the essential framework for data transmission, enabling computers to communicate across diverse networks.

HTTP, or Hypertext Transfer Protocol, represents another key protocol that operates at a higher level in the network stack. It is the foundation of data communication on the World Wide Web and governs the transfer of hypertext, which includes text, images, and multimedia content. HTTP operates on top of the TCP/IP stack, utilizing the reliable transport services provided by TCP. Over time, various versions of HTTP have emerged, with HTTP/1.1 and the more recent HTTP/2 being the most widely adopted. HTTP/2, in particular, introduces improvements in performance, allowing for more efficient utilization of network resources through techniques like multiplexing and header compression.

Moving beyond the web-specific domain, several protocols cater to diverse communication needs. The File Transfer Protocol (FTP) is instrumental in transferring files between computers on a network. It operates over the TCP/IP stack and employs separate channels for control and data transfer. FTP has seen various iterations, such as FTPS (FTP Secure) and SFTP (SSH File Transfer Protocol), which incorporate encryption for enhanced security during file transfers.

The Simple Mail Transfer Protocol (SMTP) is dedicated to electronic mail transmission. It defines the rules for sending emails between servers, outlining the interaction between the sender's and recipient's mail servers. SMTP works in tandem with the Post Office Protocol (POP) or Internet Message Access Protocol (IMAP), which enable email clients to retrieve messages from the server. POP typically downloads and removes messages from the server, while IMAP allows users to manage their messages on the server itself.

In the realm of real-time communication, the Real-Time Transport Protocol (RTP) takes center stage. RTP is designed to transmit audio and video over IP networks, facilitating applications like voice over IP (VoIP) and video conferencing. It operates on top of UDP (User Datagram Protocol), prioritizing low latency over reliability, which is crucial for real-time applications where delays can impact the user experience.

For secure communication, the Secure Sockets Layer (SSL) and its successor, the Transport Layer Security (TLS), provide cryptographic protocols that ensure the confidentiality and integrity of data exchanged over a network. TLS has become the standard for securing web communication, encrypting data during transmission and offering protection against eavesdropping and tampering.

Network Time Protocol (NTP) serves a different yet crucial purpose by synchronizing the clocks of computers within a network. Accurate timekeeping is essential for various applications, including financial transactions, network logging, and coordination among distributed systems. NTP helps maintain temporal consistency across devices, ensuring coherence in time-sensitive operations.

As the Internet of Things (IoT) continues to proliferate, protocols like Message Queuing Telemetry Transport (MQTT) have gained prominence. MQTT is a lightweight and efficient protocol designed for low-bandwidth, high-latency, or unreliable networks. It is particularly well-suited for IoT devices, allowing them to exchange messages and updates in a publish-subscribe model, minimizing overhead and conserving resources.

In conclusion, communication protocols form the backbone of modern connectivity, facilitating the exchange of data across networks with precision and reliability. TCP/IP stands as the cornerstone, providing the foundation for internet communication, while HTTP governs the transfer of data on the World Wide Web. Various specialized protocols cater to specific needs, from file transfer with FTP to secure communication with TLS. As technology evolves, new protocols emerge to address the demands of emerging paradigms, such as real-time communication with RTP and IoT connectivity with MQTT. Understanding these protocols is essential for navigating the intricate web of modern digital communication and ensuring the seamless flow of information across diverse networks.

Importance of standardized message formats in distributed communication.

Standardized message formats play a pivotal role in the realm of distributed communication, providing a common language that facilitates seamless interaction and interoperability among diverse systems and devices. In the complex landscape of distributed computing, where various components may be developed by different vendors, operate on disparate platforms, and handle diverse functionalities, the adoption of standardized message formats becomes paramount for achieving cohesion and reliability. These formats define the structure, syntax, and semantics of messages exchanged between entities, ensuring a consistent and universally understandable means of communication.

One of the primary benefits of standardized message formats lies in their ability to establish a shared understanding between communicating parties. By adhering to a predefined format, systems can accurately interpret and process incoming messages, mitigating the risks of misinterpretation or data corruption. This common ground enables disparate systems, ranging from software applications to hardware devices, to communicate effectively without the need for extensive customization or bespoke integration efforts. As a result, interoperability becomes achievable on a broader scale, fostering a more interconnected and collaborative ecosystem.

In distributed systems, where components may be geographically dispersed and operate independently, standardized message formats serve as the lingua franca that transcends geographical and organizational boundaries. This universal communication medium enhances collaboration by enabling seamless data exchange between entities regardless of their physical location or the organizational structures governing their development. The significance of this interoperability is particularly evident in modern, globally distributed applications, where components may be hosted on cloud platforms, edge devices, or traditional data centers.

Moreover, standardized message formats contribute to the longevity and sustainability of distributed systems. As technology evolves and software undergoes updates or replacements, the underlying message formats provide a stable interface that shields communicating entities from the intricacies of internal changes. This decoupling of communication from internal implementations fosters system resilience and ease of maintenance, allowing organizations to innovate and adapt without compromising the integrity of existing interactions.

A crucial aspect of standardized message formats is their role in fostering a loosely coupled architecture, a fundamental principle in distributed systems design. Loosely coupled systems are characterized by components that operate independently and are unaware of the internal workings of other components. Standardized message formats enable this separation by defining a clear contract for communication, allowing each component to focus on its specific responsibilities without being burdened by the internal details of others. This architectural flexibility enhances scalability and facilitates the evolution of systems over time.

Interchangeability is another key advantage facilitated by standardized message formats. In distributed environments, there is a continuous evolution of technologies and platforms. Standardized formats enable the substitution of components or services with minimal friction, as long as they adhere to the established communication standards. This adaptability is crucial for organizations seeking to leverage emerging technologies, upgrade infrastructure, or integrate third-party solutions seamlessly.

Security and resilience are paramount concerns in distributed systems, and standardized message formats contribute significantly to addressing these challenges. Security protocols and mechanisms can be consistently applied and enforced at the message level, ensuring the confidentiality, integrity, and authenticity of communication across the distributed environment. Moreover, in the face of failures or disruptions, standardized formats facilitate the implementation of robust error handling and recovery mechanisms, enhancing the overall resilience of the system.

The standardization of message formats also plays a central role in enhancing traceability and monitoring capabilities in distributed systems. With a predefined structure for messages, it becomes easier to log, analyze, and trace the flow of data throughout the system. This not only aids in debugging and troubleshooting but also supports compliance requirements, providing a transparent view of data interactions for auditing purposes.

Furthermore, standardized message formats contribute to the overall efficiency of distributed systems. By defining a common structure, the overhead associated with parsing and interpreting messages is reduced, promoting faster processing and lower latency. This efficiency is particularly crucial in scenarios where real-time communication or rapid response times are imperative, such as financial transactions, healthcare systems, or industrial automation.

In conclusion, the importance of standardized message formats in distributed communication cannot be overstated. They serve as the linchpin for establishing a shared understanding, enabling interoperability, and fostering a cohesive and resilient distributed ecosystem. Through the establishment of a common language, these formats facilitate the seamless exchange of data, promote architectural flexibility, and contribute to the overall efficiency and security of distributed systems. As technology continues to advance, the role of standardized message formats remains foundational, providing a timeless framework that transcends the complexities of evolving technologies and diverse landscapes in the ever-expanding realm of distributed communication.

Exploring serialization techniques for efficient data transmission.

Serialization techniques play a crucial role in the realm of data transmission, serving as the bridge between in-memory data structures and their binary or textual representations for efficient communication across networks. In the context of distributed systems, where data must traverse diverse environments and devices, the choice of serialization method becomes paramount in optimizing transmission speed, bandwidth utilization, and overall system performance. One widely adopted serialization technique is Binary Serialization, which encodes data in a binary format for efficient storage and transmission. This method is particularly advantageous in scenarios where both the sender and receiver understand the binary format, enabling faster serialization and deserialization processes compared to human-readable formats.

Text-based serialization, on the other hand, involves encoding data in a human-readable format such as JSON (JavaScript Object Notation) or XML (eXtensible Markup Language). These formats provide readability and ease of debugging, making them popular choices for data interchange in web applications and APIs. JSON, in particular, has gained widespread adoption due to its simplicity and lightweight structure, making it suitable for a variety of use cases. However, text-based serialization typically incurs higher overhead compared to binary formats, as the textual representation introduces additional characters, leading to larger payload sizes and increased transmission times.

Another serialization technique worth exploring is Protocol Buffers, a binary serialization format developed by Google. Protocol Buffers offer a compact binary representation, resulting in smaller message sizes and faster transmission compared to human-readable formats. The schema is defined in a language-agnostic protocol file, allowing for easy interoperability between systems implemented in different programming languages. Protocol Buffers are well-suited for scenarios where bandwidth is limited, and efficiency is paramount, making them a popular choice in distributed systems and microservices architectures.

MessagePack is yet another binary serialization format designed for optimal efficiency and minimal overhead. Similar to Protocol Buffers, MessagePack represents data in a binary format but focuses on achieving even smaller message sizes. It is particularly suitable for environments where bandwidth is a critical resource, such as IoT (Internet of Things) devices and real-time communication systems.

MessagePack's compact representation contributes to reduced network latency and improved overall system performance.

Avro, developed within the Apache Hadoop project, is a binary serialization framework designed for high-performance data serialization. Avro employs a schema to define the structure of data, allowing for dynamic typing and schema evolution. This flexibility makes Avro well-suited for scenarios where data schemas may evolve over time, as it accommodates changes without requiring updates to all components in the system. Additionally, Avro's compact binary format contributes to efficient data transmission, making it a popular choice in big data processing frameworks.

CBOR (Concise Binary Object Representation) is a binary serialization format that strikes a balance between efficiency and human readability. CBOR's binary encoding is more compact than JSON, resulting in reduced payload sizes, while still maintaining a level of readability when necessary. CBOR is often used in resource-constrained environments or scenarios where both efficiency and ease of debugging are important considerations.

Efficient data transmission also involves considering the context of the application and the specific requirements of the data being serialized. For instance, BSON (Binary JSON) is a binary serialization format designed to closely resemble JSON while providing a more efficient binary representation. BSON is commonly used in MongoDB, a NoSQL database, as it aligns with the document-oriented nature of MongoDB's data model.

In addition to the aforementioned serialization techniques, FlatBuffers and Cap'n Proto are notable for their focus on achieving high-performance serialization and deserialization. These frameworks are designed for scenarios where low latency and minimal memory overhead are critical, such as in gaming applications and real-time communication systems. FlatBuffers, developed by Google, employs a zero-copy deserialization approach, minimizing memory allocation and enhancing performance. Cap'n Proto, inspired by FlatBuffers, also emphasizes zero-copy deserialization and supports schema evolution, making it suitable for dynamic and evolving data structures.

The choice of a serialization technique depends on various factors, including the specific requirements of the application, the nature of the data being transmitted, and the performance characteristics desired. Binary serialization formats excel in scenarios where efficiency and minimal overhead are paramount, while text-based formats offer readability and ease of debugging. Each serialization technique comes with its trade-offs, and the optimal choice often depends on the unique constraints and goals of the system at hand. Regardless of the technique chosen, the overarching goal is to strike a balance between efficient data transmission, system performance, and the ease of development and maintenance in distributed and networked environments.

Defining RPC and its role in distributed computing.

Remote Procedure Call (RPC) is a fundamental concept in distributed computing, serving as a mechanism for enabling communication and coordination between processes or components that exist on different machines within a networked environment. At its core, RPC allows a program to execute procedures or functions on a remote server as if they were local, abstracting the complexities of inter-process communication and facilitating the development of distributed applications. The idea behind RPC is rooted in the desire to make the invocation of procedures across a network as transparent and straightforward as invoking local procedures, thus allowing developers to design and implement distributed systems without delving into the intricacies of low-level network communication protocols.

In a typical RPC scenario, there are two main entities involved: the client and the server. The client initiates the RPC by invoking a procedure, which may reside on a remote server. The client and server communicate over the network, and the server executes the requested procedure. The result, if any, is then transmitted back to the client. This process abstracts the complexities of network communication, making it appear as if the procedure invocation is a local operation for the client. Various RPC frameworks and libraries, such as Java RMI (Remote Method Invocation), gRPC, and Apache Thrift, provide tools and abstractions to implement RPC in a seamless and language-agnostic manner.

The role of RPC in distributed computing is multifaceted and pivotal for building scalable, efficient, and maintainable distributed systems. One of its primary roles is to hide the details of communication between processes, allowing developers to focus on the logic of their applications rather than the intricacies of network protocols. This abstraction simplifies the development process, fostering productivity and reducing the likelihood of errors that may arise from dealing with low-level communication nuances.

Scalability is another critical aspect where RPC plays a vital role. In a distributed system, components may be spread across multiple servers to handle increased load or achieve fault tolerance. RPC enables the seamless distribution of procedures across these servers, allowing the system to scale horizontally by adding more machines to the network. This ability to scale is essential for handling growing workloads and ensuring that the distributed application remains responsive and performant.

Furthermore, RPC contributes to the modularity and maintainability of distributed systems. By encapsulating procedures as services that can be invoked remotely, RPC fosters a modular design where components can be developed, tested, and maintained independently. This modular approach facilitates code reuse and simplifies updates or changes to specific functionalities without affecting the entire system. This is particularly advantageous in large-scale distributed applications where different teams may be responsible for different services or components.

RPC also plays a crucial role in achieving loose coupling between distributed components. Loose coupling is a design principle that emphasizes minimizing the dependencies between different parts of a system. RPC achieves this by abstracting the communication between client and server, allowing them to evolve independently. As long as the contract defined by the RPC interface remains unchanged, clients and servers can be updated or replaced without affecting the overall functionality of the system. This decoupling is essential for building distributed systems that are resilient to changes and can adapt to evolving requirements.

Moreover, RPC contributes to fault tolerance in distributed computing. In a networked environment, failures are inevitable, and systems must be designed to handle them gracefully. RPC frameworks often provide mechanisms for handling errors, retries, and timeouts, allowing distributed applications to recover from transient failures and continue functioning. Additionally, some RPC frameworks support features like load balancing and service discovery, further enhancing the resilience of distributed systems by distributing workloads and redirecting requests in the face of failures.

Security is another critical consideration in distributed computing, and RPC plays a role in ensuring secure communication between distributed components. Many RPC frameworks support encryption and authentication mechanisms to safeguard data transmitted over the network. This is particularly crucial in scenarios where sensitive information is exchanged between the client and server. By incorporating security features, RPC contributes to the overall integrity and confidentiality of communication in distributed systems.

While RPC offers numerous benefits, it is not without challenges and considerations. Network latency and reliability become prominent factors, as the performance of RPC calls is influenced by the quality of the network. As a result, developers must carefully design their distributed systems, considering factors like asynchronous communication and caching to mitigate the impact of network latency. Additionally, ensuring backward compatibility of RPC interfaces is essential, especially in systems where clients and servers may be running different versions of the software.

In conclusion, RPC plays a foundational and integral role in distributed computing, providing a mechanism for transparent and efficient communication between components across a network. By abstracting the complexities of inter-process communication, RPC enables developers to design and implement distributed systems with a focus on modularity, scalability, and maintainability. Its contribution to loose coupling, fault tolerance, security, and scalability makes RPC a cornerstone in the development of robust and responsive distributed applications. As the landscape of distributed computing continues to evolve, RPC remains a key enabler, empowering developers to harness the potential of networked environments while abstracting away the intricacies of communication protocols.

Implementing RPC in different programming paradigms.

Implementing Remote Procedure Call (RPC) across different programming paradigms is a multifaceted endeavor that involves adapting the principles of RPC to the specific characteristics and constraints of each paradigm. In the realm of procedural programming, which emphasizes the step-by-step execution of procedures or routines, implementing RPC involves defining a clear interface for remote procedures and establishing a communication mechanism between the client and server. The procedural paradigm's emphasis on modularity aligns well with RPC's goal of encapsulating functionality into callable procedures, making it conducive to the integration of RPC frameworks such as Java RMI (Remote Method Invocation) or gRPC.

Object-oriented programming (OOP), with its focus on encapsulation, inheritance, and polymorphism, introduces unique considerations when implementing RPC. In an OOP context, RPC often manifests as Remote Method Invocation, where methods of remote objects can be invoked as if they were local. Implementing RPC in an object-oriented paradigm requires the definition of remote interfaces that extend from a common interface, providing a blueprint for the methods that can be invoked remotely. Java RMI exemplifies this approach, allowing objects to be passed between client and server, enabling the invocation of methods on remote objects seamlessly.

The functional programming paradigm, characterized by a focus on immutability and higher-order functions, presents its own set of challenges and opportunities when implementing RPC. In functional programming languages, where functions are first-class citizens, RPC can be expressed as remote function calls. The challenge lies in managing statelessness and ensuring referential transparency when invoking functions remotely. Distributed computing frameworks designed for functional languages, such as Erlang's distribution mechanism, embrace the principles of RPC by allowing the invocation of functions on remote nodes. However, ensuring that functions maintain their purity and lack side effects becomes a central consideration in this paradigm.

Event-driven programming, prevalent in graphical user interfaces and reactive systems, introduces a different dimension to RPC implementation. In event-driven systems, where components communicate through events and listeners, RPC may take the form of remote event handling. The challenge lies in orchestrating the asynchronous nature of event-driven systems with the synchronous nature of RPC. Frameworks like Java's RMI or messaging systems like Apache Kafka adapt to this paradigm by providing mechanisms for remote event handling, allowing components to react to events across distributed environments.

Implementing RPC in the declarative programming paradigm, where the emphasis is on expressing what the program should accomplish rather than specifying how to achieve it, requires a shift in mindset. Declarative languages often focus on expressing relationships and constraints, making it essential to define a clear contract for remote interactions. In this context, GraphQL, a query language for APIs, exemplifies a declarative approach to RPC by allowing clients to request precisely the data they need, enabling efficient communication between clients and servers in a declarative manner.

The concurrent programming paradigm, where multiple tasks execute independently and may overlap in time, presents challenges in coordinating remote procedures without introducing race conditions or deadlocks. RPC frameworks designed for concurrent programming must address issues related to thread safety, synchronization, and parallelism. gRPC, with its support for asynchronous communication and streaming, caters to the concurrent programming paradigm by allowing clients and servers to communicate in a nonblocking fashion, accommodating the concurrent execution of multiple procedures.

In the reactive programming paradigm, which focuses on building systems that react to changes and events, RPC takes on the form of reactive communication. Reactive systems often involve the propagation of changes through a stream of events, and RPC frameworks must align with the reactive principles of responsiveness and elasticity. Reactive RPC frameworks, such as RSocket, provide support for reactive streams, enabling bidirectional communication and efficient handling of asynchronous events in distributed systems.

Serverless computing, a paradigm where developers deploy and run individual functions without managing the underlying infrastructure, presents a unique context for implementing RPC. In a serverless environment, where functions are ephemeral and stateless, RPC frameworks must adapt to the event-driven nature of serverless platforms. AWS Lambda, for example, integrates with API Gateway to facilitate RPC-style communication, allowing functions to be invoked remotely via HTTP requests. The stateless nature of serverless functions aligns with the principles of RPC, where procedures are invoked independently and do not rely on shared state.

Microservices architecture, characterized by the decomposition of applications into small, independently deployable services, places specific demands on RPC implementation. Microservices often communicate through APIs, and RPC frameworks must support the creation of well-defined interfaces for remote service interactions. gRPC, designed with support for service definition and code generation, aligns with the microservices paradigm by enabling the definition of service contracts, automatic code generation, and efficient communication between microservices.

In conclusion, implementing Remote Procedure Call (RPC) across different programming paradigms requires a nuanced approach that considers the specific characteristics and principles of each paradigm. Whether in procedural, object-oriented, functional, event-driven, declarative, concurrent, reactive, serverless, or microservices programming, the adaptation of RPC involves defining clear interfaces, managing state and synchronization, addressing asynchronous communication, and aligning with the principles of the respective paradigms. The flexibility of RPC frameworks, such as gRPC, Java RMI, and others, allows developers to seamlessly integrate remote procedure invocation into a wide array of programming paradigms, enabling the development of scalable, modular, and responsive distributed systems.

Overview of RESTful architecture in distributed systems.

Representational State Transfer (REST) has emerged as a predominant architectural style in the design of distributed systems, providing a set of principles and constraints that guide the development of scalable, maintainable, and interoperable web services. At its core, REST leverages the principles of simplicity, scalability, and statelessness to facilitate communication between distributed components. The central tenet of REST is resource-centricity, where resources are identified by URIs (Uniform Resource Identifiers) and are manipulated using standard HTTP methods. This resource-oriented approach fosters a uniform and standardized interface, making RESTful services intuitive and accessible.

In a RESTful architecture, resources encapsulate data or services, and interactions are performed through standard HTTP methods, such as GET, POST, PUT, and DELETE. The state of a resource is represented in a format, typically JSON or XML, allowing clients to request and manipulate resource representations. The statelessness of REST is a fundamental constraint that ensures each request from a client to a server is independent and self-contained. This statelessness simplifies the design, enhances scalability, and promotes the reusability of components.

One of the key characteristics of RESTful systems is the concept of a uniform interface, which is achieved through a set of constraints. The constraints include resource identification through URIs, manipulation through standard methods, representation of resource state, hypermedia as the engine of application state (HATEOAS), and a stateless communication model. These constraints guide developers in creating consistent and predictable APIs, fostering a standardized approach that enhances interoperability and simplifies the integration of diverse components in a distributed environment.

Resource identification through URIs plays a pivotal role in REST, providing a unique identifier for each resource. URIs serve as the means by which clients locate and interact with resources. The structure of URIs is designed to reflect the hierarchical nature of resources and the relationships between them. By adhering to a RESTful URI design, developers establish a clear and predictable structure, simplifying resource discovery and navigation for clients.

HTTP methods, including GET, POST, PUT, and DELETE, are employed in RESTful architectures to perform operations on resources. The idempotent nature of these methods ensures that repeated requests have the same effect as a single request, contributing to the reliability and predictability of the system. For example, the GET method retrieves the representation of a resource, POST creates a new resource, PUT updates an existing resource, and DELETE removes a resource.

Representation of resource state is a core aspect of RESTful design. Resources are represented in a format, such as JSON or XML, which encapsulates their current state. This representation can be transmitted between clients and servers, enabling the exchange of information in a standardized manner. The choice of representation format is often based on factors such as readability, ease of parsing, and compatibility with existing tools.

HATEOAS is a unique and powerful constraint in REST that allows clients to navigate a system dynamically by following hypermedia links embedded in resource representations. This self-discoverability aspect reduces the coupling between clients and servers, enabling changes to the server's URI structure without affecting clients. HATEOAS promotes a more flexible and evolvable system, where clients can adapt to changes in the service's behavior without relying on hardcoded URIs.

Statelessness, a foundational principle in REST, ensures that each client request contains all the information needed to process that request. The server does not maintain any client state between requests, simplifying server design, improving scalability, and allowing for easier fault tolerance. This stateless model aligns with the principles of the web, where each HTTP request from a client is an independent transaction.

RESTful architectures have found extensive application in the development of web services and APIs. The simplicity, scalability, and ease of integration associated with REST make it a preferred choice for building distributed systems that need to expose services over the internet. RESTful APIs, serving as the interface between clients and servers, are widely adopted for their straightforward design, making them accessible to developers across various platforms and programming languages.

The concept of resources in REST can represent a wide range of entities, from data objects to services, and their interactions can span a multitude of use cases. For instance, in a social media application, user profiles, posts, and comments could be modeled as resources, each identified by a unique URI. Clients can then perform operations on these resources using HTTP methods, such as retrieving a user profile with a GET request or creating a new post with a POST request.

Despite its widespread adoption, it's important to note that REST is not a one-size-fits-all solution, and its suitability depends on the specific requirements of a given application. As systems evolve, the need for real-time communication, bidirectional data flow, and support for more complex interactions has led to the rise of alternative architectural styles, such as GraphQL and WebSocket-based systems. However, the enduring principles of simplicity, resource-centricity, and statelessness embedded in REST continue to influence and shape the design of distributed systems, making it a lasting and foundational paradigm in the ever-evolving landscape of web development.

Design principles for creating scalable and maintainable APIs.

Designing scalable and maintainable APIs is a complex and critical task that requires careful consideration of various factors to ensure long-term success, adaptability, and ease of use. A fundamental principle in this endeavor is adhering to a RESTful architecture, which leverages a set of constraints to provide a scalable and maintainable foundation. REST, or Representational State Transfer, emphasizes resource-centric design, statelessness, and a uniform interface, fostering a standardized approach to building APIs that are scalable and easily maintainable.

Resource-centric design is a cornerstone in creating scalable and maintainable APIs. Resources, representing entities or services, should be identified by unique URIs (Uniform Resource Identifiers). By establishing a clear hierarchy and structure for resources, developers create a predictable and intuitive system that is easy to navigate and understand. Resource-centric APIs enable clients to interact with specific entities or services using standard HTTP methods, such as GET for retrieval, POST for creation, PUT for updating, and DELETE for removal. This consistent approach to resource management simplifies the API's usage and contributes to its maintainability.

The statelessness principle inherent in RESTful design is vital for scalability and maintainability. Each client request to the API should be independent and self-contained, with all the information necessary for the server to understand and process the request. The server should not retain any client state between requests. This statelessness simplifies server design, enhances scalability by allowing for horizontal scaling (adding more servers to handle increased load), and facilitates better fault tolerance. Stateless APIs are easier to manage and adapt, making them more maintainable in the long run.

Another key principle is the uniform interface, which encompasses a set of constraints that standardize the interaction between clients and servers. Adhering to a uniform interface promotes consistency, predictability, and ease of use. The use of standard HTTP methods for CRUD operations (Create, Read, Update, Delete) on resources contributes to a straightforward and recognizable design. Additionally, representing resource state in standard formats like JSON or XML fosters interoperability and simplifies client-server communication. The uniform interface principle enables developers to create APIs that are not only scalable but also maintainable by providing a standardized and intuitive way to interact with the system.

Versioning is a crucial design consideration for maintaining compatibility and supporting gradual system evolution. As APIs evolve over time, it is essential to introduce changes without breaking existing client implementations. API versioning allows for the coexistence of multiple versions, providing developers with the flexibility to migrate at their own pace. Versioning strategies may include using version numbers in the URI, custom headers, or query parameters. Thoughtful versioning practices contribute to API maintainability by facilitating the introduction of new features, improvements, and bug fixes without disrupting existing integrations.

Consistent error handling is paramount in ensuring a positive developer experience and facilitating maintainability. API responses should include standardized error codes, clear error messages, and guidance on resolving issues. By establishing a consistent error-handling approach, developers can easily diagnose and address problems. Additionally, API responses should include appropriate HTTP status codes to indicate the success or failure of a request. A well-defined error-handling strategy enhances the API's maintainability by providing clear feedback to developers and reducing the likelihood of misinterpretation or misuse.

Pagination and filtering mechanisms contribute to API scalability by managing large datasets effectively. APIs that return a large number of resources can strain both server resources and client bandwidth. Pagination involves breaking up large result sets into smaller, manageable chunks, enabling clients to request and display data incrementally. Similarly, filtering allows clients to specify criteria for the data they need, reducing the amount of unnecessary information transmitted over the network. Implementing pagination and filtering mechanisms ensures that APIs remain performant and scalable, even when dealing with substantial datasets, contributing to long-term maintainability.

Effective documentation is a linchpin for creating maintainable APIs. Comprehensive and user-friendly documentation serves as a guide for developers, helping them understand how to use the API, its available resources, endpoints, and the expected request and response formats. Documentation should include clear examples, explanations of error handling, and any authentication requirements. Well-documented APIs are easier to maintain because developers can quickly grasp how the API works and troubleshoot issues. Investing time in creating thorough documentation pays dividends in the form of reduced support overhead and increased developer satisfaction.

Authentication and authorization mechanisms are crucial aspects of API design, ensuring that only authorized users and applications can access protected resources. Scalable APIs should support various authentication methods, such as API keys, OAuth, or token-based authentication. Authorization mechanisms, on the other hand, define what actions authenticated users are allowed to perform. A robust authentication and authorization strategy enhances the security and maintainability of APIs by safeguarding against unauthorized access and misuse.

Rate limiting is an essential consideration for preventing abuse, ensuring fair usage, and maintaining system stability. By imposing limits on the number of requests a client can make within a specific time frame, rate limiting protects APIs from excessive traffic, potential denial-of-service attacks, and ensures a consistent quality of service for all users. Well-designed rate limiting mechanisms contribute to the scalability and maintainability of APIs by preventing resource exhaustion, optimizing server resources, and maintaining system stability during periods of high demand.

Webhooks provide a mechanism for real-time communication between systems, enabling event-driven architectures. Instead of relying solely on polling, where clients repeatedly request updates, webhooks allow servers to notify clients when specific events occur. This push-based approach reduces unnecessary polling and minimizes the load on both clients and servers. Implementing webhooks enhances API scalability by providing a more efficient and responsive means of communication. Moreover, it contributes to maintainability by reducing the need for continuous polling and facilitating timely updates.

Caching mechanisms play a pivotal role in optimizing API performance and reducing server load by storing and reusing previously retrieved data. By utilizing caching headers and strategies, APIs can instruct clients to cache responses locally for a specified duration. This reduces the need for redundant requests, minimizes latency, and conserves server resources. Effective caching contributes to API scalability by improving response times and reducing the load on backend systems. It also enhances maintainability by mitigating the impact of sudden spikes in traffic.

In conclusion, designing scalable and maintainable APIs involves a holistic consideration of architectural principles, constraints, and best practices. Adhering to RESTful principles, such as resource-centric design, statelessness, and a uniform interface, provides a solid foundation for creating scalable APIs that are intuitive and interoperable. Additional considerations, including versioning, error handling, pagination, and filtering, contribute to both scalability and maintainability by ensuring compatibility, effective issue resolution, and efficient data management. Authentication, authorization, rate limiting, documentation, webhooks, and caching mechanisms further enhance the security, usability, and efficiency of APIs. By carefully balancing these design principles, developers can create APIs that not only meet immediate requirements but also adapt and evolve seamlessly over time, ensuring scalability and maintainability in the dynamic landscape of distributed systems.

Understanding event-driven communication in distributed systems.

Event-driven communication is a fundamental paradigm in distributed systems that centers around the propagation and handling of events, enabling loosely coupled interactions among distributed components. In an event-driven architecture, components communicate primarily through the generation, detection, and reaction to events—significant occurrences or changes in the system. This approach contrasts with traditional request-response models, offering a more responsive, scalable, and decoupled alternative. Events can represent various system activities, such as user interactions, changes in data, or the occurrence of specific conditions, and they serve as the triggers for communication between different parts of the distributed system.

A key aspect of event-driven communication is the decoupling of components, which allows them to operate independently and asynchronously. In a traditional, tightly coupled system, components often need to be aware of each other's existence and state, leading to intricate dependencies that hinder system flexibility and scalability. In contrast, event-driven systems promote loose coupling by decoupling the producer of an event (the entity that generates the event) from the consumers (entities interested in reacting to the event). This decoupling enables components to evolve independently, supporting greater flexibility, maintainability, and scalability in distributed systems.

Event-driven communication is underpinned by the concept of an event bus or message broker, a central mechanism responsible for collecting, managing, and disseminating events throughout the system. The event bus serves as a communication medium that facilitates the flow of events from producers to consumers. Producers publish events to the bus without being aware of who or what will consume them, and consumers express interest in specific types of events without direct knowledge of the producers. This loose coupling ensures that changes to one part of the system do not necessitate modifications in all interconnected components, enhancing the overall adaptability and resilience of distributed systems.

The flexibility of event-driven communication becomes particularly evident in scenarios where real-time responsiveness is essential. Applications that require timely reactions to user interactions or dynamic changes in data benefit significantly from the asynchronous nature of event-driven systems. For instance, in a web application, user actions such as button clicks or form submissions can trigger events that are broadcasted via the event bus. Various components, such as UI elements, backend services, or external integrations, can then subscribe to relevant events and respond accordingly. This asynchronous nature of event-driven communication enables systems to provide near real-time feedback, enhancing user experience and responsiveness.

Moreover, event-driven architectures excel in scenarios where multiple components or services must collaborate without introducing tight dependencies. Microservices, a popular architectural style for building distributed systems, often leverage event-driven communication to facilitate interaction between independent services. When a microservice produces an event, it can broadcast it to the event bus, and other microservices interested in that event can react accordingly. This decoupled communication model allows microservices to evolve independently, supporting the scalability and maintainability goals inherent in microservices architectures.

Event-driven communication also plays a pivotal role in ensuring system resilience and fault tolerance. By decoupling components and relying on asynchronous communication, event-driven systems can gracefully handle failures and recover from disruptions. In the event of a failure, messages on the event bus can be retried or persisted for later processing, preventing the loss of critical information. Additionally, event-driven architectures can incorporate patterns such as event sourcing, where the state of the system is derived from a sequence of events, enabling reliable recovery and reconstruction of system state after failures.

The concept of event-driven communication extends beyond internal system interactions to encompass external integrations and collaborations. In a distributed environment, where systems often need to interact with external services or third-party applications, event-driven communication provides a flexible and extensible model. For instance, an e-commerce platform may integrate with a payment gateway through event-driven communication. When a customer successfully completes a purchase, the e-commerce system can generate a "payment successful" event, triggering subsequent actions such as order fulfillment. This approach allows distributed systems to seamlessly integrate with external services while maintaining loose coupling and adaptability.

As the complexity of distributed systems continues to grow, event-driven communication becomes essential for managing and coordinating interactions across diverse components. The publish-subscribe pattern, a prevalent model in event-driven architectures, exemplifies this communication style. In this pattern, components subscribe to specific types of events, and producers publish events to the corresponding channels. This loose coupling allows for dynamic and extensible systems, where components can be added or removed without disrupting the overall functionality. Additionally, event-driven communication facilitates the implementation of event-driven patterns such as event-driven sagas, where a sequence of related events represents a long-running process that spans multiple components.

Challenges in event-driven communication include ensuring message delivery guarantees, handling event ordering, and managing the potential for event-driven systems to become overly complex. Implementing mechanisms for reliable message delivery, such as acknowledgments and retries, is crucial to prevent message loss. Event ordering, especially in scenarios where strict sequencing is essential, demands careful consideration and may require additional coordination mechanisms. Moreover, as the number of events and subscribers grows, managing the overall complexity of the event-driven system becomes a concern. Proper tooling, monitoring, and governance are essential to maintain a clear understanding of the interactions and ensure the system's maintainability over time.

In conclusion, event-driven communication represents a powerful paradigm in the design of distributed systems, providing a flexible, scalable, and decoupled approach to managing interactions between components. The use of event buses, asynchronous communication, and the publish-subscribe pattern enables systems to achieve loose coupling, real-time responsiveness, and adaptability. Event-driven architectures excel in scenarios ranging from microservices to external integrations, supporting the evolution and scalability of distributed systems. While challenges exist, addressing issues related to message delivery, event ordering, and system complexity ensures that event-driven communication remains a cornerstone for building resilient, responsive, and maintainable distributed systems in the dynamic landscape of modern software development.

Exploring messaging queues, publish-subscribe models, and event-driven architectures.

Messaging queues, publish-subscribe models, and event-driven architectures constitute foundational components in the realm of distributed systems, offering versatile solutions to manage communication, coordination, and data flow between disparate components. Messaging queues serve as key intermediaries, enabling asynchronous communication between producers and consumers. In a messaging queue, messages are placed in a queue by producers and consumed by consumers in a decoupled manner. This decoupling facilitates the distribution of workloads, enhances system resilience, and enables disparate components to communicate without direct dependencies. Messaging queues play a pivotal role in scenarios where scalability, fault tolerance, and efficient task distribution are paramount, such as in microservices architectures or when integrating with external systems.

The publish-subscribe model is a prevalent communication pattern that underlies many distributed systems, emphasizing the dissemination of messages to multiple subscribers based on their interests. In a publish-subscribe model, components act as publishers that produce messages and subscribers that express interest in specific types of messages. Publishers broadcast messages to a central hub or topic, and subscribers receive messages based on their subscriptions. This model fosters loose coupling between components, allowing publishers and subscribers to evolve independently. Publish-subscribe architectures excel in scenarios where real-time updates, event-driven communication, and dynamic extensibility are crucial. The model supports a scalable and flexible system design, enabling the creation of dynamic and responsive distributed applications.

Event-driven architectures, often built on the foundations of messaging queues and publish-subscribe models, represent a paradigm where the flow of information is triggered by events—significant occurrences or changes in the system. Events serve as the catalyst for communication and coordination among distributed components. The event-driven approach is characterized by components that react asynchronously to events, ensuring a decoupled and responsive system. Event-driven architectures find application in a wide array of scenarios, including microservices, external integrations, real-time analytics, and complex business processes. By embracing an event-driven model, systems can achieve scalability, maintainability, and adaptability, responding dynamically to changes and interactions within the environment.

Messaging queues, as a foundational concept, provide a reliable and efficient means for asynchronous communication between distributed components. A messaging queue acts as an intermediary that temporarily stores messages until they are consumed by the intended recipients. This decouples producers and consumers, allowing them to operate independently without direct awareness of each other's state or availability. Producers enqueue messages into the queue, and consumers dequeue and process them at their own pace. This asynchronous communication model provides several advantages, including improved fault tolerance, reduced latency, and enhanced scalability.

In practical terms, messaging queues are employed in various scenarios, ranging from task distribution in microservices architectures to managing event-driven communication between disparate services. For example, in a microservices environment, different services may produce messages representing tasks or events, which are then placed in a messaging queue. Other services can independently consume these messages from the queue, enabling efficient workload distribution and allowing each microservice to scale independently. Messaging queues also contribute to the reliability of communication, as they can serve as buffers that temporarily hold messages during system downtimes or temporary spikes in load.

The publish-subscribe model extends the capabilities of messaging queues by introducing a pattern where components express interest in specific types of messages and receive only the messages they are interested in. In this model, components are categorized into two main roles: publishers and subscribers. Publishers generate messages and broadcast them to a central hub or topic, while subscribers express interest in specific topics and receive relevant messages. This decoupling of producers and consumers based on topics or channels fosters a more dynamic and extensible communication model.

In a publish-subscribe architecture, the central hub or topic acts as a mediator, ensuring that messages are efficiently delivered to the interested subscribers. This model enables a flexible and scalable design where new components can seamlessly join the system as subscribers without impacting existing components. Similarly, publishers can produce messages without being aware of the specific subscribers or their locations. This loose coupling promotes a responsive and adaptable system, making publish-subscribe architectures well-suited for scenarios requiring real-time updates, event broadcasting, and collaboration among distributed components.

Consider a scenario in which a news application employs a publish-subscribe model to deliver personalized updates to its users. Different components within the application act as publishers, generating news articles or updates. Subscribers, representing individual users with specific interests, subscribe to topics relevant to their preferences, such as sports, technology, or entertainment. When a new article is published, the corresponding publisher broadcasts the message to the relevant topic, and only subscribers interested in that topic receive the update. This ensures that users receive personalized and real-time news updates without overwhelming the system with unnecessary information.

Event-driven architectures encompass the principles of messaging queues and publish-subscribe models, emphasizing the central role of events as triggers for communication and coordination. Events represent significant occurrences or changes in the system and serve as the driving force behind the interactions between distributed components. In an event-driven architecture, components react asynchronously to events, allowing for a more responsive and decoupled system. The flow of information is determined by the occurrence of events, enabling components to dynamically adapt to changes in the environment.

Events in an event-driven architecture are often categorized into different types, each signaling a specific occurrence or state change. Components can act as event producers, generating events, and event consumers, reacting to events based on their specific responsibilities or interests. The event-driven approach provides a mechanism for distributed components to communicate without direct dependencies, promoting loose coupling and facilitating the development of scalable and maintainable systems.

Consider an e-commerce application as an example of an event-driven architecture. Various components within the application, such as inventory management, order processing, and payment services, may act as event producers. Events could include changes in product availability, order placements, or payment confirmations. Components interested in specific events, such as the order fulfillment service, can act as event consumers. When a new order is placed, the order processing service produces an "order placed" event, and the order fulfillment service, subscribed to this event, reacts accordingly by initiating the shipping process. This event-driven communication model allows different services to evolve independently, supporting the scalability and adaptability of the e-commerce system.

The advantages of event-driven architectures extend to scenarios beyond microservices and internal system interactions. Event-driven communication is well-suited for external integrations with third-party services, enabling seamless collaboration between distributed systems. External systems can produce events, and a subscribing system can react to these events, creating a loosely coupled and extensible integration model. This flexibility is particularly valuable in scenarios where systems need to interact with external services, such as payment gateways, notification services, or external APIs.

Despite the benefits, challenges exist in implementing and managing event-driven architectures. Ensuring the reliable delivery of events, handling event ordering when necessary, and managing the potential complexity of event-driven systems are critical considerations. Mechanisms such as acknowledgments, retries, and event persistence can be implemented to enhance the reliability of event delivery. In scenarios where strict event ordering is essential, additional coordination mechanisms may be required. Proper tooling, monitoring, and governance are essential to maintain a clear understanding of the interactions and ensure the maintainability of event-driven systems over time.

In conclusion, messaging queues, publish-subscribe models, and event-driven architectures represent integral components in the design and implementation of distributed systems. Messaging queues offer an asynchronous communication mechanism that enhances scalability, fault tolerance, and task distribution. Publish-subscribe models extend this by introducing dynamic communication patterns based on interests and topics, fostering loose coupling and flexibility. Event-driven architectures build upon these concepts, emphasizing the centrality of events as triggers for communication and coordination. These paradigms collectively enable the development of distributed systems that are responsive, scalable, and adaptable to the dynamic nature of modern software development.

Chapter 5: Fault Tolerance and Resilience Strategies

Defining fault tolerance and its significance in distributed computing.

Fault tolerance is a critical concept in distributed computing, referring to the system's ability to continue functioning seamlessly in the face of faults or failures. These faults can manifest in various forms, including hardware failures, network issues, or software errors. The significance of fault tolerance in distributed computing lies in its capacity to ensure system reliability, availability, and resilience. In a distributed environment where multiple interconnected components collaborate to achieve a common goal, the risk of failures is inherently higher. By incorporating fault tolerance mechanisms, distributed systems can mitigate the impact of failures and maintain functionality, thereby enhancing overall system robustness.

One fundamental aspect of fault tolerance is the ability to detect faults promptly. Detection mechanisms, ranging from simple heartbeat checks to more sophisticated algorithms, play a crucial role in identifying abnormalities or deviations from expected behavior. Once a fault is detected, the system must respond effectively. This involves isolating the faulty component, redistributing tasks among healthy components, and, in some cases, initiating recovery procedures. The goal is to minimize downtime and service disruption, ensuring that users experience continuity despite the presence of faults.

Distributed systems often face challenges arising from the inherent complexity of their architecture. The interconnected nature of components introduces dependencies and interdependencies, making it imperative to address faults comprehensively. Redundancy is a key strategy in fault tolerance, involving the duplication of critical components or data across different nodes. This redundancy ensures that if one component fails, a backup can seamlessly take over, preventing a single point of failure from jeopardizing the entire system. Redundancy can be implemented at various levels, including hardware redundancy, where duplicate hardware components are deployed, and data redundancy, where data is replicated across multiple nodes.

Consistency in distributed systems is another critical consideration for fault tolerance. In the event of a failure, maintaining data consistency becomes challenging, especially when multiple nodes are involved in parallel processing. Distributed databases and consensus algorithms, such as the Paxos or Raft protocols, address this challenge by ensuring that nodes reach an agreement on the state of the system even in the presence of faults. Consistency mechanisms contribute significantly to fault tolerance by preventing data corruption or inconsistencies that may arise due to failures during data processing.

Network failures represent a common type of fault in distributed systems, given the reliance on communication between nodes. Ensuring fault tolerance in the face of network issues involves designing protocols that can handle network partitions and recover seamlessly when connectivity is restored. Consensus algorithms, like the mentioned Paxos and Raft, facilitate coordination among nodes, enabling them to reach a consistent state despite potential network disruptions. Moreover, techniques like load balancing help distribute network traffic efficiently, preventing bottlenecks that could result from the failure of a specific network link or node.

Scalability is a crucial consideration in fault-tolerant distributed systems. As the system grows and evolves, it should be capable of accommodating an increasing number of nodes and users without compromising its fault tolerance. Scalability involves designing architectures that can handle higher workloads while maintaining fault-tolerance mechanisms that scale along with the system. This adaptability ensures that the distributed system remains resilient and reliable even as it undergoes changes in scale and complexity.

Security is an integral component of fault tolerance in distributed computing. Fault tolerance mechanisms must not only address accidental faults but also protect the system against intentional attacks. Intrusion detection systems, encryption, and access controls play vital roles in safeguarding the integrity and availability of the distributed system. Security breaches, if not handled with a fault-tolerant mindset, can lead to catastrophic consequences, making it essential to integrate security measures seamlessly into the overall fault tolerance strategy.

In addition to detecting and responding to faults, distributed systems must also focus on recovery and restoration. Recovery mechanisms involve restoring the system to a consistent and functional state after a fault has been addressed. Checkpointing, a technique where the system periodically saves its state, allows for faster recovery by enabling the system to restart from a known, stable point in the event of a failure. Automated recovery procedures further contribute to the efficiency of fault tolerance, minimizing the need for manual intervention and reducing downtime.

The significance of fault tolerance extends beyond mere system survival; it directly impacts user experience and business continuity. Users expect seamless and uninterrupted access to services, and organizations rely on distributed systems to support critical business processes. A fault-tolerant system ensures that these expectations are met, even in the face of challenges. Businesses that operate in a global and interconnected landscape cannot afford prolonged downtime or service disruptions, as they may result in financial losses, damage to reputation, and legal consequences. Therefore, the value of fault tolerance in distributed computing is closely tied to its role in preserving the reliability and integrity of services essential to organizations and end-users alike.

Moreover, fault tolerance contributes significantly to achieving high levels of system performance and efficiency. By reducing the impact of faults on system functionality, organizations can maintain a consistent and predictable level of service. This predictability is essential for resource planning, capacity management, and meeting service-level agreements. In scenarios where distributed systems support real-time applications, such as financial transactions or streaming services, the need for fault tolerance becomes even more pronounced. A delay or interruption in these time-sensitive processes can have immediate and tangible consequences, reinforcing the critical role of fault tolerance in ensuring the continuous and reliable operation of distributed systems.

In conclusion, fault tolerance is a cornerstone principle in the design and operation of distributed computing systems. Its significance lies in the assurance of system reliability, availability, and resilience in the face of faults or failures. By incorporating fault tolerance mechanisms, such as redundancy, consistency, scalability, security, and recovery, distributed systems can withstand challenges and continue to provide uninterrupted services. The impact of fault tolerance extends beyond technical considerations, influencing user experience, business continuity, and overall system performance. As organizations increasingly rely on distributed systems to support their operations, the importance of fault tolerance in ensuring the robustness and dependability of these systems continues to grow.

Types of faults and their impact on system reliability.

Various types of faults can affect the reliability of a system, each with its own distinct characteristics and impact on overall performance. Hardware faults, encompassing issues with physical components, are a common category. These faults may include failures in central processing units (CPUs), memory modules, storage devices, or network interfaces. Hardware faults can lead to system crashes, data corruption, or performance degradation. For instance, a malfunctioning CPU may cause processing errors, disrupting the execution of critical tasks and compromising the system's ability to deliver consistent and reliable results.

Network faults represent another significant category, affecting the communication links between different components in a distributed system. Network faults can result from issues such as packet loss, latency, or complete network outages. These faults impact the system's ability to transmit data reliably and in a timely manner, leading to disruptions in communication between nodes. In distributed computing, where collaboration and data exchange between nodes are essential, network faults can hinder the overall system performance and compromise its reliability.

Software faults, ranging from bugs and coding errors to more complex design flaws, pose a substantial threat to system reliability. Programming errors can lead to unexpected behaviors, crashes, or security vulnerabilities. In distributed systems, the impact of software faults is magnified due to the interconnected nature of components. A software bug in one module may propagate through the network, affecting multiple nodes and potentially causing widespread system instability. Ensuring the reliability of distributed systems requires rigorous testing, debugging, and continuous improvement of software components.

Power faults, including power outages, fluctuations, or surges, can have severe consequences for system reliability. Power failures can result in sudden shutdowns, data loss, and damage to hardware components. In critical environments, such as data centers or industrial settings, where uninterrupted power is essential, power faults pose a significant risk to system reliability. Implementing uninterruptible power supply (UPS) systems, backup generators, and other power management mechanisms is crucial to mitigate the impact of power faults on distributed systems.

Environmental faults, encompassing factors like temperature extremes, humidity, and physical contaminants, can also affect system reliability. Overheating due to inadequate cooling mechanisms can lead to hardware failures, while exposure to humidity or contaminants can corrode components and degrade performance over time. In distributed systems, especially those deployed in diverse environments, accounting for environmental factors is essential for maintaining long-term reliability and preventing premature component degradation.

Human errors represent a significant and often underestimated source of faults in distributed systems. Misconfigurations, improper maintenance procedures, or accidental data deletions can introduce faults that compromise system reliability. In complex distributed environments, where multiple individuals may be involved in system administration and maintenance, the risk of human errors increases. Establishing robust processes, implementing access controls, and providing training to personnel are essential measures to minimize the impact of human errors on system reliability.

Security faults, including cyber-attacks, unauthorized access, and data breaches, pose a critical threat to system reliability. In an interconnected world, where distributed systems often process sensitive and valuable data, security faults can have far-reaching consequences. Malicious activities, such as denial-of-service attacks or the exploitation of vulnerabilities, can disrupt services, compromise data integrity, and erode user trust. Implementing robust security measures, including encryption, access controls, and intrusion detection systems, is imperative for safeguarding the reliability of distributed systems against security threats.

Furthermore, configuration faults, related to the improper setup or parameterization of system components, can introduce vulnerabilities and impact system reliability. Misconfigurations in network settings, security policies, or application configurations can lead to unexpected behaviors and compromise the overall system performance. Regular audits, automated configuration management tools, and adherence to best practices are essential for minimizing the risk of configuration faults in distributed systems.

Additionally, temporal faults, referring to faults that occur at specific points in time, can impact system reliability. These faults may include intermittent hardware failures, transient network issues, or time-sensitive software bugs. Temporal faults are challenging to detect and reproduce, making them particularly elusive. Implementing robust monitoring and logging mechanisms, coupled with thorough testing and analysis, is crucial for identifying and mitigating the impact of temporal faults on the reliability of distributed systems.

In conclusion, the reliability of distributed systems is susceptible to a diverse array of faults, each with its unique characteristics and potential consequences. Hardware faults, network issues, software bugs, power disruptions, environmental factors, human errors, security threats, configuration vulnerabilities, and temporal anomalies all contribute to the complexity of ensuring system reliability. Mitigating the impact of these faults requires a comprehensive and multifaceted approach, involving thorough testing, continuous monitoring, fault-tolerant design principles, and proactive measures to address specific fault categories. As distributed systems play an increasingly vital role in supporting critical applications and services, understanding and addressing the various types of faults is paramount to achieving and maintaining a high level of system reliability.

Exploring replication as a strategy for enhancing fault tolerance.

Replication is a strategic approach employed in distributed computing to enhance fault tolerance by creating redundant copies of critical components, data, or services across multiple nodes within the system. This technique aims to mitigate the impact of faults, such as hardware failures, network issues, or software errors, by ensuring that if one copy of a resource becomes unavailable, a backup copy can seamlessly take over. The fundamental principle underlying replication is to distribute the workload and responsibilities across multiple nodes, reducing the likelihood of a single point of failure jeopardizing the entire system.

One of the primary applications of replication is in the context of data storage. Replicating data involves maintaining duplicate copies across different nodes or storage locations. This redundancy ensures that even if one storage location experiences a fault or becomes inaccessible, the data remains available from other replicas. Replication contributes to data durability and availability, vital aspects of fault tolerance. In distributed databases, for example, replicating data across multiple nodes allows for continued access to information, even in the face of node failures or network disruptions.

The concept of replication extends beyond data storage to encompass the redundancy of entire services or applications. By replicating services, organizations can ensure that critical functionalities remain accessible even if individual instances of the service encounter issues. Load balancers play a crucial role in distributing incoming requests among replicated service instances, enhancing fault tolerance by preventing overload on a specific node and ensuring that the system can handle increased workloads.

Furthermore, replication is instrumental in addressing the challenges posed by network faults. In a distributed system, where nodes communicate with each other over a network, the potential for network disruptions is significant. Replicating services or components across nodes enables the system to reroute traffic to healthy nodes in the event of network failures or partitions. This redirection of traffic ensures that the system maintains its operational capacity, providing a seamless experience for users even during network-related challenges.

Consistency is a critical consideration when implementing replication strategies. Maintaining consistency among replicas ensures that users receive coherent and up-to-date information regardless of which replica they access. However, achieving consistency in a distributed system with replication introduces challenges. Different replication models, such as eventual consistency or strong consistency, offer trade-offs between availability and consistency. Eventual consistency allows replicas to diverge temporarily but guarantees eventual convergence, while strong consistency ensures immediate consistency but may impact availability during updates. Choosing the appropriate replication model depends on the specific requirements of the application and the desired balance between consistency and fault tolerance.

Replication also plays a vital role in enhancing fault tolerance in the context of system scalability. As the demand for services grows, replicating components allows the system to scale horizontally by adding more nodes. Horizontal scaling, achieved through replication, enables distributed systems to accommodate increased workloads, ensuring that performance remains consistent even as the user base expands. This scalability is particularly advantageous in cloud computing environments, where the ability to dynamically allocate resources based on demand is crucial.

Security considerations are paramount when implementing replication strategies. Replicating data or services across nodes introduces additional attack vectors, as compromising one replica may affect the entire system. Ensuring the integrity and confidentiality of replicated data is essential to prevent security breaches. Encryption, secure communication protocols, and access controls are vital components of a robust security strategy for replicated systems. Additionally, organizations must address challenges related to consistency and synchronization, as security measures may impact the replication process.

The impact of replication on fault tolerance is exemplified in distributed systems that prioritize high availability and continuous operation. In scenarios where system downtime is not permissible, such as in financial transactions or real-time applications, replication becomes a cornerstone strategy. The use of redundant components, whether in the form of replicated servers, load balancers, or data stores, ensures that the system can seamlessly transition between replicas in the event of faults, maintaining uninterrupted service delivery.

Checkpointing is a complementary technique often used in conjunction with replication to enhance fault tolerance. Checkpointing involves periodically saving the state of a system, allowing it to recover from a known, stable point in the event of a failure. Combining replication with checkpointing reinforces fault tolerance by providing not only redundancy but also a mechanism for efficient recovery. The periodic snapshots created through checkpointing enable the system to resume operations quickly after a fault, minimizing downtime and reducing the impact on users.

Despite its benefits, replication introduces challenges, particularly in terms of managing and synchronizing multiple replicas. Consistency models, as mentioned earlier, influence the trade-offs between availability and consistency, requiring careful consideration based on the specific requirements of the system. Additionally, the overhead associated with maintaining and updating replicas, as well as the increased network traffic resulting from synchronization, must be managed effectively to ensure the efficiency of replication strategies.

In conclusion, replication stands as a powerful strategy for enhancing fault tolerance in distributed computing. By creating redundant copies of critical components, data, or services across multiple nodes, replication mitigates the impact of faults, contributes to data durability, ensures continuous availability, and supports system scalability. Whether applied to data storage, service replication, or entire application instances, replication is instrumental in creating resilient distributed systems that can withstand hardware failures, network issues, and other challenges. Balancing the trade-offs between consistency and availability, addressing security considerations, and leveraging complementary techniques like checkpointing are integral aspects of implementing effective replication strategies in the pursuit of fault tolerance. As distributed systems continue to play a central role in supporting critical applications and services, the importance of replication in ensuring their reliability and resilience remains paramount.

The role of redundancy in ensuring continuous system operation.

Redundancy plays a pivotal role in ensuring the continuous operation of systems, providing a strategic and proactive approach to mitigate the impact of faults and failures. In the realm of computing and engineering, redundancy involves the inclusion of additional components, resources, or mechanisms beyond what is strictly necessary for normal operation. This surplus serves as a safeguard against potential disruptions, aiming to maintain system functionality even in the face of unexpected challenges. The overarching goal of redundancy is to enhance reliability, availability, and fault tolerance, reinforcing the resilience of systems across various domains.

In the context of hardware, redundancy is a fundamental principle applied to critical components such as processors, memory modules, power supplies, and storage devices. By duplicating these components, a system can continue to operate seamlessly even if one of them experiences a failure. This approach is particularly crucial in environments where downtime is unacceptable, such as data centers, telecommunications networks, and industrial control systems. Redundant hardware configurations, often implemented using techniques like mirroring or hot standby, ensure that the failure of a single component does not disrupt the overall system, thereby contributing to continuous operation.

Network redundancy is another essential aspect, acknowledging the vital role of communication pathways in interconnected systems. Multiple network paths, routers, and links are strategically deployed to create redundant communication channels. In the event of a network failure or congestion, traffic can be rerouted through alternative paths, preventing disruptions to data transmission and maintaining connectivity. Redundant network architectures, including techniques like mesh topology or dual-homed configurations, are prevalent in mission-critical systems where uninterrupted communication is imperative.

Data redundancy is employed to safeguard against data loss or corruption, a concern prevalent in storage and database systems. Redundant data storage involves maintaining multiple copies of the same data across different locations or devices. RAID (Redundant Array of Independent Disks) configurations exemplify this approach by distributing data across multiple disks, ensuring that if one disk fails, the data can be reconstructed from the redundant information stored on other disks. In distributed databases, data replication across nodes provides a similar redundancy mechanism, allowing for continuous access to data even if some nodes become unavailable.

The redundancy concept extends to the software layer as well, where redundant processes, services, or application instances can ensure uninterrupted operation. Load balancing, a technique that distributes incoming requests across multiple servers, not only optimizes resource utilization but also enhances fault tolerance by preventing overload on individual servers. In cloud computing environments, where services may run on a virtualized infrastructure, redundancy is often achieved through the deployment of multiple instances across different physical hosts or availability zones, safeguarding against host failures and optimizing resource allocation.

Power redundancy is critical for systems that demand continuous and stable power supply. Uninterruptible Power Supply (UPS) systems, generators, and redundant power distribution units contribute to ensuring that a system remains operational in the event of power outages or fluctuations. Redundant power sources provide a seamless transition during power failures, preventing disruptions and allowing systems to continue running on backup power until normal power is restored.

Redundancy is not only about duplicating components but also about creating failover mechanisms and backup strategies. In the case of server clusters, failover mechanisms automatically redirect incoming requests to healthy servers when a server within the cluster fails. This ensures that users experience minimal downtime and uninterrupted service. Redundant backup systems, whether for data or entire server instances, are crucial for disaster recovery. These backups can be employed to restore a system to a known, stable state in the aftermath of a catastrophic failure, ensuring that operations can resume swiftly and with minimal data loss.

Despite its significant advantages, redundancy introduces challenges that must be carefully managed. Cost implications, both in terms of hardware and operational overhead, must be weighed against the benefits of continuous operation. Balancing the level of redundancy with the criticality of the system and its components is a key consideration in designing a reliable and cost-effective solution. Additionally, ensuring that redundant components remain synchronized and up-to-date requires robust mechanisms for coordination and consistency.

In dynamic environments, where system configurations may change, managing and updating redundancy configurations becomes a non-trivial task. Automated tools and orchestration mechanisms play a crucial role in maintaining and adjusting redundancy settings to adapt to evolving system requirements. Regular testing of redundancy mechanisms through simulations or controlled failure scenarios is imperative to validate their effectiveness and identify potential weaknesses before they manifest in real-world scenarios.

Redundancy is not a one-size-fits-all solution, and its application should be tailored to the specific requirements and characteristics of the system at hand. The level of redundancy needed for a critical financial transaction system may differ from that required for a less critical information-sharing platform. Strategic decision-making involves understanding the trade-offs between cost, complexity, and the desired level of continuous operation.

In conclusion, redundancy stands as a fundamental strategy for ensuring continuous system operation by mitigating the impact of faults and failures. Whether applied to hardware components, network infrastructure, data storage, or software services, redundancy reinforces the reliability, availability, and fault tolerance of systems across diverse domains. The resilience provided by redundancy is particularly crucial in environments where uninterrupted operation is paramount, such as in data centers, telecommunications networks, and critical industrial systems. However, achieving effective redundancy requires a careful balance between the associated costs, system complexity, and the specific operational requirements of the system. As technology continues to advance and systems become increasingly interconnected, the role of redundancy remains indispensable in building and maintaining robust and continuously operational systems.

The concept of checkpointing to ensure data consistency.

Checkpointing is a fundamental concept in distributed computing aimed at ensuring data consistency, a crucial aspect for maintaining the integrity and reliability of systems. The essence of checkpointing lies in periodically capturing the state of a distributed system and storing it in a persistent and stable manner. This captured state, referred to as a checkpoint, serves as a reference point that can be used for system recovery in the event of failures or faults. The primary goal of checkpointing is to provide a mechanism through which a system can resume operation from a known and consistent state after a failure, minimizing the impact on data integrity and system reliability.

In distributed systems, where multiple nodes collaborate to perform complex tasks, ensuring data consistency becomes a significant challenge due to the potential for failures or interruptions during data processing. Checkpointing addresses this challenge by creating snapshots of the system's state at regular intervals, allowing the system to revert to a consistent state following a failure. The checkpointing process involves capturing not only the data but also the state of processes, application variables, and any other relevant information needed for a complete recovery.

The frequency at which checkpoints are created depends on the specific requirements of the system and the trade-offs between consistency and performance. In scenarios where data changes rapidly, more frequent checkpointing may be necessary to minimize the potential loss of recent updates. However, frequent checkpointing introduces additional overhead due to the need to save and manage checkpoints, impacting overall system performance. Striking a balance between the need for consistent data and the overhead of checkpointing is a critical consideration in checkpointing design.

One of the challenges in implementing checkpointing is the coordination and synchronization of the distributed processes to create a consistent global snapshot. Consistent global checkpoints ensure that the entire system can be restored to a coherent state, avoiding inconsistencies that may arise from the varying states of individual nodes. Techniques such as coordinated checkpointing involve synchronizing the processes across all nodes to ensure that they reach a consensus on when to create a global checkpoint. This coordination is essential for guaranteeing the consistency of the captured state and preventing the emergence of data anomalies during recovery.

In addition to coordination, the order in which checkpoints are taken is crucial for achieving consistency. Some distributed systems employ a technique known as incremental checkpointing, where only the changes made since the last checkpoint are saved. This reduces the overhead associated with checkpointing but requires careful management of dependencies between checkpoints to ensure that the system can be reconstructed accurately. In contrast, periodic checkpointing involves capturing the entire state of the system at regular intervals, simplifying the recovery process but potentially incurring higher overhead.

The choice between consistent and inconsistent checkpoints further influences the design of checkpointing mechanisms. Consistent checkpoints ensure that the captured state reflects a valid global state of the system, preventing partial or corrupted recovery. However, achieving consistent checkpoints often requires pausing the execution of processes temporarily, which may impact system performance. Inconsistent checkpoints, on the other hand, allow processes to continue execution during checkpoint creation, reducing the interruption but potentially leading to recovery challenges, especially when dependencies among processes are not correctly captured.

Checkpointing mechanisms are closely intertwined with fault tolerance strategies in distributed systems. In the event of a failure, the system can use the latest consistent checkpoint as a starting point for recovery. This involves rolling back the system to the checkpointed state and replaying the operations or transactions that occurred after the checkpoint. This rollback and replay process ensures that the system reconstructs a consistent state, minimizing the impact of the failure on data integrity and preserving the correctness of the distributed computation.

The implementation of checkpointing is not only influenced by the technical aspects of data consistency but also by the specific characteristics of the distributed system. For example, in parallel computing environments, where multiple processors collaborate on a common task, coordinated checkpointing may involve complex communication patterns to ensure that all processors reach a consistent state simultaneously. In contrast, in distributed databases, checkpointing strategies may focus on capturing the state of multiple nodes and ensuring that transactions across nodes are coordinated to maintain data consistency.

Advancements in distributed systems, including cloud computing and containerization technologies, introduce new considerations for checkpointing. In cloud environments, where virtualized resources may be dynamically allocated or de-allocated, checkpointing strategies must adapt to the ephemeral nature of virtual machines. Container orchestration platforms, such as Kubernetes, introduce additional complexities in managing checkpoints, as containers can be rapidly scaled, migrated, or restarted.

The concept of checkpointing extends beyond traditional distributed systems to include distributed storage systems, file systems, and even distributed machine learning frameworks. In distributed storage, checkpointing ensures the durability and consistency of stored data, preventing data loss or corruption in the face of node failures. In file systems, periodic snapshots through checkpointing allow users to recover files or directories to specific points in time. In distributed machine learning, where large-scale models are trained across multiple nodes, checkpointing is essential for resuming training after interruptions or failures without starting the training process from scratch.

Despite the benefits of checkpointing, it is not a one-size-fits-all solution, and its implementation must align with the specific requirements and characteristics of the distributed system. The choice of checkpointing strategy, the frequency of checkpoints, and the coordination mechanisms employed all depend on factors such as system architecture, application requirements, and the desired level of fault tolerance. Additionally, the impact of checkpointing on system performance, storage requirements, and recovery times must be carefully considered to strike an optimal balance between data consistency and operational efficiency.

In conclusion, checkpointing stands as a fundamental concept in distributed computing to ensure data consistency and enhance fault tolerance. By creating periodic snapshots of the system's state, checkpointing provides a mechanism for restoring a distributed system to a known and consistent state in the event of failures. The coordination, synchronization, and order of checkpoints are crucial considerations in achieving global consistency, while the choice between consistent and inconsistent checkpoints introduces trade-offs between interruption and complexity. As distributed systems continue to evolve, encompassing cloud computing, containerization, and advanced data processing paradigms, the role of checkpointing remains integral in preserving the reliability, integrity, and continuity of distributed computations and data processing.

Strategies for efficient checkpointing and recovery in distributed environments.

Efficient checkpointing and recovery strategies are paramount in ensuring the resilience and fault tolerance of distributed environments, where multiple interconnected nodes collaborate on complex tasks. These strategies play a crucial role in capturing and managing the system's state, allowing for rapid and reliable recovery in the event of failures. One key approach for efficient checkpointing involves the use of incremental techniques, where only the changes made since the last checkpoint are saved. This minimizes the storage overhead associated with storing complete snapshots while still providing a comprehensive record of system changes. Incremental checkpointing is particularly advantageous in scenarios where frequent checkpoints are necessary to capture rapidly changing data, as it reduces the time and resources required for checkpoint creation.

Coordination and synchronization are essential aspects of efficient checkpointing in distributed environments. Coordinated checkpointing ensures that all nodes within the system reach a consensus on when to create checkpoints, contributing to the creation of globally consistent snapshots. Various coordination algorithms, such as the Chandy-Lamport snapshot algorithm, have been developed to synchronize processes and ensure that they collectively agree on the checkpointing instants. These coordinated approaches are instrumental in preventing inconsistencies during recovery and maintaining the integrity of the distributed system.

In addition to coordination, the order in which checkpoints are taken significantly impacts the efficiency of the checkpointing process. Initiatives like uncoordinated or independent checkpointing acknowledge the autonomy of each node in deciding when to create checkpoints. While this approach reduces the coordination overhead, it may lead to inconsistencies in the captured state, requiring careful consideration of dependencies during recovery. Balancing the trade-offs between coordination overhead and consistency is a key consideration in designing efficient checkpointing strategies tailored to the specific requirements of the distributed environment.

Periodic checkpointing is another strategy employed for efficient state capture in distributed systems. This approach involves creating complete snapshots of the entire system at regular intervals. While periodic checkpointing simplifies recovery processes, it may incur higher overhead due to the storage requirements and potential disruption in system performance during checkpoint creation. Optimizing the frequency of periodic checkpoints is crucial, as an excessively high rate may burden the system with unnecessary overhead, while an infrequent rate may compromise the granularity of captured states.

The concept of message logging is integral to efficient checkpointing and recovery strategies. In distributed systems, processes communicate through message passing, and logging the exchanged messages provides a valuable record for recovery purposes. Message logging facilitates the reconstruction of communication patterns and helps restore the state of the system accurately. Moreover, coupling message logging with checkpoints allows for the identification of consistent global states, enhancing the efficiency and reliability of the recovery process.

Storage optimization is a critical consideration in designing efficient checkpointing strategies. The storage requirements for maintaining checkpoints can become substantial, particularly in large-scale distributed systems. Techniques such as compression and deduplication can be employed to minimize the storage footprint of checkpoints without sacrificing the completeness of captured states. Additionally, leveraging distributed storage systems or cloud-based solutions can enhance scalability and efficiency in managing checkpoint data, ensuring that storage constraints do not hinder the implementation of effective checkpointing mechanisms.

Implementing efficient recovery strategies is as crucial as creating efficient checkpoints. Rollback recovery, a prevalent approach, involves reverting the system to a previous checkpoint and re-executing operations from that point forward. Coordinated recovery mechanisms, such as global rollback or selective rollback, ensure that all nodes collectively transition to a consistent state. Conversely, optimistic recovery allows nodes to continue processing after a failure while concurrently attempting to reconcile inconsistent states. The selection of a recovery strategy depends on factors such as the specific characteristics of the distributed system, the desired level of consistency, and the acceptable recovery time.

In dynamic and cloud-based distributed environments, where resource allocation and node management are fluid, checkpointing strategies must adapt accordingly. Techniques such as migration-aware checkpointing consider the mobility of virtual machines or containers, ensuring that checkpoints capture the state of both the application and its associated resources. This adaptability is crucial in environments where nodes may be dynamically added or removed, requiring checkpointing and recovery strategies to align with the fluidity of resource allocation.

Ensuring the efficiency of checkpointing and recovery strategies involves rigorous testing and performance evaluation. Simulations and controlled experiments enable system designers to assess the impact of different checkpointing frequencies, coordination mechanisms, and recovery strategies on overall system performance. These evaluations help identify optimal configurations that strike a balance between reliability, consistency, and operational efficiency.

In summary, efficient checkpointing and recovery strategies are indispensable components of fault tolerance in distributed environments. Incremental checkpointing minimizes overhead by capturing only the changes since the last checkpoint, while coordination and synchronization mechanisms, whether coordinated or independent, ensure the creation of consistent global snapshots. Periodic checkpointing simplifies recovery processes, but careful consideration of storage and performance implications is necessary. Message logging enhances recovery accuracy by preserving communication patterns, and storage optimization techniques, such as compression and deduplication, minimize storage requirements. The selection of recovery strategies, whether rollback, optimistic, or coordinated, depends on the specific characteristics and requirements of the distributed system. Adapting checkpointing strategies to dynamic and cloud-based environments is crucial for ensuring resilience in the face of resource mobility. Rigorous testing and performance evaluation contribute to the refinement and optimization of checkpointing and recovery mechanisms, ultimately enhancing the overall fault tolerance and reliability of distributed systems.

Techniques for detecting failures in distributed systems.

Detecting failures in distributed systems is a critical aspect of ensuring their reliability, availability, and fault tolerance. Various techniques and strategies are employed to identify and respond to failures, ranging from hardware malfunctions to software errors and network disruptions. One fundamental approach is the use of heartbeat mechanisms, where nodes periodically exchange signals to confirm their operational status. If a node fails to send or respond to heartbeats within a predefined time frame, it is deemed as failed, triggering appropriate recovery measures. Heartbeat-based failure detection is simple yet effective, providing a mechanism for quickly identifying unresponsive nodes and initiating corrective actions.

Another technique for detecting failures in distributed systems involves the use of timeout mechanisms. When nodes engage in communication or coordination tasks, a predefined timeout period is established. If a response is not received within this timeframe, the system assumes a failure and takes appropriate measures. Timeout-based detection is versatile and applicable to various communication scenarios, but setting appropriate timeout values requires a balance to avoid false positives and negatives. Dynamic adjustment of timeouts based on network conditions or system load can enhance the accuracy of failure detection.

In distributed databases and storage systems, a common failure detection method is through the use of quorum-based approaches. These systems often replicate data across multiple nodes, and the failure of a subset of nodes may compromise data consistency. Quorum-based techniques involve defining a minimum number of nodes that must agree on a transaction or operation for it to be considered successful. If the required quorum is not reached, it indicates a potential failure, prompting the system to initiate recovery or reconfiguration processes. Quorum-based approaches contribute to fault tolerance by preventing inconsistent states that may arise from partial failures.

Failure detectors, as a dedicated component within a distributed system, actively monitor the liveness or health of nodes. These detectors use algorithms to distinguish between crashed nodes and nodes experiencing delays or network partitions. The Eventually Perfect Failure Detector (EPFD) is an example that guarantees eventual detection of node failures while allowing for temporary delays or partitions. EPFDs are particularly useful in scenarios where timely and accurate failure detection is critical, such as in consensus algorithms like Paxos or Raft.

Consensus algorithms themselves can be leveraged for failure detection. By requiring nodes to agree on a common decision, consensus protocols inherently involve communication and coordination. Nodes that deviate from the expected behavior are identified through the consensus process, signaling potential failures. Consensus-based failure detection, as seen in algorithms like Viewstamped Replication and Virtual Synchrony, provides a distributed and fault-tolerant approach to identifying faulty nodes and maintaining system consistency.

Anomaly detection techniques are gaining prominence for failure detection in distributed systems. Machine learning algorithms, when trained on normal system behavior, can identify deviations that may indicate potential failures or abnormal conditions. Anomalies could manifest as unexpected resource consumption, unusual network patterns, or deviations from historical performance metrics.

Leveraging machine learning for anomaly detection enables systems to adapt to evolving environments and identify subtle failure indicators that may go unnoticed by traditional methods.

In network-centric distributed systems, such as those based on microservices or cloud architectures, monitoring and observability play a crucial role in failure detection. Instrumenting applications and infrastructure components with metrics, logs, and traces provides real-time insights into system behavior. Automated monitoring tools can analyze these data streams, detect abnormal patterns, and trigger alerts or actions in response to potential failures. The combination of telemetry data and intelligent analysis enhances the system's ability to detect and respond to failures promptly.

Redundancy and diversity are essential strategies for failure detection and recovery. By deploying redundant components or services across different nodes or data centers, a distributed system can detect discrepancies or inconsistencies between replicas, signaling potential failures. Redundancy allows the system to continue operation even if individual components fail, minimizing the impact on overall system reliability. Diversity, in terms of using different hardware, software implementations, or communication paths, further strengthens the system's ability to detect and mitigate failures.

For detecting transient failures or intermittent issues, health checks and probing mechanisms are effective techniques. Periodic health checks involve actively testing the functionality of nodes or services, ensuring that they respond as expected. Probing involves sending test messages or queries to nodes to evaluate their responsiveness. These mechanisms help identify nodes that may experience intermittent failures or temporary issues, allowing the system to take corrective actions before the problems escalate.

In scenarios where the failure detection process itself may be susceptible to faults, techniques like Byzantine fault tolerance (BFT) can be employed. BFT ensures that even if a subset of nodes behaves maliciously or provides incorrect information about the health of the system, correct nodes can still reach a consensus. This approach is particularly relevant in distributed systems where nodes may be compromised or provide misleading information, safeguarding against the potential for false or malicious failure detection.

Moreover, leveraging historical data and predictive analytics can enhance failure detection capabilities. By analyzing patterns of past failures, the system can anticipate potential issues and proactively take preventive measures. Predictive analytics enable the identification of trends or indicators that precede failures, allowing the system to intervene before faults escalate. This forward-looking approach aligns with the goal of minimizing downtime and ensuring continuous operation in distributed systems.

In conclusion, detecting failures in distributed systems is a multifaceted challenge addressed through a combination of techniques and strategies. Heartbeat mechanisms, timeout-based approaches, quorum-based techniques, failure detectors, and consensus algorithms contribute to the identification of node failures and deviations from expected behavior. Anomaly detection, monitoring, and observability enable the system to respond to abnormal patterns indicative of potential failures. Redundancy and diversity provide resilience against failures, while health checks, probing, and Byzantine fault tolerance address transient or malicious failure scenarios. Leveraging historical data and predictive analytics adds a proactive dimension to failure detection, allowing systems to anticipate and mitigate potential issues. As distributed systems continue to evolve, the integration of these diverse techniques remains integral to building robust, fault-tolerant architectures capable of delivering continuous and reliable services.

Designing robust handling mechanisms for various failure scenarios.

Designing robust handling mechanisms for various failure scenarios is a critical aspect of building resilient and fault-tolerant systems, particularly in distributed environments where failures can be diverse and unpredictable. Robust handling mechanisms encompass a range of strategies and techniques to detect, respond to, and recover from failures, ensuring the continued operation and integrity of a distributed system.

One fundamental principle in designing robust handling mechanisms is embracing the inevitability of failures and adopting a fail-fast approach. By assuming that failures will occur and designing the system to detect them promptly, it becomes possible to initiate recovery measures swiftly. This proactive mindset informs the architecture and implementation choices, fostering a resilient system that can gracefully degrade or adapt to changing conditions.

Redundancy is a cornerstone of robust handling mechanisms, providing a safety net against various failure scenarios. Duplication of critical components, services, or data across multiple nodes ensures that the system can continue functioning even if individual elements fail. Redundancy is often implemented in conjunction with load balancing to distribute workloads efficiently and prevent overloading specific nodes. The use of backup systems, hot standby configurations, or active-active setups contributes to fault tolerance by enabling seamless transitions in the event of component failures.

In the context of failure detection, robust handling mechanisms include techniques such as heartbeat monitoring, where nodes regularly exchange signals to verify their operational status. If a node fails to send or respond to heartbeats within a predefined timeframe, it triggers the initiation of recovery processes. Timeouts and health checks are additional tools in the failure detection arsenal, allowing the system to identify unresponsive components and take corrective actions.

Moreover, the design of robust handling mechanisms must account for the distinction between permanent and transient failures. Permanent failures, such as hardware malfunctions or irreversible software errors, may require more comprehensive recovery measures, including the replacement of faulty components. In contrast, transient failures, which are temporary disruptions in service, may be addressed through mechanisms like retrying failed operations or rerouting traffic to alternative paths. Recognizing and differentiating between these failure types is crucial for tailoring appropriate handling strategies.

Failover mechanisms play a vital role in robust handling, especially in scenarios where a primary component or node becomes unavailable. During failover, the system automatically redirects operations to backup or secondary components, ensuring continuity of service. This is particularly relevant in distributed databases, storage systems, or applications where data consistency and availability are paramount. Failover strategies need to be carefully designed to minimize downtime, avoid data inconsistencies, and maintain the overall integrity of the system.

Rollback and recovery mechanisms are integral parts of handling failures, providing a way to revert the system to a known and consistent state after a failure occurs. Checkpointing, a technique involving the periodic capture of the system's state, facilitates efficient rollback and recovery. When a failure is detected, the system can roll back to the latest consistent checkpoint and replay operations or transactions to reconstruct the state. The efficiency of rollback and recovery mechanisms is crucial for minimizing the impact of failures on system performance and maintaining data integrity.

In distributed systems, where communication is central to operation, handling network failures is a critical aspect. Network partitions, packet loss, or connectivity issues can lead to communication breakdowns between nodes. Robust handling mechanisms for network failures may involve the use of consensus algorithms, such as Paxos or Raft, to ensure that nodes collectively agree on decisions even in the presence of network partitions. Additionally, techniques like exponential backoff and jitter in retry mechanisms help mitigate the impact of transient network failures by progressively adjusting the intervals between retries.

Dynamic adaptation to changing conditions is a hallmark of robust handling mechanisms. This adaptability is particularly crucial in cloud-based or containerized environments where resource allocation, scaling, and load balancing are dynamic. Auto-scaling mechanisms, for instance, enable the system to automatically adjust the number of instances or resources based on demand. Dynamic reconfiguration and rebalancing strategies allow the system to adapt to shifting workloads, optimizing performance and resource utilization even in the face of failures.

Security considerations are paramount in the design of robust handling mechanisms, as failures can be exploited by malicious actors. Handling mechanisms must include measures to detect and respond to security breaches, such as intrusion detection systems, access controls, and encryption. Additionally, the principle of least privilege should guide the design, limiting the impact of potential breaches and ensuring that only necessary permissions are granted to system components.

Human intervention and operational procedures are essential components of robust handling mechanisms. Well-defined and tested runbooks or playbooks provide guidelines for responding to specific failure scenarios. Incident response teams equipped with the necessary training and tools play a crucial role in coordinating and executing recovery measures. Regular drills and simulations help ensure that human responses are aligned with the designed handling mechanisms, minimizing the time to detect and recover from failures.

Furthermore, the design of robust handling mechanisms should consider the impact of cascading failures, where the failure of one component triggers a chain reaction affecting other interconnected components. Techniques like circuit breakers, inspired by the electrical engineering concept, can isolate faulty components or services to prevent the propagation of failures. Throttling mechanisms and load shedding strategies can also be employed to prioritize critical operations and shed non-essential tasks during periods of increased load or system stress.

Machine learning and predictive analytics contribute to the evolution of robust handling mechanisms by enabling systems to learn from historical data and predict potential failure scenarios. Anomaly detection algorithms, when trained on normal system behavior, can identify deviations indicative of impending failures. Predictive analytics allow the system to anticipate issues, trigger proactive interventions, and optimize resource allocation to prevent failures before they occur.

In conclusion, designing robust handling mechanisms for various failure scenarios is a multifaceted endeavor that requires a comprehensive and proactive approach. Embracing the inevitability of failures, incorporating redundancy, failover mechanisms, and rollback strategies, and adapting to dynamic conditions are key principles. Failure detection techniques, security considerations, and human intervention play critical roles in ensuring the reliability and resilience of distributed systems. The ability to distinguish between permanent and transient failures, address network issues, and prevent cascading failures adds layers of complexity to the design. As technology evolves, the integration of machine learning, predictive analytics, and advanced automation further refines the art of designing robust handling mechanisms, paving the way for more adaptive, self-healing, and fault-tolerant distributed systems.

Overview of distributed consensus algorithms.

Distributed consensus algorithms form the backbone of many distributed systems, enabling a set of nodes to reach an agreement on a common decision despite the potential for individual node failures or network partitions. These algorithms address the challenges of achieving consistency, fault tolerance, and reliability in scenarios where nodes collaborate to maintain a shared state or make coordinated decisions. One of the foundational distributed consensus algorithms is the Paxos algorithm, introduced by Leslie Lamport in 1989. Paxos employs a two-phase process, known as the prepare and accept phases, to ensure that a majority of nodes agree on a single value. It can tolerate failures of some nodes and continues to function even in the presence of asynchronous communication delays. Although Paxos provides a robust foundation for consensus, its complexity has led to the development of variations and optimizations, such as Multi-Paxos, Fast Paxos, and Flexible Paxos, each tailored to specific use cases and requirements.

The Raft consensus algorithm, introduced by Diego Ongaro and John Ousterhout in 2013, offers a more intuitive and understandable approach to distributed consensus. Raft divides the consensus process into leader election, log replication, and safety properties, simplifying the algorithm's comprehension and implementation. In Raft, nodes elect a leader to coordinate the consensus process, and the leader replicates its log entries to followers. Raft's emphasis on simplicity and understandability has contributed to its widespread adoption, particularly in scenarios where ease of implementation and maintenance is crucial. Additionally, Raft's safety guarantees ensure that nodes agree on the same sequence of commands, maintaining consistency across the distributed system.

Practical Byzantine Fault Tolerance (PBFT), introduced by Miguel Castro and Barbara Liskov in 1999, extends consensus algorithms to address Byzantine failures, where nodes may exhibit arbitrary and malicious behavior. PBFT uses a voting mechanism to reach consensus on a proposed value, and it can tolerate up to one-third of Byzantine-faulty nodes. This makes PBFT suitable for applications where the trustworthiness of nodes cannot be assumed, such as in permissioned blockchain networks. However, PBFT's performance is influenced by the communication overhead introduced by the need for nodes to exchange messages, making it more suitable for environments with lower latency requirements.

The HoneyBadgerBFT algorithm, proposed by Miller et al. in 2016, represents a significant advancement in Byzantine fault-tolerant consensus. It introduces a novel approach called asynchronous binary consensus, allowing nodes to reach consensus on binary decisions without relying on synchronized clocks or timing assumptions. HoneyBadgerBFT leverages cryptographic techniques, including threshold signatures and verifiable secret sharing, to provide robust Byzantine fault tolerance. This makes it suitable for permissionless blockchain networks and other scenarios where adversarial nodes may actively attempt to disrupt the consensus process.

Blockchain technology has popularized consensus algorithms as a critical component of decentralized systems. Proof-of-Work (PoW), the consensus algorithm underlying Bitcoin, relies on miners solving computationally intensive puzzles to validate transactions and add blocks to the blockchain. PoW's security model is based on the assumption that a majority of computational power in the network is controlled by honest nodes. However, PoW has faced criticism due to its energy consumption and scalability challenges. In contrast, Proof-of-Stake (PoS) consensus algorithms, such as those used by Ethereum 2.0, select validators to create new blocks based on their ownership or staking of cryptocurrency. PoS aims to be more energy-efficient than PoW while promoting decentralization and security.

Variations of Practical Byzantine Fault Tolerance, such as Tendermint and BFT-SMaRt, have gained traction in the development of permissioned blockchain networks. Tendermint combines Byzantine fault tolerance with a consensus mechanism inspired by PoS, allowing a set of validators to propose and vote on new blocks. BFT-SMaRt, on the other hand, emphasizes modularity and flexibility, enabling users to customize the consensus logic based on their specific requirements. These consensus algorithms aim to strike a balance between the trust assumptions of participants and the efficiency of the consensus process in environments where a degree of centralization is acceptable.

Asynchronous consensus algorithms, including the Asynchronous BFT (ABFT) algorithm proposed by Amir et al. in 2005, focus on achieving consensus without relying on timing assumptions or synchronized clocks. ABFT uses cryptographic techniques to tolerate arbitrary node failures and asynchronous communication delays. The algorithm ensures that nodes agree on the order of executed commands, even in the presence of Byzantine failures. Asynchronous consensus algorithms are particularly relevant in scenarios where network conditions may vary widely, making it challenging to establish precise timing assumptions.

The introduction of decentralized finance (DeFi) applications and blockchain networks with smart contract functionality has given rise to consensus algorithms tailored for such environments. The Avalanche consensus algorithm, proposed by Emin Gün Sirer and others in 2018, employs a novel approach called Avalanche consensus, where nodes repeatedly query each other to reach rapid and probabilistic agreement. Avalanche's design aims to provide fast finality, low latency, and high throughput, making it suitable for decentralized applications that require near-instantaneous transaction confirmation.

In summary, distributed consensus algorithms play a pivotal role in the reliability and integrity of distributed systems by enabling nodes to agree on a common decision despite the potential for failures and adversarial behavior. Paxos and its variants, Raft, PBFT, HoneyBadgerBFT, PoW, PoS, and newer algorithms like Avalanche each bring unique characteristics and trade-offs to the table, catering to diverse use cases and requirements. The ongoing evolution of distributed consensus algorithms reflects the dynamic nature of distributed systems and the continuous pursuit of more efficient, secure, and scalable solutions in the ever-changing landscape of distributed computing.

Examining consensus protocols like Paxos and Raft.

Examining consensus protocols like Paxos and Raft provides insights into the foundational principles and mechanisms employed to achieve agreement among distributed nodes in the face of potential failures. Paxos, introduced by Leslie Lamport in 1989, stands as one of the earliest and most influential consensus algorithms. The Paxos protocol is designed to work in an asynchronous environment, where nodes may fail, messages may be delayed, and the system may experience arbitrary faults. Paxos operates through a two-phase process: the prepare phase, where nodes propose a value and obtain promises from a majority of nodes not to accept any lower-numbered proposal, and the accept phase, where a node can accept a proposal if it receives promises from a majority. This process ensures that a majority of nodes eventually agree on a single value, guaranteeing consensus. While Paxos provides a robust foundation for consensus, its intricate nature and the challenge of understanding its nuances have led to variations and optimizations, including Multi-Paxos and Flexible Paxos.

Raft, introduced by Diego Ongaro and John Ousterhout in 2013, represents a departure from the complexity of Paxos. Raft is designed with a focus on simplicity and understandability, making it more accessible for implementation and maintenance. The Raft consensus protocol divides the consensus process into three main components: leader election, log replication, and safety properties.

In Raft, nodes elect a leader to coordinate the consensus process, and the leader replicates its log entries to followers. This simplicity has contributed to Raft's widespread adoption, particularly in scenarios where ease of implementation and maintenance is crucial. The safety guarantees of Raft ensure that nodes agree on the same sequence of commands, maintaining consistency across the distributed system.

Paxos and Raft share common objectives – achieving consensus in a distributed system – but they differ significantly in their approaches and the conceptual models they employ. Paxos, with its complex two-phase approach and promise-based mechanism, addresses the challenges of asynchronous communication and node failures. However, this complexity has led to challenges in understanding, implementing, and maintaining Paxos-based systems. In contrast, Raft's leader-based approach simplifies the consensus process, making it more intuitive and easier to comprehend. Raft's design choices, such as leader election and log replication, contribute to its ease of implementation, which has led to its adoption in various practical applications.

One crucial aspect of consensus protocols is leader election, as the role of a leader is pivotal in coordinating the consensus process. In Paxos, leader election is implicitly addressed through the prepare and accept phases. Any node that successfully completes the accept phase becomes the leader for subsequent rounds. However, the lack of a dedicated leader election phase in Paxos can lead to inefficiencies and increased communication overhead. Raft, on the other hand, introduces a dedicated leader election mechanism where nodes periodically send heartbeats to signal their availability. If a node does not receive a heartbeat within a specified timeframe, it initiates a new leader election. This explicit leader election process simplifies the handling of leadership changes and contributes to Raft's clarity.

Log replication is a fundamental component of consensus protocols, ensuring that all nodes in the system maintain an identical sequence of commands or transactions. In Paxos, the log replication mechanism is implicit in the accept phase, where nodes agree on the sequence of commands proposed by the leader. The leader ensures that followers replicate its log entries, ensuring consistency. In Raft, log replication is a distinct and well-defined process. The leader sends AppendEntries messages to followers, containing its log entries, and followers replicate these entries. Raft's log replication mechanism, with its explicit and separate design, enhances the clarity of the protocol and facilitates ease of implementation.

Achieving safety properties is a critical goal in consensus protocols to ensure that nodes agree on the same sequence of commands or transactions. Paxos guarantees safety through its two-phase process, where nodes promise not to accept lower-numbered proposals. This promise-based mechanism prevents conflicts and ensures that a majority of nodes agree on a single value. Raft achieves safety through a combination of leader election, log replication, and commit mechanisms. The leader ensures that followers replicate its log entries, and a command is considered committed when it has been replicated by a majority of nodes. Raft's safety properties contribute to its suitability for various distributed systems where consistency is paramount.

Both Paxos and Raft exhibit fault-tolerant characteristics, allowing them to function correctly even in the presence of node failures. In Paxos, the protocol is designed to tolerate up to n/2 - 1 failed nodes, where n is the total number of nodes. As long as a majority of nodes remain operational, Paxos can continue to make progress. However, Paxos does not explicitly address Byzantine failures, where nodes may exhibit arbitrary and malicious behavior. Raft, while not initially designed to handle Byzantine failures, can tolerate network partitions and node failures as long as a majority of nodes remain available. The simplicity of Raft's design facilitates the understanding and implementation of fault-tolerant systems.

Understanding the trade-offs between Paxos and Raft requires considering factors such as clarity, ease of implementation, and the context in which each protocol is applied. Paxos, with its promise-based approach and intricate two-phase process, provides a robust foundation for consensus in asynchronous environments. However, the complexity of Paxos has led to challenges in comprehension and implementation. Raft addresses these challenges by prioritizing simplicity and understandability. Its leader-based approach, explicit leader election, and distinct log replication mechanism contribute to its clarity and ease of implementation. The choice between Paxos and Raft often depends on the specific requirements of a distributed system and the trade-offs deemed acceptable in terms of complexity, clarity, and fault tolerance.

The evolution of consensus protocols has extended beyond Paxos and Raft, with newer algorithms addressing specific challenges and requirements in different contexts. Innovations like Practical Byzantine Fault Tolerance (PBFT) and HoneyBadgerBFT aim to provide fault tolerance in the presence of Byzantine failures. PBFT, introduced by Miguel Castro and Barbara Liskov in 1999, uses a voting mechanism to achieve consensus on a proposed value and can tolerate up to one-third of Byzantine-faulty nodes. HoneyBadgerBFT, proposed by Miller et al. in 2016, introduces asynchronous binary consensus, allowing nodes to reach consensus on binary decisions without relying on synchronized clocks. These advancements cater to scenarios where adversarial nodes may actively attempt to disrupt the consensus process.

The application of consensus protocols extends to the domain of blockchain technology, where decentralized networks rely on agreement mechanisms to validate transactions and maintain a consistent ledger. Proof-of-Work (PoW), the consensus algorithm underlying Bitcoin, leverages computational puzzles and miners' competition to validate transactions and add blocks to the blockchain. While PoW provides security based on computational power, it has faced criticism due to its energy consumption and scalability challenges. Proof-of-Stake (PoS) consensus algorithms, such as those used in Ethereum 2.0, select validators to create new blocks based on their ownership or staking of cryptocurrency. PoS aims to be more energy-efficient than PoW while promoting decentralization and security.

Variations of consensus protocols, like Tendermint and BFT-SMaRt, have gained prominence in the development of permissioned blockchain networks. Tendermint combines Byzantine fault tolerance with a consensus mechanism inspired by PoS, allowing a set of validators to propose and vote on new blocks. BFT-SMaRt, on the other hand, emphasizes modularity and flexibility, enabling users to customize the consensus logic based on their specific requirements. These consensus algorithms cater to scenarios where a degree of centralization is acceptable, offering alternatives to traditional blockchain models.

The landscape of consensus protocols continues to evolve, driven by the dynamic nature of distributed systems, emerging technologies, and the diverse requirements of applications and platforms. The ongoing quest for consensus protocols that balance simplicity, clarity, fault tolerance, and scalability reflects the complexity of distributed computing. As researchers and practitioners explore new frontiers, the understanding and implementation of consensus protocols like Paxos and Raft remain foundational in the broader exploration of reliable, fault-tolerant, and scalable distributed systems.

Chapter 6: Scalability Challenges and Solutions

Defining scalability and its critical role in distributed system design.

Scalability, in the context of distributed systems, is a fundamental attribute that measures the system's ability to handle an increasing workload or growing demand while maintaining or improving performance. It is a crucial aspect of system design that directly impacts the system's capacity to adapt to changing requirements, accommodate a higher number of users, and efficiently process a larger volume of data or transactions. The concept of scalability encompasses both vertical scalability, achieved by adding resources to a single node such as increasing CPU or memory, and horizontal scalability, achieved by adding more nodes to a distributed system. Horizontal scalability is particularly emphasized in distributed systems, allowing them to expand by distributing the workload across multiple nodes, which can be added or removed dynamically.

The critical role of scalability in distributed system design becomes evident when considering the ever-increasing demands imposed by modern applications and services. As user bases grow, data volumes expand, and computational requirements become more complex, the ability of a distributed system to scale horizontally becomes paramount. Scalability directly influences the system's performance, responsiveness, and overall efficiency, ensuring that it can handle the load effectively without compromising its functionality. This is especially crucial in scenarios where the system must accommodate variable workloads, unpredictable spikes in demand, or the dynamic nature of cloud-based environments.

One of the key benefits of scalability in distributed systems is the ability to achieve high availability. By distributing the workload across multiple nodes, the system becomes more resilient to failures or disruptions affecting individual components. Horizontal scalability, in particular, supports the creation of redundant and geographically distributed instances, reducing the risk of a single point of failure. This redundancy ensures that even if some nodes experience issues or go offline, the remaining nodes can continue to serve requests, maintaining continuous operation and mitigating the impact of failures on the overall system.

Scalability is closely tied to the concept of elasticity, which refers to a system's ability to dynamically adapt its resource allocation based on the current workload. In cloud computing environments, where resources can be provisioned or de-provisioned on-demand, elasticity allows distributed systems to scale in or out in response to changes in demand. This dynamic adjustment of resources ensures efficient resource utilization, cost-effectiveness, and the ability to handle sudden increases or decreases in workload without manual intervention. Elasticity enhances the overall responsiveness and agility of distributed systems, aligning resource allocation with the system's actual requirements.

The design considerations for achieving scalability in distributed systems encompass several key principles. Firstly, the architecture should be modular and decoupled, allowing components to scale independently. Microservices architecture, for example, promotes scalability by breaking down a system into small, independently deployable services that can be scaled individually based on demand. Secondly, effective load balancing is essential to distribute incoming requests evenly across the available nodes. Load balancers play a critical role in optimizing resource utilization, preventing overloading of specific nodes, and ensuring that the entire system scales harmoniously.

Scalability is closely related to performance, and considerations for scalability often overlap with strategies for optimizing system performance. Caching mechanisms, for instance, can enhance scalability by reducing the need to repeatedly process the same data or computations. By caching frequently accessed data or results, distributed systems can respond more quickly to requests, improving overall performance and reducing the load on backend services. Content delivery networks (CDNs) also contribute to scalability by caching and delivering content from strategically located servers, minimizing latency and improving the responsiveness of distributed systems, particularly for geographically dispersed user bases.

Database scalability is a critical aspect of overall system scalability, as the database often constitutes a central component of distributed systems. Horizontal partitioning, also known as sharding, involves distributing the data across multiple database instances or nodes based on a defined criterion. This allows the system to scale horizontally, accommodating larger datasets and higher transaction volumes. NoSQL databases, designed with scalability in mind, often adopt distributed architectures that support easy horizontal scaling. Additionally, database replication and data consistency mechanisms play crucial roles in ensuring that data remains available and consistent across distributed nodes, further contributing to the overall scalability of the system.

Scalability considerations extend to communication patterns within distributed systems. As the number of nodes increases, efficient and scalable communication becomes essential. Messaging patterns, such as publish-subscribe or event-driven architectures, enable loosely coupled communication between components, allowing them to scale independently. Message queues and event-driven approaches decouple producers and consumers, enabling more flexible and scalable communication patterns. Similarly, distributed systems may leverage asynchronous communication to improve scalability by avoiding synchronous bottlenecks and allowing nodes to process tasks independently.

In the realm of distributed computing, scalability is particularly crucial in the context of parallel and distributed processing. Parallel scalability involves efficiently utilizing multiple processors or cores within a single node, optimizing performance for computationally intensive tasks. Distributed scalability, on the other hand, focuses on scaling across multiple nodes to handle larger workloads collectively. Techniques like MapReduce, introduced by Google and popularized by frameworks like Apache Hadoop, exemplify distributed scalability by enabling the parallel processing of large datasets across a cluster of nodes. This approach facilitates the efficient utilization of resources and the ability to tackle complex computational tasks that would be impractical for a single machine.

Scalability also intersects with the concept of statelessness in distributed systems. Stateless architectures, where each request is processed independently without relying on stored state information, facilitate horizontal scalability. Stateless components can be replicated and distributed across nodes, allowing the system to scale out by adding more instances as needed. Statelessness enhances fault tolerance and simplifies the management of distributed systems, contributing to their ability to dynamically adapt to changing workloads.

While scalability is a cornerstone of distributed system design, it is important to acknowledge the challenges and trade-offs associated with achieving scalable architectures. The introduction of additional nodes introduces complexities related to coordination, communication overhead, and consistency maintenance. Distributed systems must contend with issues such as load balancing, partition tolerance, and the intricacies of data synchronization. Moreover, achieving linear scalability, where adding more resources results in a proportional increase in performance, is often challenging due to bottlenecks, contention, or the nature of the workload.

In conclusion, scalability is a fundamental and multifaceted aspect of distributed system design, playing a pivotal role in ensuring the adaptability, efficiency, and resilience of systems in the face of growing demands. Horizontal scalability, elastic resource allocation, modular architectures, efficient load balancing, and considerations for statelessness collectively contribute to the scalability of distributed systems. The ability to handle increased workloads, accommodate dynamic changes, and provide high availability enhances the overall performance and responsiveness of distributed systems. As technology continues to advance, scalability remains a focal point in the pursuit of designing distributed systems that can effectively scale to meet the evolving requirements of modern applications and services.

Understanding the difference between horizontal and vertical scalability.

Understanding the difference between horizontal and vertical scalability is pivotal in the realm of system architecture, particularly in the context of distributed computing and the design of scalable applications. Horizontal scalability, often referred to as scaling out, involves adding more machines or nodes to a system to handle increased load or demand. This approach aims to distribute the workload across multiple instances, allowing the system to accommodate higher traffic, process more transactions, or store larger datasets. In horizontally scalable architectures, the emphasis is on adding identical or similar resources, such as servers, to expand the system's capacity. This approach is particularly beneficial when the workload can be divided into independent tasks that can be processed concurrently across multiple nodes. Cloud computing environments and containerized applications frequently leverage horizontal scalability to dynamically allocate and de-allocate resources based on fluctuating demand.

On the other hand, vertical scalability, often termed scaling up, involves increasing the resources of a single machine or node to enhance its capacity. This approach aims to augment the power of existing hardware by adding more CPU, memory, storage, or other resources to a single instance. Vertical scalability is characterized by a focus on improving the performance and capabilities of individual components rather than distributing the workload across multiple instances. This approach is suitable for scenarios where a single, powerful machine can handle the entire workload effectively. Vertical scalability is often associated with monolithic architectures, where a centralized server is responsible for executing various tasks, and scaling up involves upgrading the hardware specifications of that central server.

The distinction between horizontal and vertical scalability becomes more apparent when considering their implications on system design, flexibility, and overall performance. Horizontal scalability aligns with the principles of distributed computing, promoting modularity, fault tolerance, and the ability to adapt to varying workloads dynamically. As more nodes are added horizontally, the system gains the capability to handle increased traffic, balance loads, and mitigate the risk of a single point of failure. This distributed nature makes horizontal scalability particularly well-suited for applications with unpredictable demand patterns, allowing for efficient resource utilization and elasticity in cloud-based environments.

In contrast, vertical scalability is often associated with a more monolithic or centralized approach, where scaling up involves enhancing the capabilities of a single, robust machine. While vertical scalability may offer immediate performance improvements for specific tasks, it has inherent limitations. There is a threshold beyond which it becomes impractical or cost-prohibitive to further upgrade individual components. Additionally, vertical scalability may introduce challenges related to the risk of a single point of failure, as the entire system's capacity relies on the capabilities of a solitary node. Maintenance, upgrades, and hardware replacements in vertically scalable systems may require downtime, impacting overall availability.

Horizontal scalability is exemplified in architectures like microservices and container orchestration, where workloads are distributed across numerous instances that can independently handle specific tasks. Cloud-native applications often leverage horizontal scalability to ensure resilience, high availability, and the ability to scale in response to dynamic demands. Technologies like Kubernetes, Docker, and serverless computing platforms facilitate the horizontal scaling of services, enabling applications to respond dynamically to varying loads and ensuring consistent performance across a distributed infrastructure.

In vertical scalability, the focus is on augmenting the capacity of individual machines or servers. This approach is prominent in traditional, monolithic architectures where a single, powerful server handles all tasks. Vertical scalability can be advantageous for certain workloads where a singular, high-performance instance suffices. For instance, databases with vertical scalability can be scaled up by adding more powerful hardware to a single node, allowing it to handle larger datasets and process more complex queries. However, the limitations arise when scaling up becomes impractical or cost-ineffective, especially if the workload continues to grow exponentially.

One of the key considerations in understanding the difference between horizontal and vertical scalability is the trade-off between flexibility and immediate performance gains. Horizontal scalability excels in scenarios where flexibility, fault tolerance, and dynamic resource allocation are critical. Cloud environments, particularly those based on a pay-as-you-go model, align well with horizontal scalability as organizations can scale their applications horizontally based on usage patterns, optimizing costs and efficiency. In contrast, vertical scalability may provide immediate performance enhancements for specific tasks but may not be as agile or adaptable to changing conditions.

Horizontal scalability is often associated with distributed databases, where data is partitioned across multiple nodes to enable parallel processing and accommodate larger datasets. NoSQL databases, designed for horizontal scalability, distribute data across a cluster of nodes, allowing them to handle increasing read and write operations efficiently. This approach aligns with the principles of NoSQL databases like Cassandra, MongoDB, or Amazon DynamoDB, where data is distributed across nodes, and the system can scale horizontally to meet growing demands.

Vertical scalability is common in scenarios where a single, powerful machine can address the entire workload effectively. In traditional relational databases, vertical scalability involves upgrading the hardware specifications of a central server to handle increased database transactions, complex queries, or larger datasets. This approach aligns with the scalability strategies of relational databases like MySQL or PostgreSQL, where vertical scaling may be employed to address specific performance bottlenecks.

A crucial factor in the decision between horizontal and vertical scalability is the nature of the workload and the architectural requirements of the application. Applications with a modular, microservices-based architecture that can leverage horizontal scalability benefit from the advantages of distributed systems, including fault tolerance and adaptability. In contrast, legacy systems or applications with specific hardware dependencies may find vertical scalability more suitable, especially when immediate performance improvements are essential, and the system can operate effectively within the constraints of a single, powerful node.

The evolving landscape of modern applications often leans towards horizontal scalability due to its alignment with cloud-native principles, containerization, and microservices architectures. The ability to distribute workloads, dynamically allocate resources, and seamlessly respond to changes in demand positions horizontal scalability as a key enabler of agility and efficiency. Vertical scalability, while still relevant in certain scenarios, may be associated with challenges related to scalability ceilings, cost implications, and limitations in adapting to the dynamic nature of contemporary computing environments.

In conclusion, understanding the difference between horizontal and vertical scalability is fundamental to making informed decisions in system design, especially in the context of distributed computing. Horizontal scalability, with its emphasis on distributed, modular, and fault-tolerant architectures, aligns with the principles of cloud computing and modern application development. It facilitates adaptability, dynamic resource allocation, and responsiveness to changing workloads. Vertical scalability, while offering immediate performance gains for specific tasks, has inherent limitations and may not align as well with the flexibility and efficiency requirements of contemporary distributed systems. The choice between horizontal and vertical scalability depends on factors such as application architecture, workload characteristics, and the need for flexibility, and it underscores the dynamic nature of designing scalable systems in the ever-evolving landscape of technology.

Strategies for scaling databases in distributed environments.

Strategies for scaling databases in distributed environments are essential to address the increasing demands of modern applications, where data volumes and transaction rates can grow exponentially. One prevalent approach is horizontal scaling, which involves distributing the database across multiple nodes to handle a larger workload collectively. This strategy is particularly effective for read-intensive workloads and scenarios where data partitioning can be employed. NoSQL databases, such as Cassandra and MongoDB, are designed with horizontal scalability in mind. They utilize techniques like sharding, where data is partitioned and distributed across nodes, enabling parallel processing and efficient utilization of resources. Horizontal scaling allows organizations to add more nodes dynamically, adapting to changing demands and providing a cost-effective means of expanding database capacity.

Another strategy involves the use of distributed database management systems (DDBMS), which are specifically designed to operate in distributed environments. DDBMS distributes data across multiple nodes, providing transparency to users and applications by presenting a unified interface. Examples include Amazon DynamoDB and Google Cloud Spanner. These systems employ various mechanisms for data distribution, consistency, and fault tolerance. DynamoDB, for instance, replicates data across multiple Availability Zones to ensure high availability and durability. Distributed databases offer the advantage of seamless scalability, allowing organizations to add more nodes as needed without significant disruptions.

Closely related to distributed databases is the concept of NewSQL databases, which combine elements of traditional relational databases with the benefits of distributed architectures. NewSQL databases, such as Google Cloud Spanner and CockroachDB, aim to provide the consistency and transactional capabilities of traditional SQL databases while offering horizontal scalability. Google Cloud Spanner employs a globally distributed architecture with synchronized clocks to provide strong consistency across geographically dispersed nodes. CockroachDB uses a distributed, strongly consistent, and transactional model while allowing for horizontal scaling. These databases offer a middle ground between the familiarity of SQL databases and the scalability of NoSQL databases.

Partitioning is a fundamental technique in scaling databases, involving the division of large datasets into smaller, more manageable partitions. This strategy facilitates parallel processing and enables the database to scale horizontally. Range partitioning, hash partitioning, and list partitioning are common partitioning methods. Range partitioning involves dividing data based on a range of values, such as date ranges. Hash partitioning distributes data based on a hash function, ensuring an even distribution across partitions. List partitioning involves explicitly specifying which values belong to each partition. Partitioning can be applied to both relational and NoSQL databases, allowing organizations to optimize data storage and retrieval based on specific criteria.

Caching is an effective strategy to enhance database scalability by reducing the need to repeatedly fetch data from the underlying storage. In-memory caching systems, such as Redis and Memcached, store frequently accessed data in memory, allowing for rapid retrieval and reducing the load on the database. Caching mechanisms can be implemented at various levels, including application-level caching and database-level caching. Application-level caching involves caching data within the application code, while database-level caching, often referred to as query caching, caches the results of frequent database queries. Caching enhances overall system performance, especially for read-heavy workloads, and contributes to improved scalability.

Data denormalization is a strategy that involves intentionally introducing redundancy into the database schema to optimize for specific queries and enhance read performance. While normalization aims to minimize redundancy and maintain data integrity, denormalization sacrifices some of these benefits in favor of improved query performance. In distributed environments, denormalization can be particularly useful for scenarios where certain queries are executed frequently, and the cost of redundant storage is outweighed by the performance gains. This strategy is commonly applied in data warehousing and analytics use cases, where complex queries are prevalent.

Sharding, a form of horizontal partitioning, involves dividing a database into smaller, independent pieces called shards. Each shard operates as a separate database instance, managing a subset of the overall data. Sharding is effective for both read and write scalability, as each shard can handle its own transactions independently. However, managing distributed transactions and ensuring consistency across shards can introduce complexities. Database sharding is commonly employed in scenarios where the dataset is too large for a single database instance to handle or when geographical distribution of data is necessary. Sharding is widely used in systems like MongoDB, which supports automatic sharding for horizontal scaling.

Replication is a strategy that involves creating and maintaining copies of data across multiple nodes in a distributed environment. Replication enhances data availability, fault tolerance, and read scalability. In a master-slave replication model, a single node (the master) handles write operations, while multiple nodes (the slaves) replicate the data for read operations. This model is effective for read-heavy workloads but introduces the challenge of ensuring consistency between the master and slaves. Multi-master replication allows multiple nodes to handle both read and write operations, providing better write scalability but requiring mechanisms to handle conflicts and maintain consistency. Database systems like MySQL and PostgreSQL support various replication configurations to achieve scalability and high availability.

Distributed caching, often integrated with distributed databases, involves caching data across multiple nodes to improve read performance and reduce the load on the database. Distributed caching systems, such as Hazelcast and Apache Ignite, operate by storing copies of frequently accessed data in memory across multiple nodes. This approach contributes to horizontal scalability, as each node in the cache cluster can handle a portion of the read requests independently. Distributed caching is beneficial for scenarios where low-latency access to frequently accessed data is crucial, such as in web applications serving dynamic content.

Data archiving and tiered storage are strategies that involve organizing data based on its access frequency and prioritizing storage resources accordingly. Frequently accessed or "hot" data can be stored on high-performance storage, while less frequently accessed or "cold" data can be moved to lower-cost, lower-performance storage. This tiered storage approach allows organizations to optimize costs and resource utilization while maintaining the ability to scale the storage infrastructure as needed. Cloud providers often offer tiered storage solutions that automatically migrate data between different storage classes based on access patterns.

Containerization and microservices architectures contribute to the scalability of databases by promoting modular, independent components that can be scaled individually. Container orchestration platforms like Kubernetes facilitate the deployment and management of containerized database instances, allowing for dynamic scaling based on resource requirements. Microservices architectures enable organizations to develop and deploy discrete services, each with its own database, allowing for independent scaling of services based on their specific demands. This approach aligns well with the principles of horizontal scalability and adaptability to changing workloads.

Load balancing is a critical strategy for achieving scalability in distributed database environments. Load balancers distribute incoming database queries or transactions across multiple nodes, ensuring even utilization of resources and preventing overloading of specific nodes. Load balancing enhances both read and write scalability by distributing the workload efficiently. Database clusters, managed by load balancers, can automatically redirect requests to nodes with lower loads, optimizing resource usage and improving overall system performance. Load balancing is an integral component of horizontally scalable architectures, allowing organizations to seamlessly add or remove nodes based on demand.

Automated scaling, often employed in cloud environments, enables organizations to automatically adjust the number of database nodes based on predefined criteria such as CPU utilization, memory usage, or query latency. Cloud services like Amazon Aurora and Google Cloud Spanner offer automated scaling features, allowing database clusters to dynamically adapt to changing workloads without manual intervention. Automated scaling enhances efficiency, reduces operational overhead, and ensures that the database infrastructure aligns with the organization's performance and cost requirements.

In conclusion, strategies for scaling databases in distributed environments encompass a diverse range of techniques and technologies, each addressing specific aspects of scalability, performance, and adaptability. Horizontal scaling, distributed databases, partitioning, caching, denormalization, sharding, replication, distributed caching, data archiving, containerization, microservices architectures, load balancing, and automated scaling collectively contribute to the design and operation of scalable database systems. The choice of a particular strategy depends on the specific requirements of the application, workload characteristics, and the organization's goals in terms of performance, availability, and cost efficiency. The continuous evolution of technology and the dynamic nature of distributed computing environments underscore the importance of employing a combination of these strategies to meet the challenges and opportunities presented by ever-growing data volumes and increasingly complex applications.

Sharding, partitioning, and replication techniques.

Sharding, partitioning, and replication represent fundamental techniques in the realm of distributed databases, each addressing specific challenges and requirements related to scalability, performance, and fault tolerance. Sharding, also known as horizontal partitioning, involves dividing a database into smaller, independent units called shards, where each shard operates as a self-contained database instance. This approach is particularly useful in handling large datasets or high transaction volumes by distributing the workload across multiple nodes. Sharding can be based on various criteria, such as range sharding, where data is partitioned based on a range of values, or hash sharding, where a hash function determines the placement of data into shards. Sharding contributes to horizontal scalability, enabling organizations to add more shards dynamically to accommodate growing workloads. However, managing distributed transactions, ensuring data consistency, and handling potential hotspots or imbalances between shards require careful consideration and implementation.

Partitioning, a broader term that encompasses both horizontal and vertical partitioning, involves organizing data within a database based on specific criteria to enhance manageability and performance. Horizontal partitioning, or sharding, distributes data across multiple nodes, while vertical partitioning involves dividing a table into smaller tables based on columns. Vertical partitioning can be particularly useful when certain columns are accessed more frequently than others, allowing organizations to optimize storage and retrieval based on access patterns. Partitioning is a crucial strategy for achieving scalability, as it facilitates parallel processing and efficient resource utilization. Additionally, partitioning supports the implementation of other techniques, such as sharding and replication, to further enhance the overall performance and resilience of distributed databases.

Replication, a technique that involves creating and maintaining copies of data across multiple nodes, plays a pivotal role in achieving fault tolerance, high availability, and improved read scalability. In a master-slave replication model, a single node (the master) handles write operations, while multiple nodes (the slaves) replicate the data for read operations. This model is effective for read-heavy workloads but introduces challenges related to ensuring consistency between the master and slaves. Multi-master replication allows multiple nodes to handle both read and write operations, providing better write scalability but requiring mechanisms to handle conflicts and maintain consistency. Replication is crucial for ensuring data availability, as it allows for continued operation even if some nodes experience failures. However, managing replication lag, conflict resolution, and data consistency across distributed nodes are essential considerations in the implementation of replication techniques.

These techniques, while distinct, often work in tandem to address the complexities of distributed database systems. Sharding, partitioning, and replication contribute to achieving horizontal scalability, where the ability to add more nodes or shards dynamically allows the system to handle increasing workloads. Horizontal scalability aligns with the principles of distributed computing, promoting modularity, fault tolerance, and the ability to adapt to varying workloads dynamically. Sharding, as a specific form of partitioning, facilitates the distribution of data across multiple nodes, enabling parallel processing and efficient utilization of resources. In scenarios where datasets are too large for a single node or where geographical distribution of data is necessary, sharding becomes an effective strategy.

Furthermore, these techniques are often applied in conjunction with other strategies to optimize various aspects of distributed databases. For instance, the combination of sharding and replication enhances both read and write scalability, as sharding allows for parallel processing of read and write operations, while replication ensures data availability and fault tolerance. The use of partitioning, whether horizontal or vertical, contributes to efficient data organization and retrieval, aligning with the principles of modularity and adaptability. These techniques are essential considerations in the design and implementation of modern database systems, especially in the context of cloud-native applications and dynamically changing workloads.

One notable application of these techniques is in the domain of NoSQL databases, where they are commonly employed to address the challenges posed by large-scale, distributed architectures. NoSQL databases, such as MongoDB and Cassandra, leverage sharding to distribute data across multiple nodes, allowing for horizontal scalability and improved performance. Partitioning is often applied to optimize storage and retrieval based on specific access patterns, while replication ensures high availability and fault tolerance. These databases are designed to handle unstructured or semi-structured data and are well-suited for scenarios where traditional relational databases may encounter limitations in terms of scalability and performance.

In the context of partitioning, it is crucial to consider the impact on query performance and the potential for data skew or imbalances between partitions. Effective partitioning strategies take into account the distribution of data and access patterns to avoid hotspots that could lead to performance bottlenecks. Range partitioning, where data is divided based on a range of values, is suitable for scenarios where data can be evenly distributed across partitions. Hash partitioning, on the other hand, involves using a hash function to determine the placement of data, offering a more even distribution and reducing the risk of hotspots.

While sharding and partitioning contribute to scalability and parallel processing, replication addresses concerns related to fault tolerance and data availability. In distributed systems, where nodes may experience failures or disruptions, maintaining consistency and ensuring continuous operation become critical requirements. Replication mitigates the impact of node failures by providing redundant copies of data that can be used for read operations, ensuring that the system remains operational even if some nodes are unavailable. However, managing the trade-offs between consistency, availability, and partition tolerance (CAP theorem) becomes a central consideration in designing distributed systems.

The implementation of these techniques requires careful planning, taking into account the specific characteristics of the application, workload patterns, and performance requirements. Additionally, the choice between these techniques may depend on factors such as the type of data being managed, the desired level of consistency, and the overall architecture of the distributed system. In scenarios where read scalability is a primary concern, replication and sharding can be combined to optimize performance. For write-intensive workloads, a well-designed partitioning strategy may be more effective, allowing for parallel processing of write operations.

In conclusion, sharding, partitioning, and replication techniques play pivotal roles in addressing the challenges of scalability, performance, and fault tolerance in distributed database systems. Sharding facilitates horizontal scalability by distributing the workload across multiple nodes, while partitioning organizes data to optimize storage and retrieval based on specific criteria. Replication ensures fault tolerance and high availability by maintaining redundant copies of data across distributed nodes. These techniques are foundational in the design and operation of modern distributed databases, especially in the context of cloud-native applications and dynamic workloads. The successful implementation of these techniques requires a nuanced understanding of the trade-offs involved and a thoughtful approach to aligning them with the specific requirements of the application and the broader distributed system architecture.

The importance of load balancing in maintaining system performance.

The importance of load balancing in maintaining system performance cannot be overstated, as it serves as a critical mechanism for optimizing resource utilization, ensuring high availability, and enhancing the overall efficiency of complex distributed systems. Load balancing involves the distribution of incoming network traffic or computing workloads across multiple servers or resources to prevent any single component from becoming a bottleneck. In the context of web applications, for instance, load balancing plays a pivotal role in evenly distributing user requests among servers, preventing any individual server from being overwhelmed by traffic spikes or resource-intensive tasks. This distribution of workload is essential for maintaining consistent response times, minimizing latency, and avoiding performance degradation during periods of increased demand.

In distributed systems, load balancing acts as a key enabler for horizontal scalability, allowing organizations to scale their infrastructure by adding or removing resources dynamically based on workload fluctuations. This adaptability is particularly crucial in cloud environments, where applications need to respond seamlessly to varying levels of user activity and unpredictable changes in demand. Load balancers function as traffic managers, intelligently directing requests to available servers or instances, thereby optimizing resource usage and ensuring that each component operates within its capacity. This dynamic allocation of workloads promotes efficient utilization of computational resources, contributing to cost-effectiveness and the ability to scale infrastructure based on actual requirements.

One of the fundamental benefits of load balancing is the enhancement of system reliability and fault tolerance. By distributing incoming requests across multiple servers, load balancers mitigate the risk of a single point of failure. In the event that one server becomes unavailable due to maintenance, hardware failure, or other issues, the load balancer redirects traffic to the remaining healthy servers. This redundancy ensures that the system can continue to operate smoothly, maintaining continuous service availability and minimizing the impact of potential disruptions. Load balancing strategies, such as round-robin or weighted load balancing, further refine the distribution of traffic, accounting for variations in server capacity and ensuring an equitable sharing of the workload.

Load balancing is particularly vital for applications that experience dynamic and unpredictable traffic patterns. E-commerce websites during sales events, online streaming platforms during peak viewing times, or social media platforms during viral content spikes are examples where load balancing becomes indispensable. Without effective load distribution, these applications could experience performance bottlenecks, slower response times, and even service outages, leading to a degraded user experience and potential financial losses for businesses. Load balancing mechanisms, whether implemented through hardware or software solutions, intelligently manage traffic to prevent overload on specific components, contributing to a smoother, more responsive, and reliable user experience.

In the realm of application scalability, load balancing aligns closely with the principles of microservices architectures. As organizations adopt microservices-based development, where applications are decomposed into smaller, independently deployable services, load balancing becomes essential for distributing user requests across the various microservices. This approach allows each microservice to scale independently based on its specific workload, promoting modular growth and adaptability to changing requirements. Load balancing ensures that no single microservice bears an unfair share of the overall traffic, preventing bottlenecks and optimizing the responsiveness of the entire application.

Moreover, load balancing contributes significantly to the concept of elasticity in cloud computing. In cloud environments, where resources can be provisioned or de-provisioned on demand, load balancing plays a crucial role in automatically scaling the infrastructure to match the current workload. Auto-scaling configurations, often coupled with load balancers, enable organizations to dynamically adjust the number of instances or servers based on predefined criteria such as CPU utilization, memory usage, or incoming requests. This automated scaling ensures that the system efficiently allocates resources in response to changing demands, maintaining optimal performance without manual intervention.

Load balancing strategies extend beyond the distribution of incoming requests and traffic. They also encompass the optimization of backend services, databases, and other components that contribute to overall system functionality. Database load balancing, for instance, involves distributing database queries and transactions across multiple nodes, preventing any single database server from becoming a performance bottleneck. This approach is crucial for achieving efficient utilization of database resources, minimizing contention, and ensuring that data retrieval and storage operations are distributed evenly.

In the context of content delivery, load balancing is instrumental in the deployment of Content Delivery Networks (CDNs). CDNs leverage a network of strategically located servers to cache and deliver content closer to end-users, reducing latency and improving the overall performance of websites and applications. Load balancing mechanisms within CDNs ensure that user requests are directed to the nearest or least congested server, optimizing the delivery of static and dynamic content. This distributed content delivery approach enhances the user experience by accelerating page load times, reducing latency, and efficiently handling varying levels of content demand.

Load balancing algorithms and techniques vary based on the specific requirements and characteristics of the application or system. Round-robin, least connections, weighted load balancing, and session persistence are among the commonly used strategies. Round-robin evenly distributes requests in a cyclic manner, ensuring that each server receives an equal share of traffic. Least connections directs requests to the server with the fewest active connections, optimizing resource usage. Weighted load balancing allows administrators to assign different weights to servers based on their capacity, enabling a proportional distribution of traffic. Session persistence ensures that subsequent requests from the same user are directed to the same server, maintaining session state.

While load balancing brings numerous advantages, its implementation requires careful consideration of factors such as session management, data consistency, and the potential impact on application performance. Session-based applications may require specialized load balancing configurations to maintain user sessions seamlessly. Additionally, stateful applications may introduce challenges in achieving session persistence and consistent data access. Load balancers, whether hardware-based appliances or software-based solutions, need to be configured and monitored to ensure optimal performance and adaptability to changing conditions.

In conclusion, the importance of load balancing in maintaining system performance is paramount in the complex and dynamic landscape of distributed computing. Load balancing optimizes resource utilization, ensures high availability, and enhances the overall efficiency of applications and services. From distributing incoming traffic across servers to optimizing backend services and databases, load balancing strategies are foundational in achieving scalability, fault tolerance, and responsiveness. The adaptability of load balancing mechanisms to changing workloads, coupled with their role in enhancing system reliability and user experience, underscores their significance in modern computing environments. As organizations continue to navigate the challenges of evolving technologies and dynamic user demands, load balancing remains a fundamental component in the pursuit of efficient, resilient, and high-performance distributed systems.

Overview of load balancing algorithms and strategies.

An overview of load balancing algorithms and strategies is essential in understanding the diverse approaches employed to distribute incoming traffic or workloads across multiple servers or resources efficiently. One commonly used load balancing algorithm is the Round-Robin method, which evenly distributes requests among a pool of servers in a cyclic manner. This algorithm ensures that each server receives an equal share of the incoming traffic, promoting a balanced distribution of the workload. While Round-Robin is simple and easy to implement, it may not account for variations in server capacity or workload, leading to potential inefficiencies in resource utilization.

Weighted Round-Robin is an extension of the Round-Robin algorithm that introduces the concept of assigning weights to servers based on their capacity. This allows administrators to allocate a proportionate share of the workload to each server, taking into account differences in processing power, memory, or other resource factors. Weighted Round-Robin provides a more granular approach to load balancing, enabling organizations to optimize resource usage according to the capabilities of individual servers.

Least Connections is another load balancing algorithm that directs incoming requests to the server with the fewest active connections. This strategy aims to distribute the workload more evenly by sending requests to servers that are currently underutilized. While Least Connections helps prevent overloading of specific servers, it may not consider variations in server capacity or differences in the complexity of processing individual requests.

Weighted Least Connections extends the Least Connections algorithm by introducing weighted values for each server based on its capacity. This allows organizations to consider both the current load on a server and its overall capacity when making load balancing decisions. Weighted Least Connections provides a more nuanced approach to workload distribution, aligning with the principles of efficient resource utilization and adaptability to varying server capabilities.

Another load balancing algorithm is the Least Response Time strategy, which directs incoming requests to the server with the shortest response time. This approach aims to optimize user experience by selecting the server that can process requests most quickly. While Least Response Time is effective in minimizing latency and improving overall system performance, it may not consider variations in server capacity or the complexity of processing different types of requests.

The Random algorithm, as the name suggests, randomly selects a server from the pool to handle each incoming request. While simple to implement, the Random algorithm may not ensure an even distribution of the workload, and it lacks the deterministic nature of other algorithms. The lack of predictability makes Random less suitable for scenarios where precise control over workload distribution is a priority.

In scenarios where session persistence is crucial, as in applications that rely on user sessions, the Source IP Hash algorithm can be employed. This algorithm calculates a hash value based on the source IP address of the incoming request, ensuring that requests from the same client are consistently directed to the same server. Source IP Hash helps maintain session state and ensures a seamless user experience, particularly in applications where maintaining state across multiple servers is essential.

The Least Bandwidth algorithm selects the server with the least amount of bandwidth usage to handle an incoming request. This strategy aims to optimize network resources by directing traffic to servers with available bandwidth capacity. While effective in reducing network congestion, the Least Bandwidth algorithm may not consider other factors such as server processing power or memory usage, and its applicability depends on the specific requirements of the system.

The Least Requests algorithm directs incoming requests to the server with the fewest active requests. This approach is similar to the Least Connections algorithm but considers requests in progress rather than established connections. The Least Requests algorithm is effective in preventing server overload and ensuring a more even distribution of requests. However, it may not account for variations in the complexity of processing different types of requests.

Adaptive load balancing algorithms dynamically adjust the distribution of incoming requests based on real-time monitoring of server conditions. These algorithms continuously evaluate factors such as server response times, error rates, and resource utilization to make informed load balancing decisions. Adaptive algorithms, such as Least Connections with Adaptive Feedback, leverage feedback mechanisms to adapt to changing conditions and optimize workload distribution dynamically.

Load balancing strategies extend beyond algorithmic approaches to include considerations of application and system architectures. In Layer 4 load balancing, decisions are made based on information available in the network and transport layer protocols, such as IP addresses and port numbers. Layer 4 load balancers operate at the transport layer of the OSI model and are capable of efficiently distributing traffic based on network-level information. This approach is well-suited for scenarios where decisions can be made solely based on transport layer data without the need for deep application awareness.

On the other hand, Layer 7 load balancing operates at the application layer of the OSI model and considers information from the application payload, such as HTTP headers or URL paths. Layer

7 load balancers have a more granular understanding of application traffic and can make routing decisions based on specific application characteristics. This approach is beneficial for applications where routing decisions need to be based on application-level attributes, enabling more sophisticated load balancing strategies.

Global Server Load Balancing (GSLB) is a strategy that involves distributing traffic across multiple data centers or geographically dispersed server locations. GSLB ensures high availability and optimal performance by directing users to the nearest or least congested server location. This approach is particularly crucial for organizations with a global presence, where minimizing latency and ensuring continuous service availability are paramount. GSLB contributes to disaster recovery and business continuity by redirecting traffic to alternative server locations in the event of data center failures or network issues.

Load balancing can be implemented using hardware appliances, software-based solutions, or cloud-based services. Hardware load balancers are dedicated devices designed to efficiently distribute traffic across servers, often offering specialized features such as SSL termination or application-aware load balancing. Software-based load balancers, deployed as applications on general-purpose servers, provide flexibility and scalability in virtualized or cloud environments. Cloud-based load balancing services offered by major cloud providers, such as Amazon Web Services (AWS) Elastic Load Balancing or Google Cloud Load Balancing, provide automated, scalable load balancing solutions with global reach.

In conclusion, load balancing algorithms and strategies are foundational components in the design and operation of distributed systems, contributing to efficient resource utilization, high availability, and optimal user experiences. The choice of a specific load balancing algorithm depends on factors such as system architecture, application characteristics, and the desired trade-offs between simplicity, predictability, and adaptability. Whether employing traditional Round-Robin methods, adaptive algorithms, or geographically distributed strategies, load balancing remains a critical mechanism for achieving the scalability and reliability required in modern computing environments. As organizations continue to navigate the challenges of dynamic workloads, evolving technologies, and global user bases, the effective implementation of load balancing algorithms becomes paramount in delivering resilient, high-performance, and responsive systems.

Understanding the role of caching in improving system responsiveness.

Understanding the role of caching in improving system responsiveness is essential in grasping the transformative impact this mechanism has on the efficiency and performance of various computing systems. Caching, at its core, involves the temporary storage of frequently accessed or recently used data in a location that facilitates quicker retrieval. This strategic use of a high-speed storage medium, often faster than the primary storage, aims to reduce latency and enhance the responsiveness of applications and systems. In the context of web applications, caching serves as a linchpin for expediting the delivery of content, minimizing load times, and ultimately providing a seamless user experience.

One of the primary applications of caching is in web content delivery, where it plays a pivotal role in addressing the challenges posed by latency and bandwidth constraints. Content Delivery Networks (CDNs) leverage caching extensively to store copies of static or dynamic content closer to end-users in geographically distributed servers. This proximity minimizes the physical distance data must traverse, reducing latency and accelerating the retrieval of web pages, images, videos, and other resources. By strategically placing cached content at various edge locations, CDNs optimize the delivery process, ensuring that users experience faster load times and improved responsiveness, particularly in scenarios with distributed user bases.

In addition to web content caching, application-level caching is a fundamental strategy for improving system responsiveness. Caching mechanisms can be implemented at different layers of the software stack, including the application layer, database layer, and even within the user's device. In-memory caching systems, such as Redis or Memcached, store frequently accessed data in volatile memory, allowing for rapid retrieval without the need to fetch the information from the underlying storage. This approach is particularly beneficial for read-heavy workloads, as it reduces the load on databases and accelerates data access, contributing to improved application responsiveness.

Database caching is a critical aspect of system design, especially in scenarios where database queries contribute significantly to overall application latency. By caching the results of frequently executed queries, subsequent requests for the same data can be served directly from the cache, bypassing the need to recompute the query or access the underlying database. This not only reduces the time required for data retrieval but also alleviates the strain on database servers, enhancing overall system scalability. Caching strategies within databases may involve storing query results, intermediate computation results, or even precomputed aggregates to further optimize performance.

Furthermore, caching is instrumental in addressing the challenges posed by the varying speeds of different storage mediums. Storage hierarchies, encompassing fast but expensive options like RAM and slower but more economical options like disk storage, can be navigated efficiently through caching. Frequently accessed data is cached in high-speed memory, reducing the need to fetch it from slower storage mediums. This tiered approach ensures that the most critical and frequently used data is readily available in the fastest storage layer, mitigating the impact of slower storage on system responsiveness.

The concept of caching extends beyond the server-side to the client-side, where browsers and other user devices employ caching mechanisms to enhance the loading speed of websites and applications. Browser caching involves storing locally copies of static assets such as images, stylesheets, and scripts. When a user revisits a website, the browser can retrieve these assets from the local cache instead of downloading them again from the server. This not only accelerates page load times but also reduces the load on the server and conserves bandwidth. Caching on the client-side is a cornerstone of the modern web experience, fostering faster load times and a more responsive interaction with web applications.

One of the key considerations in caching strategies is cache invalidation, ensuring that cached data remains consistent with the most recent version of the underlying information. Techniques such as time-based expiration, where cached items have a predefined lifespan, or event-driven invalidation, where changes to the underlying data trigger cache updates, are employed to maintain cache accuracy. Invalidating the cache in a timely and efficient manner is crucial to preventing users from accessing outdated or stale information, striking a delicate balance between performance optimization and data consistency.

Cache hierarchies, involving multiple levels of caching with varying speeds and capacities, are a common architectural choice to further optimize responsiveness. The L1, L2, and L3 caches found in modern processors exemplify this concept, where each level is progressively larger and slower but serves as a buffer between the processor and main memory. Similar principles can be applied in distributed systems, where local caches near individual nodes or microservices complement larger, shared caches at higher levels of the infrastructure. This hierarchical caching approach maximizes the benefits of both local and shared caching, catering to the specific needs of different system components and enhancing overall responsiveness.

Another crucial aspect of caching is the distinction between full-page caching and partial or fragment caching. Full-page caching involves storing entire web pages, reducing the need for the server to generate the same page repeatedly for each user. This approach is highly effective for static content or content that changes infrequently. On the other hand, partial or fragment caching focuses on specific components of a page, such as dynamic widgets or frequently changing elements. By selectively caching only the components that contribute to latency, partial caching strikes a balance between optimizing performance and ensuring that dynamic content remains up-to-date.

Caching is not without its challenges, and cache management strategies play a critical role in maintaining optimal system performance. Cache eviction policies, determining which items to remove from the cache when it reaches its capacity, impact the effectiveness of caching. LRU (Least Recently Used), LFU (Least Frequently Used), and variations thereof are commonly employed eviction policies to ensure that the cache remains populated with the most relevant and frequently accessed items. Eviction policies need to align with the usage patterns and access characteristics of the data to avoid premature removal of valuable items or the retention of obsolete information.

Additionally, cache warming strategies are employed to prepopulate caches with frequently accessed or critical data, reducing the initial latency associated with cold caches. Proactive cache warming, performed during system initialization or in anticipation of anticipated traffic patterns, ensures that the cache is primed with the most relevant data, optimizing responsiveness from the outset. This proactive approach helps mitigate the impact of cache misses and contributes to a smoother user experience during periods of high demand.

The importance of caching in improving system responsiveness extends to the realm of microservices architectures, where modular and independent services collaborate to deliver complex applications. Caching at the microservices level allows each service to manage its own cache, minimizing dependencies and promoting autonomy. This approach is particularly relevant in scenarios where microservices have distinct data access patterns or when services operate on subsets of a shared dataset. Microservices caching enhances the overall responsiveness of the application by allowing each service to optimize its data access and reduce the need for redundant computations.

In conclusion, caching stands as a foundational strategy for improving system responsiveness across various computing environments and applications. Whether employed at the web content delivery level through CDNs, within application architectures for in-memory or database caching, or on the client-side for browser-based experiences, caching fundamentally transforms the speed and efficiency of data access. The strategic use of caching not only reduces latency and accelerates load times but also contributes to enhanced scalability, reduced server load, and improved overall user satisfaction. As organizations continue to grapple with the challenges of delivering high-performance applications and services, a nuanced understanding of caching mechanisms becomes indispensable in navigating the delicate balance between data consistency and optimal responsiveness.

Techniques for distributed caching in large-scale systems.

Distributed caching plays a pivotal role in enhancing the performance and scalability of large-scale systems by alleviating the burden on backend databases and reducing latency in data retrieval. One prominent technique employed in distributed caching is sharding, where the cache is partitioned into multiple shards, each responsible for a subset of the data. Sharding enables parallelism, allowing multiple cache nodes to handle distinct portions of the workload concurrently. This approach facilitates horizontal scaling, as additional cache nodes can be added to accommodate growing data volumes and user demands.

Consistent hashing is another fundamental technique used to distribute data across cache nodes in a way that minimizes rehashing when nodes are added or removed. By assigning a unique hash value to each cache node and key, data can be consistently routed to the appropriate node even when the number of nodes changes. This ensures that the distribution of data remains balanced, preventing hotspots and uneven loads on cache nodes.

To further enhance reliability and fault tolerance, distributed caching systems often implement replication. Replication involves creating copies of data across multiple cache nodes, reducing the risk of data loss in the event of a node failure. However, maintaining consistency among replicas introduces challenges, as updates to the cache must be synchronized. Consistency models, such as eventual consistency or strong consistency, are employed based on the specific requirements of the system.

In the context of large-scale systems, caching strategies need to consider the diverse access patterns and data access frequencies. Least Recently Used (LRU) and Least Frequently Used (LFU) are popular cache eviction policies that remove the least recently or least frequently accessed items to make room for new data. Adaptive eviction policies, such as Least Recently Used with Dynamic Aging (LRU-DA), dynamically adjust eviction priorities based on the access patterns over time, optimizing cache utilization in dynamic environments.

The concept of cache invalidation is crucial to maintaining data integrity in distributed caching systems. Invalidation mechanisms ensure that stale or outdated data is removed from the cache to prevent users from accessing inaccurate information. Time-based expiration and event-driven invalidation are two common approaches. Time-based expiration involves setting a time limit for the validity of cached data, while event-driven invalidation relies on external events or changes in the data source to trigger cache updates.

In scenarios where data consistency is paramount, distributed caching systems may integrate with distributed locking mechanisms. Distributed locks prevent multiple nodes from concurrently updating the same piece of data, avoiding race conditions and maintaining consistency. However, the use of distributed locks introduces challenges related to performance and scalability, as contention for locks can lead to bottlenecks.

As the scale of distributed systems grows, efficient communication and coordination between cache nodes become critical. Peer-to-peer communication models, such as the Gossip protocol, enable nodes to exchange information about their state and the state of the cache. This decentralized approach to communication reduces the reliance on a central coordinator, enhancing system resilience and scalability.

Load balancing is a fundamental aspect of large-scale distributed caching to ensure that each cache node receives a balanced share of the workload. DNS-based load balancing and dynamic load balancing algorithms, such as Weighted Round Robin or Least Connections, distribute incoming requests across cache nodes based on their capacity and current load. This optimizes resource utilization and prevents individual nodes from becoming performance bottlenecks.

In the context of cloud computing, serverless architectures, and microservices, distributed caching can be seamlessly integrated into the overall system design. Container orchestration platforms, like Kubernetes, provide mechanisms for deploying and managing cache containers, enabling efficient scaling and resource utilization. Additionally, caching services offered by cloud providers, such as AWS Elasticache or Azure Cache for Redis, simplify the deployment and management of distributed caches in cloud environments.

Security considerations are paramount in large-scale systems, and distributed caching introduces its own set of challenges. Strategies such as data encryption, secure communication protocols, and access controls are essential to protect sensitive information stored in the cache. Additionally, regular audits and monitoring help identify potential security vulnerabilities and ensure compliance with industry regulations.

In conclusion, distributed caching in large-scale systems involves a combination of techniques to optimize performance, scalability, reliability, and security. Sharding, consistent hashing, replication, cache eviction policies, cache invalidation mechanisms, distributed locking, peer-to-peer communication, load balancing, and integration with modern architectural paradigms all contribute to creating robust and efficient distributed caching systems. As technology continues to evolve, the landscape of distributed caching will undoubtedly witness further innovations to address the evolving needs of large-scale applications.

Exploring the relationship between microservices architecture and scalability.

The adoption of microservices architecture has significantly reshaped the landscape of modern software development, with a profound impact on the scalability of systems. Microservices, characterized by the decomposition of a monolithic application into smaller, independent services, offer a paradigm that aligns with the principles of scalability, flexibility, and resilience. The relationship between microservices architecture and scalability is multifaceted, encompassing various aspects of design, deployment, and operational considerations.

One fundamental characteristic of microservices architecture that contributes to scalability is the autonomy of individual services. Each microservice operates independently, with its own database and business logic, enabling teams to develop, deploy, and scale services autonomously. This granularity facilitates horizontal scaling, allowing organizations to add more instances of specific microservices to distribute the increasing load. This contrasts with monolithic architectures, where scaling often involves replicating the entire application, leading to inefficiencies in resource utilization.

The modular nature of microservices fosters a divide-and-conquer approach to scalability challenges. Teams can focus on optimizing the performance and scalability of individual services without being constrained by the intricacies of the entire application. This granularity not only enhances the development and deployment lifecycle but also provides the flexibility to scale specific services independently based on their unique demands, rather than scaling the entire monolith uniformly.

Scalability in microservices is also closely tied to the concept of elasticity, where the infrastructure can dynamically adapt to varying workloads. Containerization technologies, such as Docker, and container orchestration platforms like Kubernetes, play a pivotal role in enabling the elastic scaling of microservices. Containers encapsulate microservices and their dependencies, facilitating consistent deployment across diverse environments. Kubernetes, with its auto-scaling capabilities, empowers organizations to automatically adjust the number of running instances based on factors like CPU utilization or incoming request rates, ensuring optimal resource allocation.

The distributed nature of microservices introduces challenges and opportunities for scalability. While distributed systems inherently possess the potential for increased scalability, they also require robust mechanisms for inter-service communication and coordination. Asynchronous communication patterns, event-driven architectures, and message queues become essential components in managing the interactions between microservices at scale. These patterns not only enhance the scalability of individual services but also contribute to the overall resilience of the system by decoupling components and mitigating the impact of failures.

Inherent in the scalability benefits of microservices is the ability to handle diverse workloads effectively. Microservices can be specialized to cater to specific functions or user scenarios, allowing organizations to optimize the performance of each service based on its unique requirements. This specialization enables the development of lightweight, focused services that can be individually scaled to meet the demands of specific functionalities, resulting in a more efficient allocation of resources.

However, the advantages of microservices scalability come with their own set of challenges. Managing the complexities of a distributed system, ensuring data consistency across microservices, and orchestrating communication between services demand careful consideration. The implementation of effective monitoring, logging, and tracing mechanisms becomes crucial for gaining insights into the performance of individual microservices and diagnosing issues that may arise in a distributed environment.

The deployment of microservices in a scalable manner also necessitates a robust DevOps culture. Continuous integration, continuous delivery (CI/CD), and automated testing become indispensable in ensuring that changes to microservices can be seamlessly deployed and rolled back if necessary. Automation not only accelerates the development lifecycle but also enhances the reliability of deployments, a critical aspect when dealing with large-scale systems where downtime can have significant repercussions.

Security considerations are another facet of the relationship between microservices architecture and scalability. As the attack surface expands with the proliferation of microservices, implementing robust security measures becomes imperative. Techniques such as service mesh for secure communication, API gateways for access control, and the application of security best practices at both the microservice and infrastructure levels contribute to a scalable and secure architecture.

The choice of data storage mechanisms also influences the scalability of microservices. While each microservice typically manages its own database, organizations must carefully consider the trade-offs between consistency and partition tolerance in distributed databases. NoSQL databases, with their flexibility and horizontal scalability, often align well with the distributed and scalable nature of microservices.

In conclusion, the relationship between microservices architecture and scalability is characterized by a symbiotic interplay of design principles, technologies, and operational practices. The autonomy of microservices, coupled with containerization, orchestration, and elasticity, empowers organizations to scale their applications efficiently. However, realizing the full potential of microservices scalability requires a holistic approach, encompassing considerations for inter-service communication, deployment automation, monitoring, security, and data management. As organizations continue to embrace microservices, the ongoing evolution of practices and technologies will shape the landscape of scalable and resilient distributed systems.

Design principles for creating scalable microservices.

Designing scalable microservices involves a nuanced understanding of architectural principles, deployment strategies, and operational considerations. One fundamental design principle is service autonomy, which dictates that each microservice should operate independently, with its own database and business logic. This autonomy fosters a modular architecture, enabling development teams to work on individual services without being encumbered by the complexities of the entire application. By minimizing interdependencies, service autonomy facilitates horizontal scaling, allowing organizations to add more instances of specific microservices to handle increased workloads, a crucial aspect of achieving scalability.

A key aspect of scalable microservices design is the careful consideration of service boundaries. Defining clear and cohesive boundaries ensures that each microservice is focused on a specific business capability, making it easier to reason about, develop, and scale. The practice of domain-driven design (DDD) is instrumental in this regard, guiding the identification of bounded contexts and delineating the responsibilities of each microservice. Well-defined boundaries also contribute to the resilience of the overall system, as failures within one microservice are less likely to propagate to others, enhancing fault isolation and system stability.

Effective communication between microservices is paramount for scalability, and the choice of communication patterns significantly influences system performance. Asynchronous communication, facilitated by message queues or event-driven architectures, decouples services and mitigates the impact of latency. This approach not only allows microservices to operate independently but also contributes to fault tolerance, as services can continue processing events even if others experience temporary failures. However, selecting the appropriate communication pattern should be guided by the specific requirements of the application, as synchronous communication may be more suitable for certain use cases.

Scalability also hinges on the ability to efficiently manage data across microservices. Each microservice typically maintains its own database, and the choice of data storage mechanisms plays a crucial role in achieving both performance and scalability. NoSQL databases, with their flexibility and horizontal scaling capabilities, are often preferred in microservices architectures. However, the trade-offs between consistency, availability, and partition tolerance (CAP theorem) must be carefully considered, and the use of polyglot persistence allows for the selection of the most suitable database for each microservice based on its specific requirements.

Containerization technologies, such as Docker, have become integral to scalable microservices architecture. Containers encapsulate microservices and their dependencies, providing consistency across diverse environments. Container orchestration platforms, exemplified by Kubernetes, enable organizations to deploy, manage, and scale containers efficiently. The portability and isolation offered by containers simplify the scaling process, allowing organizations to seamlessly replicate and distribute microservices across clusters, whether on-premises or in the cloud.

Elasticity is a defining characteristic of scalable microservices. Leveraging auto-scaling capabilities, organizations can dynamically adjust the number of running instances based on factors like CPU utilization or incoming request rates. This ensures optimal resource allocation, preventing over-provisioning and mitigating the risk of under-provisioning during peak demand. Elastic scaling aligns with the principles of cost efficiency, allowing organizations to scale up or down based on actual usage, thereby optimizing infrastructure costs.

The implementation of effective monitoring and logging mechanisms is indispensable for maintaining scalability. Comprehensive visibility into the performance of individual microservices and the overall system is crucial for identifying bottlenecks, diagnosing issues, and optimizing resource utilization. Monitoring tools, such as Prometheus or Grafana, provide real-time insights, while centralized logging enables the aggregation of logs for analysis. Additionally, distributed tracing can help trace requests across microservices, providing a holistic view of system interactions and aiding in the identification of performance bottlenecks.

In the context of deployment, the adoption of a DevOps culture is instrumental for achieving scalable microservices architecture.

Continuous integration (CI) and continuous delivery (CD) practices streamline the deployment pipeline, enabling rapid and reliable releases. Automated testing, including unit tests, integration tests, and end-to-end tests, ensures the robustness of microservices before they are deployed. Furthermore, the use of infrastructure as code (IaC) allows for the consistent and repeatable provisioning of infrastructure, promoting agility in scaling deployments across different environments.

Security considerations are paramount in scalable microservices architecture. The distributed nature of microservices increases the attack surface, necessitating robust security measures. Implementing secure communication channels, securing APIs, and enforcing access controls are critical. Service mesh architectures, such as Istio or Linkerd, provide mechanisms for securing inter-service communication and managing policies consistently across microservices. Additionally, organizations must adopt a proactive approach to security, conducting regular audits, vulnerability assessments, and adhering to best practices for secure coding and configuration.

Polyglot microservices, where different services use different programming languages or frameworks, are a pragmatic approach to building scalable architectures. This allows teams to choose the most suitable technology stack for each microservice based on its requirements. While this introduces challenges related to skill diversity and operational overhead, the flexibility gained in selecting specialized tools for specific tasks often outweighs these challenges, contributing to enhanced scalability and adaptability in the face of evolving technology landscapes.

In conclusion, the design principles for creating scalable microservices revolve around autonomy, clear service boundaries, effective communication, data management, containerization, elasticity, monitoring, DevOps practices, security, and the adoption of polyglot architectures. These principles collectively form the foundation for building resilient, agile, and scalable microservices architectures that can meet the dynamic demands of modern applications. As technology continues to evolve, the refinement and application of these design principles will remain crucial for organizations seeking to leverage the benefits of microservices in achieving scalable and efficient systems.

Chapter 7: Security Measures in Distributed Operating Systems

Identifying unique security challenges in distributed computing.

Distributed computing, while offering numerous benefits in terms of scalability, performance, and fault tolerance, introduces a unique set of security challenges that necessitate careful consideration and robust mitigation strategies. One prominent challenge lies in the realm of network security, where the decentralized nature of distributed systems amplifies the potential attack surface. The increased number of communication channels between nodes and the exposure of data during transmission create opportunities for eavesdropping, man-in-the-middle attacks, and unauthorized access. Encrypting communication channels using secure protocols, such as TLS (Transport Layer Security), becomes imperative to safeguard sensitive data as it traverses the network. However, the complexity of managing keys, ensuring proper certificate validation, and addressing the varied communication patterns in distributed systems poses additional challenges that demand meticulous attention.

The authentication and authorization of entities within a distributed system present another formidable security challenge. In a decentralized environment, where nodes or services may be geographically dispersed and operated by different entities, establishing and maintaining trust becomes complex. Traditional centralized authentication mechanisms may not be suitable, leading to the adoption of decentralized identity management and federated authentication models. Implementing robust authentication protocols, like OAuth or OpenID Connect, and integrating identity providers for secure user authentication across distributed services are critical steps in mitigating the risks associated with unauthorized access.

Data integrity is a fundamental concern in distributed computing, where data may be distributed across multiple nodes or replicated for fault tolerance. Ensuring the consistency and integrity of data across distributed databases or storage systems poses a significant challenge, particularly in scenarios where updates occur concurrently. Distributed systems often grapple with the trade-offs between achieving strong consistency and allowing for high availability and partition tolerance, as dictated by the CAP theorem. Implementing techniques such as versioning, optimistic concurrency control, and distributed consensus algorithms (e.g., Paxos or Raft) becomes essential to maintain data integrity while navigating the complexities of distributed environments.

The shared nature of resources in distributed systems introduces the risk of resource-based attacks, where malicious actors exploit vulnerabilities in the allocation and utilization of resources. Denial-of-service (DoS) and distributed denial-of-service (DDoS) attacks pose significant threats, aiming to overwhelm system components, exhaust resources, and disrupt services. Mitigating these attacks involves implementing measures such as rate limiting, traffic filtering, and distributed load balancing. Additionally, the use of content delivery networks (CDNs) and the deployment of anti-DDoS solutions contribute to fortifying distributed systems against resource-based attacks.

Distributed systems are susceptible to a diverse array of security vulnerabilities arising from software bugs, misconfigurations, or inadequate patch management. The decentralized nature of development and deployment in distributed environments often leads to heterogeneous technology stacks and diverse programming languages, exacerbating the challenge of vulnerability management. Regular security audits, vulnerability assessments, and automated security testing are crucial for identifying and remedying vulnerabilities across the distributed landscape. Emphasizing secure coding practices, code reviews, and the timely application of patches contribute to fortifying distributed systems against potential exploits.

In the context of distributed computing, the orchestration and management of containers and microservices introduce their own set of security challenges. Container orchestration platforms, such as Kubernetes, provide powerful capabilities for deploying and scaling microservices, but their complexity can lead to misconfigurations and security oversights. Securing containerized environments involves addressing issues like container escape vulnerabilities, securing container registries, and implementing network segmentation. Additionally, the adoption of service mesh architectures, while enhancing communication security between microservices, requires diligent configuration and monitoring to prevent potential misuses and vulnerabilities.

Inter-service communication, a foundational aspect of distributed systems, introduces security challenges related to data confidentiality, integrity, and authenticity. As services communicate over networks, the potential for data exposure and interception increases. Implementing end-to-end encryption, secure APIs, and enforcing strict access controls are crucial measures to protect sensitive information. The use of service meshes, such as Istio or Linkerd, can provide additional security features like mutual TLS (mTLS) for securing communication between services within a distributed environment.

The dynamic nature of distributed systems, characterized by frequent updates, scaling events, and changes in network topologies, poses challenges in maintaining continuous security monitoring and auditing. Traditional security tools and methodologies designed for static, monolithic architectures may prove insufficient in dynamically evolving distributed environments. Implementing real-time monitoring solutions, log analysis, and anomaly detection mechanisms are vital for promptly identifying and responding to security incidents in distributed systems. The integration of security information and event management (SIEM) systems can further enhance the ability to detect and respond to security events across the distributed landscape.

Compliance and regulatory challenges add another layer of complexity to security in distributed computing. As data traverses distributed environments, organizations must navigate diverse regulatory frameworks governing data privacy, residency, and protection. Achieving and maintaining compliance with standards such as GDPR, HIPAA, or industry-specific regulations requires a comprehensive understanding of the data flow, storage, and processing within distributed systems. Implementing data anonymization, encryption, and auditing mechanisms assists organizations in meeting regulatory requirements and ensuring the lawful handling of sensitive information across distributed architectures.

The human factor introduces a nuanced dimension to security challenges in distributed systems. Decentralized development teams, varied levels of expertise, and the potential for insider threats underscore the importance of security awareness, training, and access controls. Implementing least privilege principles, role-based access controls, and conducting regular security drills contribute to mitigating the risks associated with human factors in distributed computing environments.

In conclusion, the security challenges in distributed computing span a wide spectrum, encompassing network security, authentication, data integrity, resource-based attacks, software vulnerabilities, container security, inter-service communication, dynamic monitoring, compliance, and the human factor. Addressing these challenges requires a holistic and adaptive approach, incorporating a combination of encryption, authentication protocols, distributed consensus algorithms, security testing, container orchestration security, monitoring solutions, and compliance frameworks. As organizations continue to embrace distributed computing for its myriad benefits, the ongoing evolution of security practices will be crucial in fortifying systems against evolving threats and vulnerabilities.

Overview of potential vulnerabilities and attack vectors.

The ever-expanding digital landscape has given rise to a multitude of potential vulnerabilities and attack vectors, presenting a complex and dynamic challenge for cybersecurity professionals. One prevalent avenue for exploitation lies in software vulnerabilities, where bugs, coding errors, or design flaws can be leveraged by malicious actors to compromise the integrity, confidentiality, or availability of systems. This category encompasses a diverse range of issues, from buffer overflows and injection attacks to insecure dependencies, making regular security audits, code reviews, and prompt patching essential to mitigate these vulnerabilities.

Phishing attacks represent a pervasive and insidious threat, exploiting human psychology to deceive individuals into divulging sensitive information such as passwords or financial details. Phishing techniques continue to evolve, encompassing email, social engineering, and even voice-based attacks. As organizations fortify their technical defenses, user education and awareness become critical in detecting and thwarting phishing attempts.

Credential-related vulnerabilities are a persistent concern, encompassing weak passwords, password reuse, and insufficient authentication mechanisms. Credential stuffing attacks leverage compromised credentials from one service to gain unauthorized access to others, highlighting the importance of robust password policies, multi-factor authentication (MFA), and continuous monitoring for anomalous login activities.

Web application vulnerabilities remain a lucrative target for attackers seeking to exploit flaws in web-based systems. Cross-Site Scripting (XSS) and SQL injection attacks are prevalent examples, allowing attackers to inject malicious code into web pages or manipulate databases. Web application firewalls, secure coding practices, and regular security assessments are imperative for mitigating these vulnerabilities.

As organizations increasingly adopt cloud computing, a new set of potential vulnerabilities emerges. Misconfigured cloud settings, insecure application programming interfaces (APIs), and inadequate data protection measures can expose sensitive information to unauthorized access. Cloud security requires a comprehensive approach, including secure configuration management, API security measures, and encryption to protect data in transit and at rest.

Internet of Things (IoT) devices, ranging from smart home gadgets to industrial sensors, introduce a myriad of security challenges due to their often insufficiently secured interfaces and communication protocols. Weak authentication, unencrypted communication, and the lack of regular updates make IoT devices susceptible to exploitation. Organizations must implement rigorous security standards for IoT development, including secure firmware updates, robust authentication mechanisms, and network segmentation to mitigate the potential impact of compromised devices.

Network-based attacks, such as Man-in-the-Middle (MitM) attacks, exploit vulnerabilities in network communication to intercept and manipulate data. Wi-Fi eavesdropping, session hijacking, and DNS spoofing are common techniques employed in MitM attacks. The use of secure protocols, encryption, and monitoring for anomalous network activities are crucial for detecting and preventing such attacks.

Ransomware continues to pose a significant threat to organizations worldwide. Malicious software encrypts critical data, rendering it inaccessible until a ransom is paid. Phishing emails, exploiting software vulnerabilities, or compromising remote desktop protocols are common vectors for ransomware. Robust backup strategies, network segmentation, and employee training on identifying phishing attempts are essential components of a comprehensive defense against ransomware.

Supply chain attacks leverage vulnerabilities in the interconnected ecosystem of software development, where attackers compromise the software supply chain to inject malicious code into legitimate applications. The SolarWinds incident, where a software update was manipulated to include a backdoor, exemplifies the far-reaching impact of supply chain attacks. Organizations must adopt stringent security measures, including code signing, integrity checks, and third-party risk assessments, to safeguard against supply chain vulnerabilities.

Advanced Persistent Threats (APTs) represent a sophisticated and persistent form of cyberattack, often orchestrated by well-funded and organized threat actors. APTs involve covert and prolonged intrusion into a target's network, aiming to exfiltrate sensitive data or disrupt operations. Techniques employed by APTs include zero-day exploits, spear-phishing, and lateral movement within compromised networks. Defending against APTs requires a holistic security approach, including threat intelligence, network segmentation, and continuous monitoring for anomalous activities.

Mobile devices, ubiquitous in modern society, present their own set of vulnerabilities and attack vectors. Mobile malware, insecure application permissions, and unsecured Wi-Fi connections can expose sensitive data on smartphones and tablets. Mobile device management (MDM) solutions, secure app development practices, and user education on mobile security are crucial components of mitigating vulnerabilities in the mobile ecosystem.

Social engineering attacks exploit human psychology and interpersonal relationships to manipulate individuals into divulging sensitive information or performing actions that compromise security. Techniques include pretexting, baiting, and quid pro quo, with attackers often gathering information from social media or other public sources to enhance their deceptive tactics. Regular cybersecurity training, user awareness programs, and robust incident response plans help organizations fortify their defenses against social engineering attacks.

Cryptocurrency-related vulnerabilities and attacks have become increasingly prevalent as digital currencies gain popularity. Cryptojacking, where attackers use victims' computing resources to mine cryptocurrencies, and thefts from poorly secured wallets exemplify the risks in the cryptocurrency landscape. Secure wallet management, awareness of phishing attempts targeting cryptocurrency users, and the use of reputable exchanges are essential for mitigating these risks.

Insider threats, whether intentional or unintentional, pose a significant risk to organizations. Employees with privileged access may inadvertently compromise security through negligent actions or become malicious insiders seeking to exploit vulnerabilities. Implementing least privilege principles, monitoring user activities, and conducting regular security awareness training contribute to mitigating the risks associated with insider threats.

In conclusion, the landscape of potential vulnerabilities and attack vectors is vast and continually evolving, requiring organizations to adopt a proactive and adaptive approach to cybersecurity. From software vulnerabilities and phishing attacks to supply chain compromises and insider threats, the complex interplay of technological, human, and systemic factors demands a holistic defense strategy. Continuous monitoring, threat intelligence, employee education, and the implementation of robust security measures across diverse

attack surfaces are indispensable components of a resilient cybersecurity posture in the face of an ever-changing threat landscape.

Strategies for authenticating users and entities in distributed systems.

Authentication in distributed systems involves the verification of the identity of users and entities attempting to access resources or services. The challenges posed by the decentralized nature of distributed systems necessitate the adoption of robust strategies to ensure secure and reliable authentication. One fundamental approach is the use of cryptographic techniques, such as digital signatures and certificates, to verify the authenticity of entities. Digital signatures, generated using private keys, enable the verification of the sender's identity by decrypting the signature with the corresponding public key. Certificates, issued by trusted certificate authorities, provide a means to validate the authenticity of public keys, forming the basis for secure communication in distributed environments.

The integration of decentralized identity management systems plays a pivotal role in authenticating users across distributed systems. Technologies like decentralized identifiers (DIDs) and verifiable credentials provide a framework for users to establish and control their identities without reliance on a central authority. DIDs serve as unique identifiers anchored on distributed ledgers, allowing users to assert ownership of their identity across different services. Verifiable credentials enable users to present cryptographic proofs of their attributes without revealing unnecessary details, enhancing privacy and minimizing the reliance on centralized identity providers.

In the realm of distributed systems, federated authentication emerges as a strategic approach to streamline the authentication process across multiple services or domains. Federated identity providers, such as OpenID Connect or OAuth, facilitate the seamless sharing of user authentication and authorization information between participating entities. This enables users to access various services with a single set of credentials, enhancing user experience while reducing the need for users to manage multiple accounts and passwords. Federated authentication promotes interoperability and can be instrumental in scenarios where users interact with services hosted by different organizations.

Multi-factor authentication (MFA) stands out as a cornerstone strategy for bolstering authentication security in distributed systems. MFA requires users to provide multiple forms of identification, typically a combination of something they know (e.g., a password), something they have (e.g., a mobile device), or something they are (e.g., biometric data). The use of multiple factors adds an additional layer of security, reducing the likelihood of unauthorized access even if one authentication factor is compromised. MFA is particularly effective in distributed environments, where the risk of credential-based attacks is heightened.

The adoption of OAuth (Open Authorization) as an authentication and authorization framework has become prevalent in distributed systems, particularly in scenarios involving third-party access to resources. OAuth enables users to grant limited access to their resources without disclosing their credentials directly. It is commonly employed in conjunction with OpenID Connect to provide a comprehensive identity layer, allowing for secure and standardized authentication and authorization in distributed environments. OAuth's token-based approach facilitates secure delegation of authorization across services.

For web-based applications and services within distributed systems, the use of Security Assertion Markup Language (SAML) has been a widely adopted standard for exchanging authentication and authorization data. SAML enables single sign-on (SSO) capabilities, allowing users to access multiple services with a single set of credentials. The assertion-based nature of SAML tokens provides a mechanism for communicating authentication and attribute information securely between identity providers and service providers, fostering interoperability in distributed ecosystems.

Blockchain technology introduces innovative strategies for authenticating entities in distributed systems, especially in scenarios where decentralized and tamper-resistant identity verification is essential. Decentralized identity platforms, built on blockchain, enable users to control and verify their identities without reliance on central authorities. Blockchain-based decentralized identity solutions, such as Self-Sovereign Identity (SSI), leverage distributed ledgers to provide a secure and transparent foundation for user authentication, enhancing privacy and reducing the risks associated with centralized identity management.

Biometric authentication represents a technologically advanced strategy for user and entity authentication in distributed systems. Leveraging unique biological features such as fingerprints, facial recognition, or iris scans, biometric authentication provides a high level of assurance in verifying the identity of users. Biometric data, when properly protected and encrypted, can serve as a robust authentication factor. However, the implementation of biometric authentication requires careful consideration of privacy concerns, regulatory compliance, and the potential risks associated with biometric data breaches.

The concept of risk-based authentication has gained prominence in distributed systems as a dynamic approach that adapts authentication requirements based on perceived risk factors. Risk-based authentication analyzes contextual information such as device characteristics, user behavior, and network attributes to assess the likelihood of a login attempt being fraudulent. When a login attempt is deemed higher risk, additional authentication measures may be triggered. This approach allows organizations to balance security and user convenience, adapting authentication requirements to the specific context of each interaction in distributed environments.

In scenarios where a centralized identity provider may not be suitable, decentralized identity solutions based on blockchain and distributed ledger technology offer an alternative paradigm. These solutions enable users to control and manage their identities without relying on a central authority. By anchoring identity information on a tamper-resistant and transparent ledger, decentralized identity solutions enhance privacy, reduce the risk of identity theft, and empower users to selectively disclose information as needed.

Zero Trust Security, a holistic security model, emphasizes the principle of "never trust, always verify" across all aspects of a distributed system. This model challenges the traditional perimeter-based security approach by assuming that threats may exist both outside and inside the network. Zero Trust Authentication requires continuous verification of the identity and security posture of users, devices, and entities, regardless of their location or network access. Implementing Zero Trust principles involves granular access controls, continuous monitoring, and dynamic risk assessments, providing a robust framework for securing distributed systems against evolving threats.

In conclusion, the strategies for authenticating users and entities in distributed systems encompass a diverse array of technologies and methodologies. From cryptographic techniques and federated authentication to multi-factor authentication, blockchain-based identity, and risk-based authentication, organizations must carefully select and implement a combination of these strategies based on the specific requirements and characteristics of their distributed environments. As the landscape of distributed systems continues to evolve, the ongoing refinement and integration of authentication strategies will play a crucial role in ensuring the security, privacy, and resilience of these complex and interconnected ecosystems.

Implementing authorization mechanisms for secure access control.

Implementing robust authorization mechanisms is a cornerstone in ensuring secure access control within distributed systems. Authorization is the process of determining what actions or resources a user or entity is allowed to access, and it plays a crucial role in protecting sensitive information and maintaining the integrity of systems. Role-based access control (RBAC) emerges as a fundamental approach in authorization, where access permissions are assigned based on predefined roles that users or entities hold within the system. Roles encapsulate sets of permissions, allowing for a granular and organized way to manage access rights. Organizations often leverage RBAC to simplify access control administration and ensure that users have appropriate privileges based on their responsibilities and functions within the system.

Attribute-based access control (ABAC) extends the capabilities of access control mechanisms by considering dynamic and contextual attributes in the decision-making process. ABAC takes into account various attributes such as user characteristics, environmental conditions, and resource properties when evaluating access requests. This flexibility enables organizations to implement fine-grained access policies that adapt to changing conditions. For example, an ABAC system might grant access to certain data only if the user is accessing it from a specific location during a predefined time window. Implementing ABAC requires a comprehensive understanding of the attributes relevant to access decisions and the establishment of policies that consider these attributes in a dynamic context.

OAuth (Open Authorization) stands out as a widely adopted authorization framework, especially in scenarios involving third-party access to resources. OAuth enables delegated access by allowing users to grant limited permissions to external applications or services without revealing their credentials. This is achieved through the issuance of access tokens that represent specific permissions and a defined scope. OAuth is commonly used in conjunction with OpenID Connect to provide a comprehensive identity and authorization layer. It facilitates secure and standardized authorization in distributed systems, allowing for secure delegation of access rights across services.

JSON Web Tokens (JWT) are a prevalent technology for implementing secure authorization mechanisms, particularly in the context of stateless and distributed applications. JWTs are compact, self-contained tokens that can encode information about the user, permissions, and other relevant claims. These tokens are digitally signed, ensuring their integrity and authenticity. When a user requests access to a resource, the system verifies the JWT to determine the user's identity and permissions. The use of JWTs simplifies the handling of authorization information, reduces the need for constant interaction with an authentication server, and supports the creation of stateless and scalable distributed systems.

In scenarios where authorization decisions need to be made based on complex policies or conditions, the eXtensible Access Control Markup Language (XACML) offers a standardized and expressive framework. XACML provides a policy language for defining access control policies and a request/response protocol for making authorization decisions. It allows organizations to articulate sophisticated policies that consider various attributes and conditions, enabling fine-grained access control. XACML can be integrated into distributed systems to centralize and enforce access policies consistently across different services, providing a unified approach to authorization.

Attribute-Based Encryption (ABE) is an encryption paradigm that aligns with the principles of access control. In ABE, access policies are expressed as logical predicates over attributes, and encryption keys are associated with specific attributes. Users are then able to decrypt data if their set of attributes satisfies the access policy embedded in the ciphertext. ABE is particularly useful in scenarios where access control requirements are dynamic and may depend on a combination of attributes. By integrating ABE into distributed systems, organizations can enforce access control policies at the data level, ensuring that only authorized users with the requisite attributes can decrypt and access specific information.

Implementing Time-of-Check to Time-of-Use (TOCTOU) protection is crucial for securing access control in distributed systems. TOCTOU attacks involve a time gap between the check of a user's permissions and the actual use of those permissions. During this gap, an attacker may manipulate conditions or permissions, leading to unauthorized access. Mitigating TOCTOU risks requires implementing mechanisms that minimize the time window between the authorization check and the actual use of permissions. This can involve techniques such as short-lived access tokens, frequent reevaluation of access policies, and real-time monitoring to detect and respond to suspicious activities.

Context-based access control leverages contextual information to make authorization decisions dynamically. Contextual factors, such as the user's location, device characteristics, or network conditions, are considered when determining whether to grant or deny access. This approach enhances security by tailoring access decisions to the specific context in which the user or entity operates. For example, access from an unusual location or an unrecognized device may trigger additional authentication requirements. Implementing context-based access control requires a comprehensive understanding of the relevant contextual factors and the integration of real-time monitoring and analysis into the authorization process.

Authorization in distributed systems is intricately tied to the concept of Zero Trust Security, a paradigm that challenges traditional notions of trust within networks. Zero Trust Security assumes that threats may exist both outside and inside the network, and it mandates continuous verification of the identity and security posture of users, devices, and entities, regardless of their location or network access. Implementing Zero Trust principles involves granular access controls, continuous monitoring, and dynamic risk assessments, providing a robust framework for securing distributed systems against evolving threats. By adopting a Zero Trust approach, organizations can minimize the risk of unauthorized access and data breaches in distributed environments.

Implementing dynamic authorization mechanisms is crucial for scenarios where access control requirements change rapidly based on evolving business needs or security considerations. Dynamic authorization involves the ability to update access policies in real-time without requiring a complete system overhaul. This flexibility is particularly valuable in distributed systems where services and users may have dynamic attributes and access requirements. Role-based and attribute-based approaches can be extended with dynamic policy enforcement, enabling organizations to adapt quickly to changing access control demands and enhance the agility of their distributed systems.

In the context of cloud computing, Role-Based Access Control (RBAC) plays a crucial role in managing access to resources within distributed cloud environments. Cloud services often rely on RBAC to define roles and associated permissions that govern user access to virtual machines, storage, databases, and other cloud-based resources. Organizations can implement RBAC in cloud environments to ensure that users have appropriate access levels based on their roles and responsibilities. Integrating RBAC with cloud identity management solutions enhances the scalability and manageability of access control in distributed cloud systems.

In conclusion, the implementation of authorization mechanisms for secure access control in distributed systems involves a multifaceted approach. Role-based access control, attribute-based access control, OAuth, JSON Web Tokens, XACML, Attribute-Based Encryption, Time-of-Check to Time-of-Use protection, context-based access control, Zero Trust Security, and dynamic authorization mechanisms collectively contribute to a robust and adaptive access control framework. Organizations must carefully consider their specific requirements, the nature of their distributed systems, and the evolving threat landscape to tailor and implement effective authorization strategies that balance security, flexibility, and user experience within their distributed environments.

The role of encryption in securing data during transmission. Encryption plays a pivotal role in safeguarding data during transmission, forming a critical component of modern cybersecurity strategies. At its core, encryption is the process of converting plaintext data into ciphertext using mathematical algorithms and cryptographic keys. The primary objective is to render the information unreadable to unauthorized parties, ensuring confidentiality and privacy as data traverses networks, both public and private. Securing data in transit is of paramount importance, especially in an era where the exchange of information occurs ubiquitously across diverse communication channels.

The Secure Sockets Layer (SSL) and its successor, the Transport Layer Security (TLS) protocol, exemplify the foundational role of encryption in securing data during transmission over the Internet. TLS, the de facto standard for secure communication, employs a combination of symmetric and asymmetric encryption to establish a secure and encrypted channel between two communicating parties. As data moves between a client and a server, TLS ensures that eavesdroppers or attackers cannot decipher the transmitted information, providing a secure foundation for activities such as online banking, e-commerce transactions, and sensitive data exchanges.

Public key cryptography, a key element in encryption, relies on the use of asymmetric key pairs: a public key for encryption and a private key for decryption. When a user accesses a secure website, the server presents its public key to the client's browser. The client then uses this key to encrypt data, such as login credentials or financial information, before sending it back to the server. Only the server, possessing the corresponding private key, can decrypt and access the sensitive information. This asymmetric encryption process ensures the confidentiality of data during transmission, safeguarding it from interception by malicious entities.

End-to-end encryption represents an advanced encryption paradigm that extends the protection of data confidentiality to the entire communication path. In end-to-end encryption, data is encrypted on the sender's device and can only be decrypted by the intended recipient. Even service providers facilitating the communication cannot decipher the content. Messaging applications like Signal and WhatsApp employ end-to-end encryption, ensuring that only the sender and the recipient possess the cryptographic keys necessary to access the exchanged messages. This approach fortifies the privacy of user communications, minimizing the risk of unauthorized access at any point along the communication route.

Virtual Private Networks (VPNs) leverage encryption to establish secure and private communication channels over public networks. By encrypting data as it traverses the internet, VPNs create a secure tunnel that shields the transmitted information from potential eavesdropping or interception. This is particularly valuable for remote workers or individuals accessing sensitive corporate resources over untrusted networks. The use of protocols like IPsec or SSL/TLS within VPNs exemplifies how encryption is instrumental in ensuring the confidentiality and integrity of data during its journey across potentially insecure communication paths.

In the context of wireless communication, Wi-Fi networks rely on encryption protocols to secure data transmission. WPA3 (Wi-Fi Protected Access 3), the latest standard in Wi-Fi security, introduces advanced encryption mechanisms to protect data exchanged between devices and wireless access points. WPA3 employs the Simultaneous Authentication of Equals (SAE) protocol for key exchange, enhancing the security of Wi-Fi networks and mitigating vulnerabilities associated with earlier encryption standards. By encrypting wireless communication, WPA3 ensures that unauthorized parties cannot decipher the data packets transmitted over Wi-Fi, safeguarding user privacy and preventing unauthorized access to network resources.

The Hypertext Transfer Protocol Secure (HTTPS) exemplifies the widespread adoption of encryption to secure data during web communication. In contrast to the unencrypted HTTP protocol, HTTPS incorporates SSL/TLS encryption to protect the confidentiality and integrity of data exchanged between a user's browser and a web server. Websites that handle sensitive information, such as login credentials or financial transactions, prioritize the use of HTTPS to prevent eavesdropping, man-in-the-middle attacks, and unauthorized access to user data. The encryption of web traffic through HTTPS has become a standard practice, contributing to a more secure online environment.

In the domain of email communication, the implementation of encryption is crucial to protect the confidentiality of messages and attachments. Pretty Good Privacy (PGP) and its open-source counterpart, GNU Privacy Guard (GPG), offer a robust framework for email encryption. PGP/GPG use a combination of asymmetric and symmetric encryption to secure email content and attachments. By encrypting emails at the sender's end and decrypting them at the recipient's end, PGP/GPG ensures that even if intercepted during transmission, the content remains indecipherable to unauthorized entities, enhancing the privacy of email communication.

File transfer protocols, such as the Secure File Transfer Protocol (SFTP) and Secure Copy Protocol (SCP), incorporate encryption to protect files during transit. These protocols use cryptographic mechanisms to encrypt data as it is transferred between a client and a server. SFTP, for instance, leverages the SSH (Secure Shell) protocol for secure file transfers, encrypting both the data and the commands exchanged between the client and server. This ensures the confidentiality and integrity of files as they move across networks, mitigating the risk of unauthorized access or tampering during the transfer process.

Cloud services, central to modern data storage and sharing, prioritize encryption to secure data during both transmission and storage. Cloud providers typically implement encryption in transit using protocols like SSL/TLS when users upload or download data. Additionally, they often offer mechanisms for encrypting data at rest, ensuring that stored information remains protected even if physical storage media were to be compromised. The integration of client-side encryption, where data is encrypted on the user's device before being uploaded to the cloud, further enhances the security posture by limiting the exposure of sensitive information even within the cloud environment.

The concept of Perfect Forward Secrecy (PFS) underscores the importance of continuously enhancing encryption mechanisms to protect data over time. PFS ensures that even if a long-term key is compromised, previously intercepted encrypted communications remain secure. The Diffie-Hellman key exchange algorithm, commonly used to establish secure connections, is a notable example of PFS. As technologies evolve, the integration of forward secrecy principles into encryption protocols becomes essential to mitigate the impact of potential key compromises and enhance the long-term security of data during transmission.

As the Internet of Things (IoT) proliferates, the role of encryption becomes increasingly critical in securing data exchanged between connected devices. IoT devices, ranging from smart thermostats to industrial sensors, often communicate sensitive information over networks. Implementing encryption ensures the confidentiality and integrity of this data, preventing unauthorized access or manipulation by malicious actors. Protocols like MQTT (Message Queuing Telemetry Transport) in IoT deployments commonly incorporate encryption mechanisms to protect the communication channels and the data exchanged between devices.

The use of hardware-based encryption modules, such as Trusted Platform Modules (TPMs) and Hardware Security Modules (HSMs), adds an additional layer of security to data transmission. These specialized devices store cryptographic keys securely, perform encryption and decryption operations, and ensure the integrity of the cryptographic processes. By offloading cryptographic operations to dedicated hardware, organizations enhance the resilience of their encryption infrastructure, safeguarding against potential vulnerabilities associated with software-based implementations.

Despite the critical role of encryption in securing data during transmission, organizations must also consider the management of cryptographic keys. The secure generation, storage, and distribution of encryption keys are paramount to the effectiveness of encryption mechanisms. Key management practices include the use of Key Management Services (KMS), secure key storage solutions, and periodic key rotation to mitigate the risks associated with key compromise. Robust key management ensures that even if an attacker gains access to encrypted data, the absence of the corresponding cryptographic keys renders the data indecipherable.

In conclusion, encryption serves as an indispensable tool in ensuring the security and privacy of data during transmission across diverse communication channels. From securing web communication through HTTPS to encrypting emails with PGP/GPG, and from protecting wireless networks with WPA3 to implementing end-to-end encryption in messaging applications, the broad adoption of encryption technologies underscores their critical role in modern cybersecurity. As technologies continue to evolve and threats become more sophisticated, the ongoing refinement and advancement of encryption mechanisms will remain imperative for maintaining the integrity and confidentiality of data in an interconnected and digitized world.

Strategies for implementing end-to-end encryption.

Implementing end-to-end encryption (E2EE) is a critical aspect of securing digital communications and data privacy, ensuring that only the intended recipients can access and decipher the information. Several strategies can be employed to effectively implement E2EE across various applications and platforms. Firstly, adopting a robust cryptographic framework is paramount. Utilizing well-established algorithms such as Advanced Encryption Standard (AES) for symmetric encryption and RSA or Elliptic Curve Cryptography (ECC) for asymmetric encryption provides a solid foundation for securing data at rest and in transit.

Key management plays a pivotal role in E2EE, necessitating the establishment of secure mechanisms for generating, distributing, and storing encryption keys. Public Key Infrastructure (PKI) or decentralized key management systems can be employed to facilitate secure key exchange between communicating parties. Additionally, the implementation of Perfect Forward Secrecy (PFS) ensures that even if a key is compromised, past communications remain confidential.

Furthermore, the integration of secure key exchange protocols, like the Diffie-Hellman key exchange, enhances the resilience of the E2EE system against potential attacks. Deploying robust authentication mechanisms, such as multi-factor authentication (MFA) or biometric authentication, ensures that only authorized users can access encrypted data or communications.

In the realm of messaging applications, the Signal Protocol serves as a noteworthy example of a comprehensive E2EE solution. This protocol employs a combination of symmetric and asymmetric encryption techniques, incorporating features like deniable authentication and ratcheting to continually update encryption keys. Such dynamic key management strategies bolster the overall security posture of the communication channel.

In addition to securing the content of messages, metadata protection is crucial in maintaining user privacy. Techniques like traffic analysis resistance and padding can be employed to obfuscate patterns in communication, thwarting attempts to glean information from metadata. The Tor network, for instance, exemplifies a system that leverages these principles to provide anonymous and secure communication channels.

Moreover, considerations for user experience and ease of implementation are essential to encourage widespread adoption of E2EE. Striking a balance between security and usability involves designing user-friendly interfaces, seamless key exchange processes, and transparent encryption mechanisms. Application programming interfaces (APIs) and software development kits (SDKs) that simplify the integration of E2EE into various platforms contribute to the accessibility of secure communication technologies.

Regular audits and security assessments are imperative to identify and address vulnerabilities in the E2EE implementation. Continuous monitoring and prompt patching of potential weaknesses ensure that the encryption system remains resilient against emerging threats. Collaboration with the cybersecurity community through bug bounty programs can provide an additional layer of scrutiny, fostering a proactive approach to security.

Legal and regulatory compliance must be considered in the implementation of E2EE, as some jurisdictions may have specific requirements or restrictions. Striking a balance between user privacy and lawful access to information poses a complex challenge, necessitating careful navigation of legal landscapes to ensure compliance without compromising the fundamental principles of end-to-end encryption.

In conclusion, implementing end-to-end encryption involves a multifaceted approach encompassing cryptographic foundations, key management, authentication, dynamic key exchange, metadata protection, user experience considerations, and ongoing security assessments. A comprehensive strategy, combined with a commitment to user privacy and legal compliance, ensures the creation of a robust and effective E2EE system that empowers individuals and organizations to communicate securely in the digital age.

Designing distributed firewall systems for network security.

Designing distributed firewall systems is a crucial endeavor in enhancing network security, providing a layered defense mechanism to safeguard against diverse cyber threats. The fundamental principle of distributed firewall architecture involves the deployment of firewall components across multiple points within a network, allowing for comprehensive monitoring, analysis, and control of traffic. One key aspect of this design is the strategic placement of firewall nodes at various network entry points, such as perimeter gateways and internal segments, to establish a robust defense-in-depth strategy.

To achieve effective distributed firewalling, a granular approach to rule definition and enforcement is essential. Policies must be meticulously crafted to permit or deny specific types of traffic based on factors like source and destination addresses, ports, protocols, and even application-level characteristics. The adoption of stateful inspection techniques enables the firewall to track the state of active connections, allowing for intelligent decision-making and improved security. Additionally, the integration of intrusion detection and prevention mechanisms at the firewall level adds an extra layer of defense, enabling the system to detect and respond to anomalous or malicious activities in real-time.

Centralized management and orchestration are integral components of distributed firewall systems, ensuring consistent policy enforcement and configuration across all firewall nodes. This centralized control facilitates the seamless coordination of security policies, updates, and threat intelligence across the distributed architecture. Automation plays a crucial role in this regard, enabling rapid response to emerging threats and minimizing the risk of misconfigurations. The use of Software-Defined Networking (SDN) principles can further enhance the agility and scalability of the distributed firewall infrastructure, allowing for dynamic policy adjustments in response to evolving network conditions.

In a distributed firewall system, communication and coordination between firewall nodes are pivotal for effective threat mitigation. Secure communication channels and synchronized rule databases enable the exchange of threat intelligence and the enforcement of consistent security policies. This collaborative approach ensures that the distributed firewall operates cohesively, with each node contributing to the overall network security posture.

Scalability is a critical consideration in the design of distributed firewall systems, particularly in large and complex network environments. The architecture must be scalable to accommodate the growing volume of network traffic and the increasing number of connected devices. Load balancing mechanisms can be employed to evenly distribute traffic among multiple firewall nodes, preventing bottlenecks and ensuring optimal performance. Furthermore, the use of cloud-based firewall solutions can provide elasticity, allowing the distributed firewall to adapt to changing workloads and network dynamics.

Integration with threat intelligence feeds and security information and event management (SIEM) systems is imperative for enhancing the efficacy of distributed firewall systems. Real-time updates on emerging threats, vulnerabilities, and attack patterns empower the firewall to make informed decisions and respond proactively to potential security incidents. Continuous monitoring of network traffic and the analysis of security events contribute to a proactive security stance, allowing for the identification and mitigation of threats before they can cause significant harm.

Redundancy and failover mechanisms are integral components of a resilient distributed firewall architecture. The design should account for scenarios where individual firewall nodes may become unavailable due to hardware failures, software issues, or targeted attacks. Employing techniques such as clustering and high availability configurations ensures that the loss of a single node does not compromise the overall security posture, maintaining continuous protection for the network.

Compliance with regulatory requirements and industry standards is a critical consideration in the design and implementation of distributed firewall systems. Adherence to standards such as the Payment Card Industry Data Security Standard (PCI DSS) or the Health Insurance Portability and Accountability Act (HIPAA) is essential to ensure that the network security infrastructure aligns with legal and regulatory frameworks. Additionally, robust auditing and logging mechanisms enable organizations to demonstrate compliance and facilitate post-incident analysis.

In conclusion, designing distributed firewall systems demands a holistic and strategic approach to network security. This includes meticulous rule definition, stateful inspection, intrusion detection and prevention, centralized management, secure communication between firewall nodes, scalability, integration with threat intelligence, redundancy, failover mechanisms, continuous monitoring, and regulatory compliance. A well-designed distributed firewall infrastructure fortifies the network against a spectrum of cyber threats, providing organizations with the confidence that their digital assets are protected in an ever-evolving threat landscape.

THE ROLE OF INTRUSION detection systems in distributed environments.

In distributed environments, the role of Intrusion Detection Systems (IDS) becomes paramount in fortifying network security, as these systems play a crucial role in detecting and mitigating potential threats across a network's various nodes and segments. The distributed nature of modern networks necessitates a comprehensive and adaptive approach to intrusion detection, where IDS serves as a vigilant guardian against a wide spectrum of cyber threats. The primary function of an IDS is to monitor network and system activities, analyzing patterns and anomalies that may indicate malicious behavior. This real-time scrutiny is particularly crucial in distributed environments, where the attack surface is extensive, and potential entry points are diverse.

An effective intrusion detection system in a distributed environment relies on both signature-based and anomaly-based detection methods. Signature-based detection involves the comparison of network traffic and system activities against predefined patterns or signatures of known threats. This approach is adept at identifying well-established attack patterns but may struggle with novel or sophisticated attacks. Anomaly-based detection, on the other hand, establishes a baseline of normal network behavior and triggers alerts or actions when deviations from this baseline are detected. This method is especially valuable in distributed environments where the network's dynamics can vary significantly.

The deployment of distributed IDS nodes strategically positioned throughout the network architecture is vital to ensuring comprehensive coverage. This placement includes sensors at network entry points, internal segments, and critical infrastructure nodes. Each IDS node contributes to the collective intelligence of the system, providing a holistic view of the network's security posture. In a distributed environment, these nodes must collaborate seamlessly, sharing threat intelligence and collectively responding to potential security incidents.

Centralized management and coordination are instrumental in optimizing the efficiency of distributed IDS in large and complex environments. A centralized management console enables security administrators to configure, monitor, and update the distributed IDS nodes uniformly. This centralized control ensures consistency in policies, rule sets, and response mechanisms, facilitating a coordinated and cohesive defense against potential intrusions. The coordination among distributed IDS nodes is crucial to correlate events, discern patterns of attack across multiple segments, and respond promptly to emerging threats.

Adaptive and context-aware intrusion detection mechanisms are essential in distributed environments due to the dynamic nature of modern networks. Machine learning and artificial intelligence algorithms can be integrated into IDS to enhance its ability to discern normal from abnormal behavior. This adaptive approach allows the IDS to evolve and adapt to changes in the network environment, improving its accuracy in detecting both known and novel threats. Furthermore, contextual information, such as user behavior, device characteristics, and network topology, enhances the precision of intrusion detection and reduces false positives.

In distributed environments, where data may traverse diverse network segments and geographically dispersed locations, encryption poses both a challenge and an opportunity for intrusion detection. While encrypted traffic may obscure the payload from traditional inspection, distributed IDS can leverage techniques like deep packet inspection, traffic analysis, and behavioral analytics to identify anomalous patterns even within encrypted communication. This ensures that the IDS remains effective in safeguarding against threats hidden within encrypted traffic, enhancing overall network security.

Integration with other security components, such as firewalls, antivirus solutions, and Security Information and Event Management (SIEM) systems, is essential for a holistic security posture in distributed environments. The IDS collaborates with these components to provide layered defense, where each element contributes unique insights and capabilities. For example, the IDS may trigger automated responses, such as firewall rule adjustments or blocking of malicious IP addresses, based on identified threats. Integration with SIEM systems facilitates comprehensive log analysis and correlation, enabling security teams to gain insights into the broader security landscape.

Continuous monitoring and auditing of the IDS performance are critical in distributed environments to ensure its effectiveness over time. Regular updates to threat signatures, system software, and detection algorithms are essential to keep pace with evolving threats. Periodic assessments and penetration testing help identify and address potential weaknesses in the intrusion detection system, ensuring that it remains a resilient and adaptive component of the overall network security architecture.

In conclusion, the role of intrusion detection systems in distributed environments is pivotal for maintaining the integrity and security of modern networks. Through a combination of signature-based and anomaly-based detection methods, strategic deployment of IDS nodes, centralized management and coordination, adaptive algorithms, integration with other security components, and continuous monitoring, IDS acts as a vigilant guardian against a diverse range of cyber threats. In the dynamic landscape of distributed environments, an effective IDS is not just a component but an integral part of a layered defense strategy, contributing to the resilience and security of the entire network ecosystem.

The importance of regular security audits in distributed systems.

Regular security audits in distributed systems are of paramount importance for maintaining the integrity, resilience, and effectiveness of the overall security posture in modern, complex network environments. The distributed nature of these systems, spanning across multiple nodes, networks, and geographic locations, introduces a myriad of potential vulnerabilities and points of attack. Security audits serve as a proactive and systematic approach to identifying, assessing, and mitigating these vulnerabilities, thereby reducing the risk of security breaches, data compromises, and service disruptions.

One key aspect of the importance of regular security audits lies in their role as a preventative measure against emerging threats and evolving attack vectors. As the threat landscape continually evolves, new vulnerabilities and attack methodologies surface, challenging the security mechanisms in place. Regular audits enable organizations to stay ahead of these threats by assessing the effectiveness of existing security controls, identifying potential weaknesses, and adapting the security infrastructure to address the latest risks. By proactively addressing vulnerabilities, organizations can minimize the window of opportunity for malicious actors seeking to exploit weaknesses in the distributed system.

Moreover, security audits play a crucial role in ensuring compliance with industry regulations, legal requirements, and internal policies. In distributed systems, which often handle sensitive data and diverse user interactions, compliance is not only a matter of good practice but a legal and ethical imperative. Regular audits provide organizations with the means to assess their adherence to regulatory frameworks such as GDPR, HIPAA, or industry-specific standards like PCI DSS. Demonstrating compliance not only helps avoid legal repercussions but also instills confidence among users, partners, and stakeholders in the organization's commitment to data protection and security.

The dynamic nature of distributed systems, characterized by constant changes in infrastructure, applications, and user access patterns, necessitates continuous monitoring and evaluation. Security audits offer a comprehensive examination of the entire distributed environment, including networks, servers, applications, and data repositories. This holistic assessment ensures that security controls are aligned with the evolving landscape, taking into account changes in technology, business processes, and user behavior. Regular audits, therefore, provide a mechanism for organizations to validate the relevance and effectiveness of their security measures in the face of dynamic and ever-changing conditions.

In the distributed systems paradigm, where interconnected components may have varying levels of security, regular audits serve to establish a baseline security posture and ensure consistency across the entire ecosystem. This is particularly crucial in environments where different departments or business units may have autonomy over their components. Audits help identify and rectify disparities in security practices, standardize security configurations, and enforce consistent security policies throughout the distributed infrastructure. This uniformity is essential for minimizing weak links and ensuring that security is not compromised due to inconsistencies in implementation.

Another significant aspect of security audits in distributed systems is their role in uncovering insider threats and human-related vulnerabilities. While technological safeguards are essential, human factors such as negligence, inadvertent errors, or malicious intent can introduce substantial risks. Regular audits scrutinize user access controls, authentication mechanisms, and adherence to security policies, shedding light on potential insider threats or unauthorized access. By identifying and addressing these issues promptly, organizations can mitigate the risks associated with internal vulnerabilities and establish a culture of security awareness among their workforce.

Security audits are instrumental in evaluating the effectiveness of incident response plans and disaster recovery mechanisms within distributed systems. In the event of a security incident or a system failure, the ability to respond swiftly and effectively is critical for minimizing damage and downtime. Regular audits simulate various security scenarios, allowing organizations to assess the readiness of their incident response teams, the robustness of their recovery procedures, and the efficacy of their backup and restoration mechanisms. This proactive approach ensures that, in the face of adversities, the distributed system can recover and resume operations with minimal impact on business continuity.

Furthermore, as distributed systems often leverage cloud services and third-party integrations, security audits play a vital role in scrutinizing these external dependencies. Assessing the security controls of cloud providers, third-party applications, and external APIs is essential for identifying potential risks associated with these dependencies. Regular audits enable organizations to validate that these external entities adhere to security best practices, have robust data protection measures in place, and do not introduce vulnerabilities that could compromise the overall security of the distributed system.

In conclusion, the importance of regular security audits in distributed systems cannot be overstated. These audits serve as a proactive and systematic approach to identify, assess, and mitigate vulnerabilities, ensuring that the distributed environment remains resilient against emerging threats. From addressing evolving risks and ensuring compliance to establishing baseline security postures, uncovering insider threats, and validating incident response mechanisms, security audits are a linchpin in maintaining the integrity and effectiveness of security measures within the intricate landscape of distributed systems. A proactive and comprehensive audit strategy is not merely a security best practice but an essential element of responsible and forward-thinking cybersecurity management in the ever-evolving digital landscape.

Ensuring compliance with industry standards and regulations.

Ensuring compliance with industry standards and regulations is a critical imperative for organizations operating in diverse sectors, as it establishes a foundation for responsible and secure business practices. The regulatory landscape is vast and constantly evolving, encompassing a range of industries such as finance, healthcare, technology, and more. Compliance involves adhering to a set of rules, guidelines, and standards established by regulatory bodies, governmental authorities, or industry consortiums to safeguard various facets of business operations, including data protection, financial transactions, and consumer rights.

One of the primary drivers for compliance is the protection of sensitive data, and industry standards often mandate the implementation of robust data protection measures. In sectors like finance, the Payment Card Industry Data Security Standard (PCI DSS) dictates the security requirements for organizations handling credit card transactions. Adherence to these standards not only protects consumers from financial fraud but also fosters trust in the organization's ability to handle sensitive financial information securely. Similarly, in healthcare, the Health Insurance Portability and Accountability Act (HIPAA) mandates safeguards for protected health information, ensuring the privacy and security of patient data.

Compliance also plays a pivotal role in enhancing cybersecurity. Standards such as the ISO/IEC 27001 focus on information security management systems, providing a framework for organizations to establish, implement, maintain, and continually improve their information security posture. This standard, and others like it, guide organizations in the development of comprehensive security policies, risk assessments, and incident response plans, contributing to a robust defense against cyber threats. For industries reliant on technology and interconnected systems, adherence to cybersecurity standards is integral to protecting against data breaches, ransomware attacks, and other malicious activities.

Moreover, compliance acts as a safeguard for consumer rights and privacy. The General Data Protection Regulation (GDPR) in the European Union, for example, empowers individuals with greater control over their personal data. Organizations must comply with stringent requirements regarding the collection, processing, and storage of personal information. Demonstrating GDPR compliance not only avoids legal consequences but also signals a commitment to respecting individual privacy rights, thereby fostering positive relationships with customers.

In addition to safeguarding data and privacy, compliance with industry standards mitigates financial risks for organizations. Regulatory fines and penalties for non-compliance can be substantial, and in some cases, they may lead to severe financial consequences or even business closure. Organizations that prioritize compliance not only avoid these financial risks but also demonstrate their commitment to ethical business practices, which can enhance their reputation and credibility in the eyes of investors, partners, and customers.

Ensuring compliance requires a systematic and proactive approach. Organizations often establish a compliance management framework that includes risk assessments, policy development, monitoring, and reporting mechanisms. Regular internal audits and assessments are conducted to evaluate adherence to specific standards and regulations. External audits, often performed by third-party entities, provide an unbiased evaluation of an organization's compliance status. These audits are crucial for identifying areas of improvement, validating the effectiveness of existing controls, and ensuring that the organization aligns with the evolving regulatory landscape.

However, achieving and maintaining compliance is not a one-time effort but an ongoing process. Regulations and industry standards are subject to updates and revisions, necessitating continuous monitoring and adaptation. Organizations must stay abreast of changes in the regulatory environment, assess the impact on their operations, and adjust their compliance strategies accordingly. This dynamic approach ensures that compliance efforts remain effective and aligned with the ever-evolving requirements of the business environment.

Collaboration and communication are integral components of a successful compliance strategy. Organizations often work closely with legal experts, compliance officers, and technology professionals to interpret and implement regulatory requirements. Industry associations and consortiums also play a role in shaping standards and providing guidance on best practices. Engaging with these external entities facilitates a shared understanding of compliance expectations and allows organizations to tap into collective knowledge to enhance their own compliance efforts.

For multinational corporations, navigating the complexities of global compliance is a multifaceted challenge. Different regions may have distinct regulatory frameworks, requiring organizations to develop a nuanced approach that addresses the unique requirements of each jurisdiction in which they operate. This may involve tailoring policies and procedures, adapting to varying data protection standards, and understanding cultural nuances that impact compliance expectations. International standards, such as ISO certifications, can provide a common foundation for organizations seeking to harmonize their compliance efforts across diverse regions.

In conclusion, ensuring compliance with industry standards and regulations is a multifaceted and integral aspect of responsible and ethical business practices. Compliance safeguards sensitive data, enhances cybersecurity, protects consumer rights and privacy, mitigates financial risks, and contributes to an organization's overall credibility and reputation. Through a systematic and ongoing approach, organizations can navigate the complex regulatory landscape, adapt to changes, and demonstrate a commitment to operating with integrity and accountability. As the business environment continues to evolve, maintaining compliance remains a dynamic and essential aspect of organizational governance and risk management.

Chapter 8: Future Horizons: Emerging Trends in Distributed Systems

Exploring the rise of edge computing and its impact on distributed systems.

The rise of edge computing marks a transformative shift in the landscape of computing architectures, fundamentally altering the way data is processed, stored, and managed. Unlike traditional centralized computing models, where data is processed in distant data centers, edge computing decentralizes computational resources, bringing them closer to the point of data generation or consumption. This paradigm shift is driven by the increasing demand for low-latency, high-performance applications and services, particularly in the context of the Internet of Things (IoT), real-time analytics, and immersive technologies.

Edge computing's impact on distributed systems is profound, reshaping the dynamics of data processing and communication across networks. In traditional distributed systems, data is typically transmitted to centralized servers for processing, introducing latency and potential bandwidth constraints. With edge computing, computational resources are strategically deployed at the network's periphery, enabling data processing to occur closer to the source. This localization of processing power reduces latency, enhances real-time responsiveness, and optimizes bandwidth utilization, resulting in a more efficient and responsive distributed system.

One of the key drivers behind the adoption of edge computing is its ability to address the challenges posed by the sheer volume of data generated by IoT devices. In scenarios where massive amounts of data are produced at the edge of the network, transmitting all this information to a central data center for processing becomes impractical. Edge computing mitigates this challenge by enabling data preprocessing and analysis at or near the source, allowing organizations to extract valuable insights locally before transmitting relevant data to central servers. This approach minimizes the burden on network infrastructure and optimizes resource utilization.

Furthermore, the rise of edge computing introduces a paradigm shift in data privacy and security considerations within distributed systems. By processing sensitive data locally at the edge, organizations can retain greater control over their data and reduce the exposure of sensitive information during transit to centralized data centers. This distributed approach aligns with privacy regulations and concerns, offering a more secure environment for data processing, particularly in applications where privacy and compliance are paramount.

The architecture of distributed systems is also impacted by the distributed nature of edge computing. Traditional distributed systems often rely on a hierarchical structure, with central servers orchestrating communication and computation. In contrast, edge computing introduces a more decentralized model, where nodes at the edge have increased autonomy and decision-making capabilities. This shift in architecture promotes a more resilient and adaptive system, capable of functioning even in scenarios where connectivity to central servers is compromised. Decentralization at the edge enhances the fault tolerance and scalability of distributed systems, making them more robust in dynamic and challenging environments.

As edge computing gains prominence, the role of edge devices becomes pivotal in the overall architecture of distributed systems. These devices, ranging from IoT sensors to edge servers, contribute to the distributed computing fabric by hosting applications, processing data, and facilitating communication. The edge devices act as intelligent endpoints, capable of executing tasks locally, making decisions based on real-time data, and collaborating with other edge devices to perform complex distributed computations. This evolution in the role of edge devices reshapes the traditional client-server model, distributing computational capabilities across the entire network infrastructure.

Moreover, edge computing has a profound impact on the scalability of distributed systems, offering a more flexible and scalable approach to resource provisioning. In traditional distributed systems, scaling often involves adding more resources to centralized data centers, which may encounter practical limitations. Edge computing allows for a distributed scaling approach, where additional computing resources can be deployed at the edge to meet specific demands. This flexibility in scaling is particularly advantageous in dynamic environments where workloads fluctuate, enabling organizations to adapt their computational capacity based on the needs of specific edge locations.

The integration of edge computing with cloud computing further enriches the capabilities of distributed systems. Cloud resources can complement edge devices, providing additional computational power, storage, and services. This hybrid approach, often referred to as edge-cloud computing, allows organizations to leverage the strengths of both edge and cloud computing paradigms. For example, critical data processing tasks can be offloaded to edge devices for low-latency execution, while non-latency-sensitive workloads can be processed in the cloud, offering scalability and centralized management.

The rise of edge computing also introduces new challenges for distributed systems, ranging from the management of diverse edge devices to the orchestration of distributed applications. The heterogeneity of edge devices, each with varying computing capabilities and constraints, requires sophisticated management solutions to ensure seamless integration into the distributed system. Additionally, orchestrating applications across a distributed edge environment demands advanced coordination mechanisms to optimize resource utilization, data flow, and workload distribution.

In conclusion, the rise of edge computing represents a paradigm shift with profound implications for distributed systems. This evolution decentralizes computational resources, reducing latency, improving real-time responsiveness, and optimizing bandwidth utilization. Edge computing's impact extends to data privacy, security considerations, system architecture, fault tolerance, scalability, and the role of edge devices within the distributed computing fabric. The integration of edge and cloud computing further enriches the capabilities of distributed systems, offering a hybrid approach that leverages the strengths of both paradigms. While presenting new challenges, the transformative potential of edge computing is evident in its ability to address the evolving demands of modern applications, particularly in the context of IoT, real-time analytics, and immersive technologies.

Architectural considerations for distributed edge environments.

Architectural considerations for distributed edge environments involve a holistic and strategic approach to designing systems that leverage edge computing capabilities. The distributed edge, where computational resources are strategically placed closer to the data source, introduces unique challenges and opportunities that demand careful consideration in system architecture. One fundamental consideration is the deployment of edge nodes to optimize proximity to data generation points. This strategic placement ensures low-latency data processing, enabling real-time responsiveness and enhancing the overall performance of distributed edge environments. The architectural design must accommodate the dynamic nature of edge nodes, which may include various devices such as sensors, edge servers, and IoT devices, each with varying computational capabilities and resource constraints.

Scalability is a critical aspect of architectural considerations for distributed edge environments. The architecture must be designed to scale gracefully as the number of edge nodes increases, accommodating the growing demands of data processing and application workloads. A scalable architecture ensures that distributed edge environments can handle increasing volumes of data and support the deployment of additional edge devices without compromising performance or introducing bottlenecks. Dynamic load balancing mechanisms play a crucial role in optimizing resource utilization and ensuring that computational workloads are distributed efficiently across the edge environment.

Interoperability is another essential consideration in architectural design for distributed edge environments. The heterogeneous nature of edge devices and the diversity of applications require standardized communication protocols and interfaces to facilitate seamless interaction between different components. Ensuring interoperability enables edge devices from various manufacturers to collaborate effectively, promotes the development of diverse applications, and enhances the overall flexibility of the distributed edge ecosystem. Standardization efforts, such as those within industry consortia, contribute to the establishment of common protocols for interoperability in distributed edge environments.

Security is a paramount concern in distributed edge environments, given the decentralized nature of computational resources and the potential exposure to diverse threats. The architectural design must incorporate robust security measures to protect data in transit and at rest. Encryption, secure communication protocols, and authentication mechanisms are essential components of a secure architecture for distributed edge environments. Moreover, the architecture should include intrusion detection and prevention systems at the edge nodes, ensuring early detection and mitigation of security threats. Secure boot processes and regular security updates for edge devices contribute to a resilient security posture in distributed edge environments.

Reliability and fault tolerance are critical considerations in architectural design, especially in distributed edge environments where edge nodes may operate in dynamic and challenging conditions. Redundancy mechanisms, such as deploying duplicate edge nodes or incorporating failover strategies, ensure continuous operation even in the event of hardware failures or network disruptions. The architectural design should include self-healing capabilities to automatically recover from failures and maintain the reliability of distributed edge systems. Additionally, distributed data storage and replication strategies contribute to fault tolerance by preventing data loss in case of localized failures.

Data management is a complex consideration in architectural design for distributed edge environments, encompassing issues related to data storage, processing, and synchronization. Decentralized data storage at the edge nodes minimizes the need for constant data transmission to centralized servers, reducing latency and optimizing bandwidth utilization. However, effective data synchronization mechanisms are essential to maintain consistency across distributed edge nodes. Architectural solutions must address data management challenges, including data versioning, conflict resolution, and synchronization protocols, to ensure that all edge nodes operate with accurate and up-to-date information.

The integration of edge computing with cloud computing introduces a hybrid architectural model that combines the strengths of both paradigms. In a distributed edge environment, cloud resources can be leveraged to provide additional computational power, storage, and centralized management capabilities. The architectural design should consider seamless integration between edge and cloud components, enabling the offloading of certain workloads to the cloud for scalability or resource-intensive tasks. Hybrid architectures also allow organizations to benefit from centralized monitoring, orchestration, and analytics while maintaining low-latency processing at the edge.

Machine learning and artificial intelligence (AI) at the edge present additional considerations in architectural design. Edge nodes equipped with AI capabilities can process and analyze data locally, reducing the need for transmitting large volumes of raw data to centralized servers. The architectural design must account for the deployment of lightweight machine learning models optimized for edge devices, ensuring efficient use of computational resources. Edge nodes with AI capabilities can support real-time decision-making, anomaly detection, and predictive analytics, contributing to enhanced functionality and intelligence in distributed edge environments.

Furthermore, the architectural design should prioritize energy efficiency in distributed edge environments, considering the often-constrained power resources of edge devices. Energy-efficient algorithms, low-power hardware components, and intelligent power management strategies contribute to a sustainable architecture that minimizes the environmental impact of distributed edge computing. Additionally, the architectural design should include mechanisms for optimizing energy consumption during periods of low activity, such as dynamic scaling or sleep modes for idle edge devices.

In conclusion, architectural considerations for distributed edge environments require a comprehensive approach that addresses the unique challenges and opportunities presented by the decentralization of computational resources. Designing scalable, interoperable, secure, reliable, and energy-efficient architectures ensures the effectiveness and sustainability of distributed edge systems. Incorporating mechanisms for seamless integration with cloud computing, addressing data management challenges, and accommodating machine learning at the edge contribute to a holistic architectural framework. As distributed edge environments continue to evolve, a thoughtful and adaptable architectural design remains essential to unlock the full potential of edge computing in diverse applications, ranging from IoT to real-time analytics and beyond.

Understanding the paradigm shift towards serverless computing.

The paradigm shift towards serverless computing represents a transformative evolution in the way applications are developed, deployed, and scaled in modern computing environments. Serverless computing, often referred to as Function as a Service (FaaS), abstracts the underlying infrastructure, enabling developers to focus solely on writing code for specific functions or services without the need to manage servers. This departure from traditional server-centric models has profound implications for the efficiency, scalability, and cost-effectiveness of application development and deployment.

At the core of the serverless paradigm is the concept of functions, which are discrete units of executable code designed to perform specific tasks. In a serverless architecture, these functions are executed in response to events triggered by various sources, such as HTTP requests, database updates, or messaging queues. The serverless model eliminates the need for developers to provision, manage, and maintain servers, allowing them to concentrate on writing code that addresses specific business logic or functionality. This abstraction of infrastructure management represents a significant departure from the traditional model where developers had to grapple with server provisioning, configuration, and scaling.

One of the key drivers behind the shift towards serverless computing is the inherent scalability and elasticity it offers. Traditional server-centric models often require upfront capacity planning and provisioning to accommodate peak loads, leading to underutilization of resources during periods of low demand and potential resource constraints during spikes in activity. Serverless computing, on the other hand, automatically scales functions in response to incoming events, ensuring optimal resource utilization and eliminating the need for manual scaling adjustments. This dynamic scalability enhances the agility of applications, making them more responsive to fluctuations in user demand and reducing the complexity associated with traditional scaling methods.

Cost efficiency is another compelling factor driving the adoption of serverless computing. With traditional models, organizations incur costs associated with maintaining a dedicated infrastructure, regardless of the actual workload. In contrast, serverless computing follows a pay-as-you-go model, where organizations are billed based on the actual execution of functions. This results in cost savings, especially for applications with variable workloads, as organizations are only charged for the resources consumed during active function executions. The granular pricing model aligns closely with the resource consumption patterns of applications, offering a more economical approach to infrastructure provisioning.

Furthermore, the serverless paradigm significantly accelerates the development lifecycle by abstracting away the complexities of infrastructure management. Developers can focus on writing code, deploying functions, and delivering features without the need to delve into the intricacies of server provisioning, configuration, and maintenance. This streamlined development process promotes rapid iterations, facilitates continuous deployment practices, and accelerates time-to-market for applications. The serverless model encourages a server-agnostic mindset, enabling developers to write functions without being concerned about the underlying infrastructure, fostering a more agile and efficient development culture.

Security considerations in serverless computing involve a shared responsibility model where cloud providers manage the security of the underlying infrastructure, while users are responsible for securing their code and application layer. The serverless architecture inherently benefits from the security measures implemented by cloud providers, such as access controls, encryption, and network isolation. However, developers must adhere to secure coding practices, implement proper authentication and authorization mechanisms, and stay vigilant against potential vulnerabilities in their code. While serverless computing offers security advantages, organizations must remain proactive in addressing security concerns specific to their applications and data.

The event-driven nature of serverless computing aligns well with microservices architectures, where applications are composed of small, independent services that communicate via APIs. Each function in a serverless environment encapsulates a specific piece of functionality, making it conducive to the microservices paradigm. This alignment enhances the modularity, maintainability, and scalability of applications, enabling organizations to build and deploy complex systems by composing individual functions that seamlessly interact with each other. The serverless and microservices combination fosters a more resilient and flexible architecture, where changes to one function do not necessitate alterations to the entire application, promoting a modular and agile development approach.

Despite its advantages, the serverless paradigm is not a one-size-fits-all solution and is not without challenges. Cold start latency, where functions may experience initial delays in response times, is one such challenge that can impact real-time or interactive applications. Additionally, resource constraints imposed by serverless platforms, such as execution time limits and ephemeral storage, require careful consideration and design choices. The statelessness of serverless functions also poses challenges for applications that rely heavily on maintaining state between function invocations. Developers must carefully assess the suitability of serverless computing for specific use cases, considering factors such as execution time, resource requirements, and state management.

In conclusion, the paradigm shift towards serverless computing represents a transformative leap in the evolution of cloud computing architectures. The abstraction of infrastructure management, dynamic scalability, cost efficiency, and accelerated development cycles are driving forces behind the widespread adoption of serverless computing. This model aligns well with modern application development practices, emphasizing agility, modularity, and responsiveness to varying workloads. While challenges such as cold start latency and resource constraints exist, the benefits of serverless computing are reshaping how organizations approach application development and deployment, ushering in a new era of efficiency and innovation in the realm of cloud computing.

The role of serverless architectures in distributed environments.

The role of serverless architectures in distributed environments signifies a transformative shift in the way applications are developed, deployed, and scaled. At its core, serverless computing, often referred to as Function as a Service (FaaS), represents a departure from the traditional server-centric model by abstracting the underlying infrastructure, allowing developers to focus solely on writing code for specific functions or services without the burden of server management. In the distributed landscape, where applications span across multiple nodes and networks, the serverless paradigm introduces a dynamic and scalable approach that leverages the principles of event-driven, on-demand computing.

One of the primary roles of serverless architectures in distributed environments is to enhance the scalability and elasticity of applications. Traditional server-centric models often require meticulous capacity planning to accommodate peak loads, leading to underutilization of resources during periods of low demand and potential resource constraints during spikes in activity. Serverless computing introduces an inherently scalable model where functions, encapsulating discrete units of code, automatically scale in response to incoming events. This dynamic scalability ensures optimal resource utilization, enabling applications to seamlessly adapt to varying workloads. The serverless paradigm empowers distributed environments with the ability to handle sudden surges in demand without the need for manual scaling adjustments.

Cost efficiency is another pivotal role played by serverless architectures in distributed environments. The traditional model of maintaining dedicated infrastructure incurs ongoing costs regardless of the actual workload. In contrast, serverless computing operates on a pay-as-you-go model, where organizations are billed based on the actual execution of functions. This granular pricing aligns closely with resource consumption patterns, translating to cost savings, especially for applications with variable workloads. By only charging for the resources consumed during active function executions, serverless architectures offer an economically efficient alternative to traditional infrastructure provisioning in distributed environments.

The role of serverless architectures extends beyond cost efficiency and scalability; it significantly accelerates the development lifecycle in distributed environments. Developers can concentrate on writing code, deploying functions, and delivering features without the need to grapple with server provisioning, configuration, and maintenance intricacies. This streamlined development process promotes rapid iterations, facilitates continuous deployment practices, and accelerates time-to-market for applications in distributed environments. The serverless model encourages a server-agnostic mindset, enabling developers to focus on the business logic or functionality of specific functions without being entangled in the complexities of underlying infrastructure management.

Security considerations in serverless computing within distributed environments are essential and involve a shared responsibility model. Cloud providers manage the security of the underlying infrastructure, while users are responsible for securing their code and application layer. The serverless architecture inherently benefits from the security measures implemented by cloud providers, such as access controls, encryption, and network isolation. However, developers must adhere to secure coding practices, implement proper authentication and authorization mechanisms, and remain vigilant against potential vulnerabilities in their code. While serverless computing offers security advantages, organizations must remain proactive in addressing security concerns specific to their applications and data within the distributed landscape.

The event-driven nature of serverless computing aligns seamlessly with the principles of microservices architectures in distributed environments. Microservices advocate breaking down applications into small, independent services that communicate via APIs. Each function in a serverless environment encapsulates specific functionality, making it conducive to the microservices paradigm. This alignment enhances the modularity, maintainability, and scalability of applications, enabling organizations to build and deploy complex systems by composing individual functions that seamlessly interact with each other in the distributed environment. The serverless and microservices combination fosters a more resilient and flexible architecture, where changes to one function do not necessitate alterations to the entire application, promoting a modular and agile development approach.

Furthermore, the serverless paradigm encourages a shift towards event-driven architectures in distributed environments. Functions within a serverless architecture are triggered by events, which can range from HTTP requests and database updates to messaging queues. This event-driven approach aligns with the distributed nature of modern applications, where components communicate asynchronously based on events rather than relying on synchronous and tightly coupled interactions. Event-driven architectures enhance the decoupling of components within distributed environments, promoting greater flexibility, adaptability, and responsiveness to changes in the distributed landscape.

The integration of serverless computing with cloud services further enriches its role in distributed environments. Cloud providers offer a range of managed services that seamlessly integrate with serverless architectures, providing additional capabilities such as storage, databases, authentication, and messaging. This integration simplifies the development and deployment of distributed applications, allowing developers to leverage a myriad of cloud services without the need for extensive configuration or management. The combination of serverless computing and cloud services contributes to a more comprehensive and versatile toolkit for building and scaling applications in distributed environments.

Despite its advantages, the serverless paradigm is not without challenges in distributed environments. Cold start latency, where functions may experience initial delays in response times, can impact real-time or interactive applications. Additionally, resource constraints imposed by serverless platforms, such as execution time limits and ephemeral storage, require careful consideration and design choices. The statelessness of serverless functions also poses challenges for applications that rely heavily on maintaining state between function invocations within the distributed environment. Developers must carefully assess the suitability of serverless computing for specific use cases, considering factors such as execution time, resource requirements, and state management within distributed environments.

In conclusion, the role of serverless architectures in distributed environments is multifaceted, redefining the way applications are developed, deployed, and scaled. The dynamic scalability, cost efficiency, accelerated development lifecycle, and alignment with microservices and event-driven architectures make serverless computing a compelling choice for modern distributed applications. Its integration with cloud services further enhances its versatility, offering a comprehensive toolkit for building and scaling applications in distributed environments. While challenges exist, the benefits of serverless computing are reshaping how organizations approach application development, ushering in a new era of efficiency and innovation in the realm of distributed computing.

Exploring the intersection of blockchain and distributed systems.

The intersection of blockchain and distributed systems marks a revolutionary convergence that redefines the landscape of decentralized computing and trust mechanisms. At its core, a blockchain is a distributed ledger that records transactions across a network of nodes in a secure, transparent, and tamper-resistant manner. This fundamental principle aligns with the core tenets of distributed systems, where computational tasks and data are distributed across multiple nodes to achieve resilience, fault tolerance, and scalability. Exploring this intersection requires delving into the foundational concepts of both blockchain and distributed systems, understanding their synergies, and recognizing the transformative potential they collectively offer.

Distributed systems, in their traditional sense, involve a network of interconnected nodes that collaborate to achieve a common goal. These nodes may span across geographical locations, and their coordination is essential for tasks such as data storage, computation, and communication. The decentralization inherent in distributed systems provides advantages such as fault tolerance, scalability, and improved responsiveness. However, it also introduces challenges related to consistency, coordination, and the prevention of malicious activities. Blockchain, as a distributed ledger, introduces a novel solution to some of these challenges by employing consensus algorithms and cryptographic techniques to ensure the integrity and immutability of data.

The marriage of blockchain and distributed systems manifests in the form of a decentralized and trustless ledger. In a blockchain network, each node maintains a copy of the entire ledger, and transactions are added to the ledger through a consensus mechanism, often achieved through processes like Proof of Work (PoW) or Proof of Stake (PoS). This decentralized ledger ensures that no single entity has control over the entire system, mitigating the risks associated with centralization and providing a transparent and verifiable record of transactions. The cryptographic nature of blockchain ensures that once a block of transactions is added to the chain, it is practically impossible to alter, fostering a high degree of data integrity within the distributed environment.

One of the notable intersections between blockchain and distributed systems is the concept of smart contracts. Smart contracts are self-executing contracts with the terms directly written into code. Deployed on blockchain platforms, smart contracts automate and enforce the execution of predefined rules, eliminating the need for intermediaries and reducing the potential for disputes. This paradigm aligns with the principles of distributed systems, as the execution of smart contracts occurs across the network of nodes, ensuring consensus on the outcomes. The introduction of smart contracts extends the capabilities of distributed systems by enabling programmable and decentralized execution of agreements, ranging from financial transactions to complex business processes.

Consensus algorithms play a pivotal role in both blockchain and distributed systems, serving as the mechanism through which nodes agree on the state of the system. In distributed systems, achieving consensus is essential for maintaining a consistent view of the shared data among nodes. Traditional distributed systems often employ algorithms like the Paxos or Raft consensus algorithms to ensure agreement on a single version of truth. In the realm of blockchain, consensus mechanisms are fundamental to validating transactions and adding them to the immutable ledger. Proof of Work, used by Bitcoin, requires nodes to solve complex mathematical puzzles to add a block, while Proof of Stake, used by various blockchain platforms, involves nodes staking cryptocurrency to validate transactions. The convergence of consensus mechanisms highlights the common objective of achieving agreement in decentralized and distributed environments.

Decentralized storage is another area where the intersection of blockchain and distributed systems is evident. Traditional distributed systems may utilize distributed file systems or cloud storage solutions to ensure fault tolerance and availability of data. In blockchain networks, decentralized storage solutions leverage the collective resources of network participants to store and retrieve data in a distributed manner. This approach aligns with the principles of decentralization, as no single entity has control over the storage infrastructure. Blockchain-based decentralized storage systems aim to provide data immutability, resilience, and censorship resistance, expanding the capabilities of distributed storage in the broader context of decentralized applications (DApps) and blockchain-based ecosystems.

Interoperability is a crucial consideration in exploring the intersection of blockchain and distributed systems. As the adoption of blockchain technology grows, the need for seamless communication and interaction between different blockchain networks and traditional distributed systems becomes apparent. Interoperability solutions aim to facilitate the exchange of assets, data, and information across diverse distributed environments. Projects and initiatives focused on interoperability, such as cross-chain bridges and protocols, seek to bridge the gap between distinct blockchains and traditional distributed systems, fostering a more connected and collaborative ecosystem.

Identity management and authentication represent another area where the integration of blockchain and distributed systems offers innovative solutions. Traditional identity management systems often rely on centralized authorities to verify and authenticate users. In contrast, blockchain-based identity solutions leverage decentralized and cryptographic principles to provide individuals with greater control over their identity. Users can have self-sovereign identities stored on a blockchain, enabling them to selectively disclose information without relying on a central authority. This decentralized approach aligns with the principles of distributed systems by distributing the control and verification of identities across a network of nodes, enhancing security and privacy.

In the context of financial systems, the intersection of blockchain and distributed systems has given rise to the concept of decentralized finance (DeFi). DeFi platforms leverage blockchain technology to recreate and decentralize traditional financial services such as lending, borrowing, and trading. Smart contracts on blockchain networks facilitate the execution of financial transactions without the need for intermediaries, offering transparency, security, and accessibility. The decentralized nature of these financial systems aligns with the principles of distributed systems, as the services are not reliant on a single central authority. However, challenges such as scalability, security, and regulatory compliance in the evolving landscape of DeFi underscore the complexities of integrating blockchain with distributed financial systems.

Challenges and considerations emerge at the intersection of blockchain and distributed systems. Scalability remains a prominent concern, especially as blockchain networks grow in size and transaction volume. The consensus mechanisms that contribute to the security of blockchains can also introduce latency and throughput limitations. Addressing these scalability challenges involves ongoing research and development efforts to optimize consensus algorithms, implement layer-two scaling solutions, and explore novel approaches such as sharding. Achieving a balance between decentralization, security, and scalability is a nuanced task at the intersection of these technologies.

Furthermore, the environmental impact of consensus mechanisms, particularly Proof of Work, has prompted discussions around the sustainability of blockchain networks. The energy-intensive nature of certain blockchain consensus mechanisms raises concerns about their long-term viability, especially as the demand for decentralized applications and blockchain services continues to grow. Innovations in consensus algorithms, such as the shift towards Proof of Stake and the exploration of environmentally friendly alternatives, underscore the importance of sustainable practices in the intersection of blockchain and distributed systems.

In conclusion, exploring the intersection of blockchain and distributed systems reveals a dynamic landscape where decentralized principles redefine how data is stored, transactions are executed, and trust is established. The convergence of blockchain and distributed systems introduces transformative concepts such as decentralized ledgers, smart contracts, and self-sovereign identities. The alignment in consensus mechanisms, the emergence of decentralized finance, and the pursuit of interoperability underscore the synergies between these technologies. Challenges related to scalability, sustainability, and interoperability serve as focal points for ongoing research and development. As blockchain technology continues to evolve and integrate with distributed systems, its impact on reshaping trust, transparency, and collaboration in diverse sectors becomes increasingly profound, paving the way for a decentralized future.

Applications of distributed ledger technologies beyond cryptocurrencies.

The applications of distributed ledger technologies (DLTs) extend far beyond their initial implementation in cryptocurrencies, offering innovative solutions across various industries and sectors. At the heart of these applications is the decentralized and tamper-resistant nature of distributed ledgers, which ensure transparency, trust, and immutability of recorded data. One notable domain where DLTs are making significant strides is supply chain management. By employing distributed ledgers, supply chain participants can record and track the provenance of goods throughout the entire supply chain. This transparency enhances traceability, reduces the risk of fraud, and enables quicker responses to issues such as product recalls. The decentralized and shared nature of the ledger ensures that all relevant parties in the supply chain have access to real-time, verifiable information.

In the realm of finance, DLTs, particularly blockchain, have sparked a transformative wave. Blockchain's application in trade finance, for example, streamlines complex processes by providing a shared and immutable record of transactions. This facilitates faster and more efficient cross-border trade, reduces the risk of errors and fraud, and enhances the overall transparency of financial transactions. Additionally, blockchain-based smart contracts automate the execution of predefined contractual terms, reducing the need for intermediaries and expediting settlement processes. These applications not only optimize operational efficiency but also contribute to the creation of more inclusive financial systems, allowing for greater financial access, particularly in regions with limited traditional banking infrastructure.

Healthcare is another sector witnessing the integration of DLTs to address challenges related to data management, security, and interoperability. By utilizing distributed ledgers, healthcare providers can create a secure and interoperable system for managing patient records. The decentralized nature of DLTs allows patients to have greater control over their health data while ensuring that healthcare professionals can access accurate and up-to-date information. This approach not only improves the overall quality of patient care but also enhances data security and privacy compliance. Moreover, the application of DLTs in clinical trials can streamline data sharing among researchers and ensure the integrity of trial results, ultimately accelerating the pace of medical research and drug development.

The real estate industry is experiencing a transformation through the application of DLTs, particularly in property management and land registries. Blockchain, with its decentralized and transparent ledger, provides a reliable system for recording property transactions and ownership details. This not only reduces the risk of fraudulent activities such as property fraud but also streamlines the cumbersome process of property transactions. Smart contracts on blockchain platforms automate and enforce property-related agreements, eliminating the need for intermediaries and reducing the time and costs associated with real estate transactions. The use of DLTs in real estate introduces efficiency, security, and transparency into an industry traditionally burdened by paperwork and complex legal processes.

Governance and voting systems are areas where DLTs are being explored to enhance transparency and security. Blockchain, in particular, offers a decentralized and tamper-resistant platform for conducting elections and ensuring the integrity of voting processes. By recording votes on a blockchain, the results become verifiable and immune to tampering, thereby increasing trust in electoral outcomes. The decentralized nature of DLTs reduces the risk of centralized manipulation and fraud, promoting fair and transparent governance. This application of DLTs aligns with the broader goal of leveraging technology to strengthen democratic processes and enhance citizen participation in decision-making.

The energy sector is undergoing a paradigm shift with the application of DLTs to create more efficient and sustainable energy systems. Blockchain, for instance, enables the creation of decentralized energy grids where participants can produce, sell, and consume energy directly without the need for traditional utility intermediaries. The use of smart contracts ensures automatic and transparent transactions within the energy grid, optimizing energy distribution and consumption. Additionally, DLTs facilitate the tracking of the origin and carbon footprint of energy sources, supporting the transition towards greener and more sustainable energy practices. This application of DLTs contributes to the evolution of resilient and decentralized energy ecosystems.

In the realm of intellectual property and content distribution, DLTs offer solutions for issues related to copyright, piracy, and royalty distribution. Blockchain, with its transparent and immutable ledger, provides a secure and traceable system for recording and managing intellectual property rights. Content creators can timestamp their work on the blockchain, establishing a verifiable record of ownership and creation. Smart contracts on blockchain platforms automate royalty payments, ensuring that content creators receive fair compensation for the use of their work. This application of DLTs not only protects intellectual property but also empowers creators by providing a decentralized and transparent framework for content distribution.

The application of DLTs in identity management is becoming increasingly crucial, particularly in addressing issues related to identity theft, fraud, and digital identity verification. Blockchain, with its decentralized and cryptographically secured ledger, offers a robust platform for individuals to manage their digital identities. Users can have self-sovereign identities recorded on a blockchain, allowing them to control and selectively share their identity information without relying on a centralized authority. This approach enhances privacy, reduces the risk of identity theft, and streamlines identity verification processes across various sectors, including finance, healthcare, and e-commerce.

The emergence of tokenization is a transformative application of DLTs, particularly in the representation of real-world assets as digital tokens on a blockchain. This concept extends beyond cryptocurrencies and encompasses the representation of physical assets such as real estate, art, and commodities as digital tokens. Tokenization facilitates fractional ownership, enabling individuals to invest in high-value assets with smaller capital contributions. This democratization of asset ownership not only enhances financial inclusion but also introduces liquidity to traditionally illiquid markets. The transparent and decentralized nature of DLTs ensures the integrity and traceability of tokenized assets, fostering a new era in asset management and investment.

The application of DLTs in the Internet of Things (IoT) realm is creating a more secure and efficient ecosystem for connected devices. By leveraging blockchain, IoT devices can securely record and share data in a tamper-resistant manner. The decentralized nature of DLTs enhances the security and privacy of IoT data by eliminating single points of failure and reducing the risk of unauthorized access. Additionally, blockchain-based smart contracts can automate interactions and transactions between IoT devices, enabling seamless and trustless collaboration. This application of DLTs contributes to building a more resilient and secure foundation for the growing ecosystem of interconnected devices.

Cross-border payments and remittances represent a domain where DLTs, particularly blockchain, are reshaping the financial landscape. Traditional cross-border payment systems are often plagued by inefficiencies, delays, and high transaction costs. Blockchain technology, with its decentralized and transparent ledger, provides a more streamlined and cost-effective solution. Blockchain-based cross-border payment systems enable faster and more transparent transactions, reducing the reliance on intermediaries and lowering fees. Additionally, the use of stablecoins pegged to fiat currencies on blockchain platforms offers a bridge between the benefits of blockchain and the stability of traditional currencies, making cross-border transactions more accessible and efficient.

The exploration of DLTs in the education sector is yielding innovative solutions for credential verification and secure record-keeping. Blockchain, with its decentralized and tamper-resistant ledger, provides a reliable platform for recording and verifying academic credentials. Students can have their educational achievements securely recorded on a blockchain, ensuring the authenticity and integrity of their academic records. This not only simplifies the verification process for employers and academic institutions but also mitigates the risk of credential fraud. The application of DLTs in education aligns with the broader trend of leveraging technology to enhance the transparency and efficiency of administrative processes.

In conclusion, the applications of distributed ledger technologies extend far beyond cryptocurrencies, permeating diverse sectors and industries with transformative solutions. From revolutionizing supply chain management to streamlining financial transactions, improving healthcare, and enhancing the transparency of governance, DLTs are at the forefront of driving innovation. The decentralized, transparent, and tamper-resistant nature of distributed ledgers contributes to solutions that address longstanding challenges in areas such as identity management, intellectual property, and cross-border payments. As the technology continues to evolve, the potential applications of DLTs in creating more efficient, secure, and inclusive systems are bound to expand, shaping a future where decentralized principles play a pivotal role in various facets of our interconnected world.

The integration of machine learning for intelligent decision-making.

The integration of machine learning into decision-making processes represents a transformative shift in the realm of artificial intelligence, where systems evolve beyond rule-based programming to learn from data and make intelligent decisions. At its core, machine learning is a subset of AI that empowers systems to recognize patterns, draw insights, and improve their performance over time without explicit programming. The fusion of machine learning with decision-making mechanisms offers unprecedented opportunities across diverse domains, revolutionizing industries, optimizing processes, and enhancing the quality of choices made by intelligent systems.

One of the key aspects of integrating machine learning into decision-making is the ability to leverage historical data for predictive analytics. Machine learning models, ranging from simple linear regression to sophisticated deep neural networks, can analyze vast datasets to identify patterns and relationships. This historical perspective enables decision-makers to make informed predictions about future outcomes, contributing to strategic planning, risk management, and resource allocation. For instance, in finance, machine learning algorithms analyze historical market data to predict stock prices, aiding investors in making more informed decisions.

The concept of supervised learning plays a pivotal role in training machine learning models for decision-making. During the training phase, models are provided with labeled datasets where the correct outcomes are known. The algorithm learns to map input features to the corresponding output labels, allowing it to generalize its learning to new, unseen data. This supervised learning paradigm is particularly powerful in scenarios where decision-making involves recognizing patterns, classifying data, or predicting outcomes. Applications span diverse domains, from medical diagnosis, where machine learning models analyze patient data to predict diseases, to fraud detection in finance, where algorithms learn patterns of fraudulent transactions.

Unsupervised learning is another facet of machine learning integration, especially relevant in decision-making scenarios where the structure or labels of the data are not predefined. Clustering and dimensionality reduction techniques in unsupervised learning allow systems to identify patterns and group similar data points without explicit guidance. In decision-making, this can lead to the discovery of hidden insights within data, aiding in segmentation, anomaly detection, and pattern recognition. For instance, in marketing, unsupervised learning can be employed to segment customers based on their behavior, enabling businesses to tailor their strategies more effectively.

Reinforcement learning, a paradigm where agents learn through interaction with an environment, contributes significantly to the integration of machine learning into decision-making processes. This approach is particularly powerful in scenarios where decisions are made sequentially over time, with feedback received based on the consequences of those decisions. Applications range from game-playing algorithms, where agents learn optimal strategies through trial and error, to robotics, where reinforcement learning enables machines to learn complex tasks through interactions with their surroundings. In decision-making, reinforcement learning models can adapt and improve their strategies over time, optimizing outcomes based on feedback and experience.

The interpretability of machine learning models is a critical consideration in decision-making, especially in fields where transparency and accountability are paramount. As models become more complex, such as deep neural networks, understanding the reasoning behind their decisions becomes challenging. Explainable AI (XAI) techniques aim to address this issue, providing insights into how a model arrived at a particular decision. This interpretability is crucial in applications like healthcare, where machine learning models assist in diagnosis or treatment recommendations, ensuring that healthcare professionals can trust and comprehend the decisions made by the algorithm.

The integration of machine learning into decision-making is evident in the realm of natural language processing (NLP), where algorithms analyze and understand human language to inform decisions. Sentiment analysis, for example, employs machine learning models to assess the sentiment expressed in textual data, aiding businesses in gauging public opinion, customer satisfaction, or even predicting market trends. Chatbots and virtual assistants leverage NLP to understand user queries and provide intelligent responses, enhancing the quality of decision-making in customer service and support.

The concept of ensemble learning, where multiple models are combined to make more robust and accurate predictions, further amplifies the impact of machine learning on decision-making. Techniques like bagging and boosting, which involve aggregating predictions from multiple models, contribute to improved generalization and robustness. Ensemble methods are widely used in various applications, such as in finance for portfolio optimization or in healthcare for disease prediction. The synergy of multiple models enhances the reliability and accuracy of decisions, mitigating the risks associated with relying on a single algorithm.

In the context of decision-making under uncertainty, Bayesian machine learning offers a principled framework for incorporating probabilistic reasoning. Bayesian models update their beliefs based on new evidence, allowing decision-makers to quantify uncertainty, account for prior knowledge, and make decisions that are more adaptive to changing conditions. This is particularly valuable in fields such as autonomous vehicles, where decisions must be made in real-time based on uncertain and dynamic environments. Bayesian machine learning provides a robust methodology for reasoning under uncertainty, contributing to safer and more reliable decision-making in complex scenarios.

The integration of machine learning into decision-making processes is closely tied to the concept of automated decision support systems. These systems leverage machine learning models to analyze data, provide insights, and assist human decision-makers in making more informed choices. In healthcare, for example, decision support systems can aid clinicians in diagnosing diseases, suggesting treatment plans, or predicting patient outcomes based on historical data. By augmenting human decision-making with machine-generated insights, these systems enhance accuracy, efficiency, and the overall quality of decisions in complex domains.

Ethical considerations play a significant role in the integration of machine learning into decision-making, particularly when decisions impact individuals or communities. Biases present in training data can lead to biased predictions, potentially reinforcing and perpetuating existing social inequalities. Fairness-aware machine learning techniques aim to address these biases by ensuring that decisions are equitable across different demographic groups. Ethical considerations extend to transparency, accountability, and privacy, urging the development of responsible AI frameworks that prioritize the ethical implications of machine learning in decision-making processes.

The emergence of federated learning is reshaping the landscape of machine learning for decision-making, especially in scenarios where data privacy and security are paramount. Federated learning allows models to be trained across decentralized devices or servers without exchanging raw data, preserving the privacy of sensitive information. In healthcare, for instance, federated learning enables collaborative model training across multiple healthcare institutions without sharing patient data. This approach reconciles the need for decentralized decision-making with data privacy concerns, opening avenues for secure and collaborative machine learning applications.

The integration of machine learning into decision-making is not without challenges. The "black box" nature of certain complex models raises concerns about interpretability, trust, and accountability. As machine learning models become more sophisticated, efforts to develop explainable AI and interpretability techniques are essential for ensuring that decisions made by these models are understandable and justifiable. Moreover, the need for large labeled datasets for training, the risk of biased algorithms, and the ethical considerations surrounding AI applications underscore the importance of ethical guidelines, regulatory frameworks, and ongoing research to address these challenges responsibly.

In conclusion, the integration of machine learning into decision-making processes marks a paradigm shift in how intelligent systems operate and contribute across diverse domains. From predictive analytics and unsupervised learning to reinforcement learning and ensemble methods, machine learning techniques offer versatile tools for enhancing decision-making. As AI technologies continue to advance, the ethical considerations, interpretability challenges, and the evolution of responsible AI frameworks will shape the trajectory of machine learning's role in decision-making. The ongoing collaboration between human expertise and machine intelligence promises a future where decisions are more informed, adaptive, and aligned with the complexities of our rapidly evolving world.

Enhancing distributed systems with predictive analytics and pattern recognition.

In the rapidly evolving landscape of distributed systems, the integration of predictive analytics and pattern recognition has emerged as a pivotal paradigm, ushering in a new era of efficiency, resilience, and performance. At its core, predictive analytics harnesses the power of historical data and sophisticated algorithms to forecast future trends and behaviors, enabling distributed systems to proactively address potential issues before they escalate. This foresight not only optimizes resource allocation but also enhances overall system reliability. Moreover, by leveraging pattern recognition, distributed systems can discern intricate correlations and anomalies within vast datasets, providing invaluable insights for decision-making processes.

The synergy of predictive analytics and pattern recognition bolsters fault tolerance in distributed systems, offering a preemptive shield against potential disruptions. The ability to identify and predict patterns in system behavior empowers these networks to distinguish normal operational states from abnormal ones, enabling swift responses to emerging challenges. This proactive approach to fault management minimizes downtime and mitigates the impact of unforeseen events, fostering a resilient infrastructure capable of adapting to dynamic conditions.

Furthermore, the incorporation of predictive analytics and pattern recognition into distributed systems greatly enhances scalability. By analyzing historical usage patterns and predicting future resource demands, these systems can dynamically adjust their configurations to accommodate varying workloads. This adaptability not only optimizes performance but also ensures cost-effectiveness by efficiently allocating resources in real-time. The result is a distributed ecosystem that seamlessly scales to meet the demands of ever-expanding user bases and evolving application requirements.

In the realm of resource optimization, predictive analytics plays a pivotal role in anticipating bottlenecks and potential performance constraints within distributed systems. By analyzing historical data and identifying patterns related to resource utilization, these systems can proactively allocate resources where they are most needed, preventing inefficiencies and ensuring optimal performance. This predictive resource allocation not only enhances system efficiency but also contributes to energy conservation, aligning with the growing emphasis on sustainable computing practices.

Moreover, the integration of predictive analytics and pattern recognition fosters intelligent automation within distributed systems. By leveraging insights derived from historical data and recognizing patterns in user behavior, these systems can autonomously optimize workflows, streamline processes, and adapt to changing conditions without manual intervention. This intelligent automation not only reduces the burden on human operators but also accelerates decision-making, enabling distributed systems to operate with unprecedented agility and responsiveness.

In the realm of security, predictive analytics and pattern recognition serve as formidable tools in the detection and prevention of cyber threats within distributed systems. By analyzing historical data and identifying patterns associated with malicious activities, these systems can proactively thwart potential security breaches. The ability to predict and recognize patterns indicative of cyber threats empowers distributed systems to deploy preemptive security measures, safeguarding sensitive data and preserving the integrity of the overall infrastructure.

Furthermore, the integration of machine learning algorithms into distributed systems enhances the adaptability and learning capabilities of these networks. By continuously analyzing data patterns and adapting to evolving circumstances, machine learning algorithms enable distributed systems to improve their performance over time. This self-optimization not only ensures the longevity of distributed systems but also positions them as dynamic and intelligent entities capable of evolving in tandem with technological advancements.

In conclusion, the convergence of predictive analytics and pattern recognition represents a transformative force in the realm of distributed systems. This symbiotic relationship empowers these systems with the foresight to predict and proactively address challenges, the resilience to withstand unforeseen disruptions, and the intelligence to optimize resources and adapt to dynamic conditions. As the digital landscape continues to evolve, the integration of predictive analytics and pattern recognition will undoubtedly play a pivotal role in shaping the future of distributed systems, unlocking new frontiers of efficiency, security, and innovation.

Addressing ethical considerations in the development and deployment of distributed systems.

In the intricate tapestry of technological advancement, addressing ethical considerations in the development and deployment of distributed systems is an imperative that goes beyond mere technical prowess. As these systems become integral to various aspects of our daily lives, ethical considerations emerge as crucial pillars upon which the foundation of responsible innovation rests. One paramount concern is the equitable access to distributed systems, ensuring that technological benefits are not confined to privileged segments of society. Developers and policymakers must be vigilant in crafting solutions that bridge the digital divide, fostering inclusivity and avoiding the exacerbation of existing social inequalities.

The responsible collection and use of data represent another ethical frontier in the realm of distributed systems. As these networks thrive on vast datasets to enhance their functionality, there is a pressing need to establish robust data governance frameworks. Striking a delicate balance between leveraging data for system optimization and safeguarding user privacy is paramount. Ethical data practices involve transparent communication with users about data collection purposes, providing them with control over their information, and implementing stringent security measures to thwart unauthorized access. In an era where data is often deemed the new currency, ethical considerations demand a conscientious approach to its stewardship.

Security and privacy concerns loom large in the ethical landscape of distributed systems, particularly as cyber threats become more sophisticated. Developers must embed security measures at every layer of the system architecture, ensuring the confidentiality, integrity, and availability of data. Furthermore, ethical considerations dictate that the development of distributed systems should not compromise individual privacy. Striking a delicate balance between system functionality and user privacy involves employing anonymization techniques, implementing robust encryption mechanisms, and adhering to data protection regulations. In an age where privacy breaches can have far-reaching consequences, the ethical imperative of safeguarding user information cannot be overstated.

The ethical considerations in distributed systems extend to the responsible use of artificial intelligence (AI) and machine learning algorithms. As these systems evolve to possess increasingly autonomous decision-making capabilities, ethical dilemmas arise concerning the potential biases ingrained in algorithmic decision-making. Developers must be vigilant in identifying and mitigating biases within AI models to prevent discriminatory outcomes. Ethical AI development demands transparency in algorithmic decision-making processes, enabling users to understand the basis of automated decisions. Additionally, ongoing scrutiny and evaluation of AI systems are essential to identify and rectify biases that may emerge over time.

In the deployment phase of distributed systems, the ethical responsibility extends to ensuring system resilience and reliability. Unforeseen system failures can have profound consequences, ranging from financial losses to jeopardizing public safety in critical infrastructures. Ethical considerations implore developers to implement robust testing procedures, conduct thorough risk assessments, and establish failover mechanisms to mitigate the impact of potential disruptions. Moreover, transparency in system behavior and clear communication about potential risks are ethical imperatives to empower users and stakeholders to make informed decisions.

The global nature of distributed systems introduces ethical dimensions related to international collaboration and compliance with diverse regulatory frameworks. Developers must navigate a complex landscape of legal and cultural considerations, respecting the sovereignty of nations and adhering to local regulations. Responsible development involves proactive engagement with international stakeholders, understanding diverse cultural perspectives, and adapting systems to comply with regional legal frameworks. Ethical considerations underscore the importance of fostering a global dialogue that transcends technological boundaries, promoting ethical standards that resonate across borders.

Environmental sustainability emerges as a pressing ethical concern in the era of distributed systems, where energy consumption and carbon footprints become pivotal considerations. Developers must prioritize the design and deployment of energy-efficient systems, leveraging renewable energy sources and optimizing resource utilization. Ethical considerations demand a shift towards eco-friendly practices, recognizing the environmental impact of technology and striving for sustainable solutions that minimize the ecological footprint of distributed systems.

In the ever-evolving landscape of technology, addressing ethical considerations in the development and deployment of distributed systems is an ongoing and multifaceted endeavor. It requires a holistic approach that transcends technical expertise, encompassing social responsibility, transparency, user empowerment, and environmental stewardship. As architects of the digital future, developers and stakeholders must embrace the ethical imperative, recognizing that the impact of distributed systems extends far beyond lines of code — it shapes the very fabric of society in which these technologies are embedded.

Balancing technological advancements with social responsibility.

In the relentless march of technological progress, the imperative to balance advancements with social responsibility emerges as a guiding principle that transcends the boundaries of innovation. The rapid evolution of technology has bestowed upon society a myriad of transformative tools and capabilities, from artificial intelligence to biotechnology, reshaping the very fabric of our existence. Yet, in the pursuit of innovation, it becomes incumbent upon technologists, policymakers, and society at large to navigate the delicate equilibrium between pushing the frontiers of technology and safeguarding the well-being of humanity.

At the core of balancing technological advancements with social responsibility lies the ethical consideration of how these innovations impact individuals and communities. Ethical technology development involves a conscientious effort to mitigate the unintended consequences of emerging technologies, ensuring that they contribute positively to societal well-being. As technologies like artificial intelligence gain prominence, addressing issues of bias, fairness, and accountability becomes crucial. Developers must grapple with the ethical dimensions of algorithmic decision-making, striving for fairness and transparency to prevent the perpetuation of societal inequalities.

The concept of social responsibility in technology extends to the principle of inclusive design, recognizing the diverse needs and experiences of all members of society. Innovations should not inadvertently marginalize certain groups; instead, they should be designed with accessibility in mind, accommodating a broad spectrum of users, including those with disabilities. This inclusive approach fosters an equitable distribution of technological benefits, ensuring that advancements enhance the quality of life for all, rather than exacerbating existing disparities.

Moreover, as technology becomes increasingly intertwined with personal data, the responsible handling of information emerges as a critical aspect of social responsibility. Data privacy concerns have become central to public discourse, necessitating stringent safeguards to protect individuals from unwarranted intrusion. Companies and developers must prioritize robust data protection measures, adhere to privacy regulations, and empower users with control over their personal information. This commitment to data privacy upholds the principles of autonomy and individual agency, reinforcing the ethical underpinnings of technological advancements.

In the realm of artificial intelligence, the ethical imperative involves creating systems that augment human capabilities rather than replace them. The responsible integration of AI should prioritize collaboration between humans and machines, enhancing productivity, creativity, and problem-solving. This human-centric approach to AI development mitigates fears of job displacement and emphasizes the potential for technology to complement human skills, fostering a symbiotic relationship that advances societal progress.

Social responsibility extends beyond the design phase of technology into considerations of environmental impact. As the demand for electronic devices and data storage continues to soar, the ecological footprint of technology becomes a pressing concern. Sustainable design practices, energy-efficient technologies, and responsible waste management are essential elements of balancing technological advancements with environmental stewardship. Technological progress should not come at the expense of the planet, and a commitment to eco-friendly practices is integral to upholding social responsibility in the digital age.

The responsible deployment of emerging technologies also necessitates a proactive engagement with the broader ethical implications of innovation. The development of biotechnologies, for instance, raises profound questions about the ethical boundaries of manipulating life and genetic information. A thoughtful and inclusive dialogue involving scientists, ethicists, policymakers, and the public is essential to establish ethical frameworks that guide the ethical development and deployment of these transformative technologies, ensuring that they align with societal values.

In the context of social responsibility, technology companies play a pivotal role in shaping the ethical landscape of the digital era. Corporate responsibility involves not only delivering cutting-edge products and services but also embodying ethical business practices. This includes transparency in dealings, fair labor practices, and a commitment to social and environmental sustainability. Companies are increasingly being held accountable for their impact on society, and embracing a sense of social responsibility is not just a moral imperative but a strategic necessity in the contemporary business landscape.

As we navigate the complex terrain of technological advancements, education emerges as a linchpin in fostering a socially responsible approach to technology. An informed and digitally literate populace is better equipped to understand the implications of technological innovations, question the ethical dimensions of emerging technologies, and actively participate in shaping the trajectory of technological progress. Educational institutions must cultivate a sense of digital citizenship that instills ethical values and empowers individuals to navigate the evolving technological landscape responsibly.

In conclusion, balancing technological advancements with social responsibility is an intricate dance that requires a harmonious interplay of ethical considerations, inclusive design, environmental stewardship, and corporate responsibility. As we stand at the precipice of a future shaped by unprecedented technological possibilities, the commitment to social responsibility becomes the compass guiding the trajectory of innovation. It is a call to action for technologists, policymakers, and society at large to ensure that the fruits of technological progress are shared equitably, that the potential harms are mitigated, and that the relentless march of innovation aligns with the collective well-being of humanity. In this delicate equilibrium, lies the promise of a future where technology serves as a force for positive transformation, enriching the lives of individuals and advancing the greater good.

| Page